Islam and the Culture of Modern Egypt

Telling a new story of modern Egypt, Mohammad Salama uses literary and cinematic sources to construct a clear and accessible narrative of the dynamics of Islam and culture in the first half of the twentieth century. The conflict between tradition and secular values in modern Egypt is shown in a stimulating and challenging new light as Salama bridges analysis of nationalism and its connection to Islamism and outlines the effects of secular education versus traditional Islamic teaching on varied elements of Egyptian society. These include cultural production, politics, identity, and gender relations. All of this helps to discern the harbingers that led to Egypt's social transition from the monarchy to the republic, and opens the possibility of Islam as an inspiring and inspirational force. This illuminating, provocative, and informative study will be of inestimable value to anyone interested in the period, whether general readers, students, or researchers.

MOHAMMAD SALAMA is Professor and Director of the Arabic Program at San Francisco State University. He has published numerous articles on comparative literature and Arabic literature and film, is the author of *The Qur'an and Modern Arabic Literary Criticism* (2018), *Islam, Orientalism, and Intellectual History* (2011), and is the coeditor of *German Colonialism: Race, the Holocaust, and Post-War Germany* (2011). He is the recipient of two Fulbright Scholar Awards.

Islam and the Culture of Modern Egypt

From the Monarchy to the Republic

MOHAMMAD SALAMA
San Francisco State University

CAMBRIDGE
UNIVERSITY PRESS

CAMBRIDGE
UNIVERSITY PRESS

University Printing House, Cambridge CB2 8BS, United Kingdom

One Liberty Plaza, 20th Floor, New York, NY 10006, USA

477 Williamstown Road, Port Melbourne, VIC 3207, Australia

314–321, 3rd Floor, Plot 3, Splendor Forum, Jasola District Centre, New Delhi – 110025, India

79 Anson Road, #06–04/06, Singapore 079906

Cambridge University Press is part of the University of Cambridge.

It furthers the University's mission by disseminating knowledge in the pursuit of education, learning, and research at the highest international levels of excellence.

www.cambridge.org
Information on this title: www.cambridge.org/9781108417181
DOI: 10.1017/9781108265027

First published 2018

Printed and bound in Great Britain by Clays Ltd, Elcograf S.p.A.

A catalogue record for this publication is available from the British Library.

Library of Congress Cataloging-in-Publication Data

Names: Salama, Mohammad, author.
Title: Islam and the culture of modern Egypt from the monarchy to the republic / Mohammad Salama.
Description: Cambridge : Cambridge University Press, 2018. | Includes bibliographical references and index.
Identifiers: LCCN 2018012840 | ISBN 9781108417181 (hardback : alk. paper)
Subjects: LCSH: Islam and culture—Egypt. | Islam and secularism—Egypt. | Egypt—History—20th century. | Egypt—History—21st century.
Classification: LCC BP64.E3 S263 2018 | DDC 297.0962—dc23
LC record available at https://lccn.loc.gov/2018012840

ISBN 978-1-108-41718-1 Hardback

To my children, Salma, Malachi, Aliya, Noah; my siblings, Nasser, Ahmad, Kareem, Amani; my parents, Aziza and Ramadan; and in memory of John McGuire – what I have learned from John cannot be quantified.

Contents

Acknowledgments

As befits a comparatist, this book owes its genesis to many places: the University of 'Ayn Shams in Cairo, where I studied and taught English literature; the University of Wisconsin–Madison (UW–Madison), where I studied Comparative Literature; Columbia University, where I delivered versions of these chapters on many occasions; Trent University, where I gave talks about Islam and Egyptian modernity; and of course, San Francisco State University (SFSU), where I teach and continue to learn from the ever-curious and inspiring minds of my students. SFSU and its administrators, colleagues, and staff have, as usual, provided me not only with plentiful support and encouragement but also with an enormously stimulating intellectual network.

There are people in those places to whom I owe a substantial debt of gratitude. At 'Ayn Shams University: Salwa Bahgat, Yasser Chaddad, Muhammad Nassar, Abd al-Rhaman, Abd al-Salam, Atif Bahgat, Manal Ghoneim, Yomna Saber, Amani Toma, Alladin Mahmoud, Samar Abd El Salam, Fadwa Kamal AbdelRahman, Diaa Elnaggar, Yomna Saber, Noha Faisal, Khaled Elghamry, Yasser Chaddad, Waseem Abdel Haleem, and Mayy El-Haiawy. At UW–Madison: Dustin Cowell, Hala Ghoneim, Kelley Conway, Michelle Hilmes, Max Statkiewcz, Toma Longinovic, Jan Plug, Gerhard Richter, Jacques Lezra, and Luís Madureira. At Columbia University: Muhsin al-Musawi. At Trent University: Kelly McGuire and Shaoling Wang. And at SFSU: Ayan Jiggetts, Caterina Mariotti, Pamela Vaughn, Hisham Khairy Issa, Gusatvo Calderon, Chris Wen-chao Li, Berenice Le Marchand, Midori McKeon, Larry Hanley, Mary Soliday, Ana Luengo, Gustavo Calderon, Yang Xioa-Desai, Frederik Green, Mohammad Azadpur, Mahmood Monshipouri, Beverly Voloshin, Dina Ibrahim, Mike Lunine, Maxine Chernoff, and Paul Sherwin.

I would like to give special thanks to Didi Pollock, Hanadi al-Samman, Gretchen Head, Nizar Hermes, Nuraini Abd Zabar, Michael Cooperson, Peter Gran, Hussam Eldin Raafat Ahmed, Anna

Cruz, Douja Mamelouk, Nevine El Nossery, Francesca Bell, Asaad al-Saleh, Yaseen Noorani, Abdlkarim Alamry, Terri DeYoung, Maya Yazigi, Nui Zimu, Mariam Cooke, and Suzanne Stetkevych.

I cannot end without expressing my sincerest gratitude to Zailig Pollock for all the help he has given me with editing this book, patiently reading through the entire manuscript, making countless suggestions, picking up numerous infelicities, and offering generous and insightful comments. I am grateful to Benjamin Palmer Davis for his kindness and rare editorial talent. I am deeply indebted to Jaroslav Stetkevych, the peerless Arabist, for enriching my understanding and appreciation of Egyptian culture with his keen intellect and captivating anecdotes about al-Ḥakīm, Mahfouz, and other writers included in this study. My debt to Jaroslav is boundless. I am grateful to Cambridge University Press. I would like to particularly thank the anonymous reviewers who read the manuscript and offered useful criticism. Their suggestions have been received with appreciation and generally followed. Maria Marsh helped me immeasurably with the task of nursing this manuscript to fruition. Her patience and outstanding encouragement in preparing the manuscript and her unfailing presence and efficiency are exemplary. Thanks are also due to Abigail Walkington for her expert handling of the manuscript, book cover, and design. I am grateful to Katrina Keefer for her impressive editing and diligent reading of the manuscript. My gratitude extends to Cassi Roberts, Abirami Ulaganthan, and Ian Kingston for their timely and impressive work on the manuscript during its final stages.

My deepest indebtedness and love to Kelly McGuire for her ultimate support, her infectious intellect, our endless stimulating conversations, and the gentle imprints she leaves behind so that I can follow the footprints of her ever-fascinating and beautiful mind.

Finally, my everlasting gratitude goes to my parents, Aziza and Ramadan, for bringing me to the world and for nurturing my heart and soul in a city that was not just beautiful but also charged with memories of the Egyptian past.

A Note on Transliteration and Translation

This book follows a specialized diacritical system for Arabic for all scholarly purposes. I use the standard Western spelling of terms that have entered the English language like "Arab," "Islam," and country names. I use the standard Library of Congress transliteration system for all other Arabic terms, with a few exceptions. In Arabic words such as 'Ā'isha, the (') symbolizes the Arabic letter (ع) ['ayn], while the (') symbolizes the glottal Arabic (ئ ؤ إ أ ء) [hamza]. An accented (á) symbolizes the alif maqṣūra (ى) at the end of an Arabic word, as in (على) 'alá.

The definitive (ال) is fully transcribed as (Al-/al-) regardless of whether the following letters are ḥurūf shamsiyya or ḥurūf qamariyya. In genitive iḍāfa constructions, the pronounced (ة) is transcribed as a -t- between two nouns, or as part of the full word, as in Jumhūriyya-t- Faraḥāt or Jumhūriyyat Faraḥāt. Full case endings are added to Qur'ānic and poetic quotations only. When a full case ending is necessary, in cases of tanwīn تَنْوِين or nunation, the sign (-un) indicating the nominative case, (-an) indicating the accusative case, and (-in) indicating the genitive case are all superscripted.

Dagger alif (أَلِف خَنْجَرِيَّة) [alif khanjarīyya], which is also known as symbolic alif, small alif, superscript alif, or historical alif, and which appears in Arabic script as a short vertical stroke on top of a consonant, is symbolized as a long /ā/ sound. For example: (هٰذَا) [hādhā] or (رَحْمٰن) [raḥmān]. The (ه) at the end of a transcribed Arabic word like the possessive pronoun in كتابه [his book] refers to Arabic words ending in an (h) (ه) and not with a (ة), as commonly practiced. The final (ة) is not transcribed, as in كتابة [kitāba].

Unless otherwise noted in the text or notes, all translations from Arabic and French are my own.

Preface

During the Second World War, in the summer of 1943 to be exact, a young orphan migrated north from *Ḥawḍ ʻAshara* (District 10) in the Upper Egyptian city of *Qinā* to settle in the metropolis known among Egyptians as *ʻRūs al-Baḥr al-Mutwassiṭ* (The Bride of the Mediterranean Sea). At this time, Alexandria was the most popular destination for Upper Egyptians seeking cooler weather and a more prosperous livelihood in northern Egypt. This particular man's elder brother had established himself five years earlier as a caretaker for a well-to-do family in the area of Rushdie Pasha. Fortunately, the landowning wealthy family was now seeking a nighttime guard for the house, with full board and a small stipend. They hired the younger brother for the position. To an illiterate Upper Egyptian peasant in the Farūq years, this was a golden opportunity for economic self-improvement. Soon enough, the young man moved into the small two-bedroom apartment located in the lower eastern corner of the villa's basement. To supplement his income, he was also able to find a part-time commuting job as a machine operator at the Sibahi Spinning and Weaving Company on the outskirts of Alexandria. That young man was my future father.

Twenty-two years earlier, a similar story took place when a man from the same *ṣa'īd* (Upper Egyptian) neighborhood in *Qinā* migrated to Alexandria to work for the British-owned Shell Oil Company. He soon married a young woman from Damanhūr and had three children with her before she died at a young age. The youngest of the three orphaned siblings was my mother, who married my father through the *Khātiba* (matchmaker) tradition of conservative *ṣa ʻīdī* families living in Alexandria. My mother and father were thus brought together by the ambitions of migrant working classes who elbowed their way through the economics and politics of a fading British Empire, a feeble monarchy, and a rising nationalism. It was in the summer of 1965 that my parents got married and my mother moved to live with my father in his caretaker apartment in the Rushdie villa.

Such an encounter could have happened in Alexandria or elsewhere in Metropolitan Egypt. There is, however, an important rationale for beginning my book with this glance backwards into my own prehistory. We all strive to make sense of the past as a generalized record of history open to everyone's reflections and analyses, but any such record will inevitably be colored by personal recollections. And just as with Ṭāhā Ḥusayn's autobiography, *al-Ayyām* (*The Days*), my recollections of the past stretch back beyond the point where my own childhood memories begin. For me, born as I was in the shadow of European dominion in Egypt, to a father and a mother who were toddlers in the aftermath of Ḥasan al-Bannā's establishment of the Muslim Brotherhood and adolescents when the Free Officers carried out their coup on July 23, 1952, the regime of Nasser, with which I conclude this study, falls within my own extended familial autobiography. As such, my account of this regime bears the marks of my parents' experience of the culture of modern Egypt at a period that preceded my birth, the outset of the twentieth century. And just as it reflects my preconscious experience of the Nasser years, it reflects, as well, the marks of my direct exposure to the years that have followed.

Nasser died on September 28, 1970, leaving behind him a gap and a memory. The Arabic word for memory is *dhikrà*, which derives from the three-letter root *dh. k. r.* In addition to its connection to memory and remembering, *dh. k. r.* also means to "mention." The root connects the word memory, *dhikrà*, to an enunciation in the present (the now), thus making memory an act of the present. I carry those memories with me wherever I go, as a stamp of my identity, as I strive to make sense of the past and seek solace in a somewhat blurred narrative that has a beginning, a middle, and an end, and that I call my life. Yet, I am equally aware that remembering, an arduous task of keeping one's own identity intact, will never be fully achieved in the present, but will always remain a unique and unverifiable work in progress.

As an act of *dhikrà*, this book is a memory, not only of the past and of my own interactions with, and readings of, all those narratives on Islam and the culture of modern Egypt; it is also a memory of the future, rooted in the past, yet signaling what is yet to come of Egypt, a memory that has been expressed by many authors in this study, from Haykal's romantic love to Idrīs's satirical utopia, from Mahfouz's nihilism to Chahine's nationalism, from Qutb and Bākāthīr's Islamism to al-Ḥakīm and Ḥusayn's humanism. Memory is not just about failed revolutions, the years of deprivation, the ugly reality of village medicine, or the oppression of religious institutions, although all these are important. Memory is life, embodied in the fears and aspirations of individuals in living societies, subject to the dialectic of utopia and despair, of dreams and reality, of remembering and forgetting. Memory, as the Arabic origin denotes, is a bond between the past and the present, an invocation of a lived past that thrives on vague reminiscences and hazy impressions; its rootedness in the concrete, an image, a landscape, a sweet voice, a flavor, a gesture, an object, a photo, a materiality beaten by time, hazily recorded and locked up in a mental safe, allowing us to situate the personal in a sacred assertion of, or search for, our own identities. Amidst all this haziness, Nasser occupies a similarly nebulous place in the collective memory of my generation.

Many recollections of Nasser have been eclectic and dismissive. Many historical works dwell on the famous events in Nasser's regime. Events such as the 1952 coup, the nationalization of the Suez Canal, the Agrarian Reform Law, and the wars with Europe and Israel, as well as the relationship with the Arab world and Russia, all become the focus of those histories concerned with taking these events apart to show how they functioned and how they came about. But most of those writings raise many questions about biases and interpretations, and sometimes even give profundity to a past devoid of it. Take, for example, Bernard Lewis's perspective on Nasser in his book, *The Middle East and the West*. In 1955, Bernard Lewis speaks of the "mood and wish that united many if not most Arabs" in their desire to "spite and humiliate the West." According to Lewis, the "most dramatic and satisfying expression" of this attitude was found in "Nasser's Russian arms deal in Egypt in September 1955. In the twilight world of popular myths and images, the West is the source of all evil."[1] The Nasser of Bernard Lewis's twilight zone is the antagonist of a monolithic West.

I am sure Nasser is remembered differently by his family, children, and grandchildren. Even in my own family, my father would have

[1] Bernard Lewis, *The Middle East and the West* (London: HarperCollins College Division, 1968), 20.

begged to differ with Bernard Lewis. The word "Nasser" was very important to him. Nasser is the name he chose to give to my elder brother, his first son, after which my father was always called *Abū Nāṣir* (father of Nasser) and my mother *Umm Nāṣir* (mother of Nasser). To have such popular *kunya* (a teknonymy or a practice of referring to parents by the names of their first born) as the same name of an Upper Egyptian Alexandria-born President is a glory that speaks for itself. My siblings and I grew up singing nationalist songs and listening to tapes by popular singers like Muḥammad 'Abd al-Wahhāb, Um Kulthūm, and 'Abd al-Ḥalīm Ḥāfiẓ. Ours was a radio household in a radio republic. Nationalism was fed to us, both consciously and unconsciously, by the speeches that our father would make us sit down and listen to, even if we did not understand a word or cared to, and by the rampant drums of militarism that penetrated our ears on a daily basis, as we went to school, while we lunched on the delicious falafel sandwiches of *Abū Rabī'* at Isis (Izīs/Buklà/Bolkoley) Tram Station, or when we went for a swim at Rushdie and Stanley Beaches.

I recall one of the earliest childhood memories of a photo of my father in his youth in front of his machine in the Sibahi Spinning and Weaving Factory in Kafr al-Dawwār, a suburb of Alexandria. It was a black and white shot, with my father smiling in the middle left corner of the frame, though not looking directly at the camera, while keeping busy with his hands on that huge machine that engulfed the remaining two-thirds of the photo. He looked so happy, yet too young, I later thought, to be operating such an enormous machine. I grew up with this photo magnifying my father's heroism in my eyes, though I often wondered why it would take him so long to go to work and come back, and how, with little or no education, he was able to do his daily *wardiyya* (shift) on this colossal nonstopping leviathan. It was much later, and after he got a more stable job at the Alexandria Transportation Company, that I came to learn that pre-coup textile managements intentionally located their factories far from major urban centers to better control their workforces, and that they intentionally and selectively recruited illiterate, unskilled Egyptians with no prior experience of industrial life so that they might not ask for salary increases or work-related accident compensation, or organize to improve their working conditions.

My father was lucky; he worked at the Sibahi Spinning and Weaving Company at the right time in Egypt's modern history, when

Nasser's regime cleverly restored the dignity of Egyptian peasants and factory workers while simultaneously dismantling all labor unions and labeling union organizers as communist ideologues punishable by the law. Nasser's regime thus managed to orient the workers' movements towards nationalist issues and to dissolve them in the newly forming Egyptian collective. Nationally, the regime's support for the working class was a very successful move. This, of course, was consolidated by Nasser's nationalization of the Suez Canal and the regime's emphasis on expanding modern industry. In turn, the working class grew in size and gained political legitimacy and status, but lost their unions, and with them the right to justice and legal representation. My father's employment as *'āmil mākīna* (a machine operator) in a spinning and weaving factory owned by a *mutamaṣṣir* (Egyptianized) redefined Egyptian nationalism. An Egyptian peasant in a cotton-related business, his status as a symbol of the new, hard-working, Egyptian native was somehow linked to the historical meta-narrative of Egypt's anti-colonial struggle, and to the fact that from 1882 to 1952, Egypt was subject to British colonial domination. During those times, nearly all of the large-scale employers were foreigners enjoying economic power that was enhanced and safeguarded by the monarchy, which in turn protected Britain's interests in Egypt. My father's status was perceived as part of the country's fight for self-determination and he, as a worker, was perceived as the dispossessed, native peasant coming back to reclaim his usurped rights.

This motif of the dispossessed peasant – whatever ideology it serves – is at the center of Egypt's colonial and postcolonial self-definition. It is easy to see it as a common thread throughout this book, passing from Ḥaqqī's *Virgin of Denshawai* (1906), to Haykal's *Zaynab* (1914), to Ḥusayn's *The Days* (1927), to Bākāthīr's *The Red Revolutionary* (1949), and to other works not addressed in this study, all the way up to Chahine's *Gamīla* (1958). I do not take credit for noting this: there is a peasant in every Egyptian story. However, it took me decades to connect the dots and to see the multi-gowned peasant clothed, by turn, in injustice, inequity, negligence, enslavement, fundamentalism, Islamism, nationalism, and Egyptianism as the decades went by. My father, the migrant peasant of Upper Egypt, unequipped with any kind of certificate or skill other than farming, or for that matter with anything that would make for a decent life in Metropolitan Egypt, found opportunity once he made the decision to leave the neglected south and board *wabūr al-sā 'a ithnā 'ashar* (the twelve o'clock locomotive), the overnight train that runs between Aswān and Alexandria.

My father's Islam has its beginning in Upper Egypt, Sufism of a deeply stoic nature, occasional *dhikr* nights (focused collective prayers in praise of God), daily prayers, Friday *khuṭba* (sermon), *zakā* (charity), fasting in the month of Ramadan, listening to *Idhā 'a-t-al-Qur'ān al-Karīm* (a national radio station broadcasting the Holy Qur'ān), and praying for a miracle to be able to afford *Ḥajj* (pilgrimage). Speaking of miracles, when I first read Ḥusayn's autobiography, *The Days*, in high school, I was struck by a familiar parental attitude towards the idea of Providence. The young boy's father asked him to recite the Yāsīn chapter repeatedly with the expectation or hope that God would not turn down the appeals of a blind lad reciting the Qur'ān. My father, too, prayed insistently and continually appealed for economic improvement in the form of a financial gift from God, literally a "bag of money." My father promised God, in his earnest yet simple prayers, that if He were to grant him a gift, he would use the money to build a mosque nearby for people to pray in. Anyone who has been to Alexandria or other parts of Egypt, even briefly, will not fail to see that our neighborhood, in fact the whole of Egypt, did not need any more mosques. But that was my father's pledge, a contractual hope for an act of divine generosity to be reciprocated with an act of human gratitude.

This culture of appeal and supplication is indeed the ethos of many Egyptian Muslims, including appeals for career advancement, marriage, safety, success at school, and cure from illnesses. Egypt's arch-enemies are poverty and disease. These have not changed, no matter the place, the cultural formations, the religious affiliations, or the political leanings. Of course, every generation is shaped by different cultural forces. I got onto the train of postcolonial Egypt at a different stop than my father did. I had my own expectations of what the destination would be, having missed the rough transition from monarchy to republic, which for my parents and their generation must have been the most crucial cultural turn in Egypt's modern history.

That is what I mean in this book by the *relationship* between Islam and the culture of modern Egypt. Islam in modern Egypt is a multitude – in other words, not exactly the fundamentalist hardline of the Muslim Brotherhood or even the more militant *al-Jamā 'a al-Islāmiyya*, whose members assassinated President Sadat in 1980, but rather the varied forms of cultural practices at home, greeting people, stepping into the mosque with the right foot, TV *adhān* reminders (calls for prayers), Friday exhortations, and the two Eids. The practice of Islam is more like a sanctuary from the mundane, a reminder that God will reward the good and punish evil. God is the poverty antidote, the spiritual recharge to cope with life in a police state of class privileges. My father knew very well that there are different ways of understanding Islam and the world. Shrouding Egypt and the whole world in a Quṭbian cloak of Islamism was simply detestable and unthinkable for him. Understandably enough, his 'basic' perspective on and practice of Islam seemed to be well-suited for Nasser's Egypt, which was intolerant of religious fundamentalism, less concerned with intellectual or social movements, and definitely dismissive of any principles of shared governance.

It took me decades to be able to discern how the ebbs and flows of the labor movement in Nasser's Egypt coincided with the successive upsurges of the nationalist movement. The participation of the working class in the nationalist cause, which my father represented, infused the movement for full independence and evacuation of British military forces with a radical social consciousness. Workers' strikes and demonstrations, including that of the Muslim Brotherhood – which, ironically enough, started *as* a social union – were usually directed against foreign enterprises. The labor movement was often considered to be one component in a larger nationalist movement. After 1956, Nasser's foreign policy shifted towards *al-Ḥiyād al-Ījābī* (Positive Neutralism) and *al-Tasalluḥ Ḍidd al-Isti'mār* (Militant Anti-imperialism). The tripartite attack of 1956 served to confirm for a nationalistically indoctrinated Egyptian public that the main political question of the day was still the struggle against imperialism and neo-colonialism, now augmented by the Muslim Brotherhood's failed plot to take over Egypt in 1954 and Israel's external threats after 1948 and beyond.

These issues, rather than the economy and internal class struggle, dominated Nasser's politics. There was no interest in addressing Egypt's most immediate and urgent challenges: poverty, disease, illiteracy, and dictatorship. Nor was there concern with the question of the degree to which republicanism (Egyptian republicanism that is, which Idrīs ridicules in *Farāḥāt's Republic*) and democracy can be reconciled, and with the question of whether new structures of governance can be created through legal-bureaucratic means. If the question of Egypt's democracy began with Nasser, it also ended there, and my memory of it during Sadat and Mubarak's regimes became a memory of a distant and uncertain future.

From the very beginning, the nationalist state was too narrow a framework to adequately guarantee successful economic policies and to protect Egypt against external factors – against the imperatives of the world market and the growing economic control of the United States. The development of a nation-state culture has arrived at an impasse, a horrifying realization that, of all the works discussed in this study, only Idrīs's novella is able to articulate, as early as 1956. Much was not known of Nasser's regime except through what the media granted Egyptians access to. During the Sadat years, Nasser was still referred to as *al-Rayyis* (the Leader), *Baṭal al-Thawra* (The Hero of the Revolution), but Sadat soon came to assume his new position as *baṭal al-Ḥarb wa al-Salām* (The Hero of War and Peace) and also *al-Rayyis* (the Leader). Mubarak, too, got the label of heroism, *al-Baṭal al-Qā'id* (The Leading Hero). Every new "hero" diminishes the others; in the Mubarak years, Sadat was reduced to *ṣāhib qarār al-ḥarb* (the one who made the decision to go to war [against Israel]), while Nasser was only left his bare name, sans privileges, *Nasser* – a name often uttered among Egypt's working class fellows with a sad, nostalgic sigh.

One must give credit where credit is due. Nasser's regime provided free education for all Egyptians. My mother was able to send me to public school because of Nasser. Without Nasser, I would not have been able to afford an education. Nasser's advent was thus populist as much as it was anti-monarchic and anti-Islamist, a major shift in Egypt's modern political and cultural history. It gave hope for at least the idea of a new Egypt. And this new Egypt, this particular revolutionary Egypt, would represent the only political culture that would resist the monarchy; that is, resist the royal and imperially planted rule of a sole dynasty, and take a stand in the face of subordination and authoritarianism.

There are two main reasons why the promise of the welfare republic could not hold. The first lies in the understanding of what democracy means, a question that risks disrupting the legacy and the promise of the word "democracy" from Nasser to el-Sisi. The second reason is that this democracy, or the memory of Nasser's promise of democracy, inherited by Sadat, Mubarak, Morsi (the short-tenured and currently imprisoned Islamist President), and now el-Sisi, became the refrain of presidential speeches, the speech of utopia, the irony of all ironies, uttered and celebrated by dictatorial leaders violating it and ridiculing its very meaning.

All that was needed, the Egyptian intelligentsia agreed, was stability – good, persistent stability – because our country could not afford to continue to live in poverty and constant revolutions and wars. The intelligentsia had conflicting visions of the Egyptian *fallāḥ* (peasant) and which path was the best to follow to achieve this stability. Would Egypt be better off with a return to the premodern stability of Islam? Had this stability ever existed, or had it always been only a utopia of things past? Or was it yet to be found in a modern form of Islam? If so, what would that be? Or should Egypt be secular, European, trans-Islamic? The irony is that all, including Nasser, Quṭb, Ḥusayn, and Bākāthīr, wanted an Egypt that could address the central need for welfare and stability, post-colonization, and post-Revolution. But that crucial need for *istiqrār* (stability), has in the process of realizing itself, destroyed itself, precisely by getting carried away with itself, leaving behind it a history, or rather a memory, of a series of thwarted revolutions and of straw-man heroes who squandered the aspirations for democracy on the long path toward it.

Introduction

Prelude, Considerations, and Definitions

Reading literature, we learn to learn from the singular and the unverifiable.

Gayatri Spivak, A Critique of Postcolonial Reason

Production of Violence: Reflections on an Un-mastered Past

A video of the twenty-six year-old Egyptian journalist Aḥmad Samīr ʻĀṣim's filming his own death in the aftermath of the June 30, 2013 event as the military was taking over the country is perhaps the most poignant symbol of the state of affairs in Egypt now.[1] The young man was filming the President's Republican Guards at close range while they were shooting down civilians, only to have the sniper on film realize what the young man was doing, turn the rifle onto him, and kill him on the spot. The blackness that ensued, the brief and haphazard mechanical rolling of the empty film that no longer has agency or the purpose to tilt over and show us the brave young man as he lies dead in a pool of his own blood, signifies the worst return of the same, or, if you will, the saddening descent of Egypt into a state of political chaos.

The death of Aḥmad Samīr ʻĀṣim as he was recording barbarism – like the death of many other innocent Egyptians protesting the abuses of their government – is a grim reminder that even if democracy has not yet found a stable ground on Egypt's soil, the rule of law still remains the only way out of the vacant darkness of authoritarianism. While incidents like these might make it easy for the "West" to

[1] See www.independent.co.uk/news/world/middle-east/video-shocking-footage-appears-to-capture-moment-egyptian-filmed-his-own-death-through-his-lens-8700519.html; www.telegraph.co.uk/news/worldnews/africaandindianocean/egypt/10170307/Ahmed-Assem-the-Egyptian-photographer-who-chronicled-his-own-death.html.

re-absorb the "Egyptian" narrative into the usual colonial and postcolonial pathos – the masses hungry for the "Western" fruit of "civilization" and liberal democracy undone by their own "Oriental" traits of violence, irrationality, authoritarianism – the "Other" continues to struggle to find a way out of these customary traps of representation.

The event is one among thousands of recorded cases of military brutality against Egyptian citizens; it is indeed a logical continuity of colonial violence followed immediately by postcolonial dictatorships. This alone makes writing about Egypt's modern history a source of pain. But if we were to put this current crisis in a larger context, we would see that education is the backbone of every civilized society and the foundation of civic discourse and democratic government. Just as water does not suddenly come to the boil, but reaching 100°C is rather the culmination of a gradual heating process, so too is an ongoing process of education necessary for building a democratic society. It takes decades, perhaps even centuries, to establish a sound and reliable educational base. One's indignation at the politics of the democratically elected Egyptian president and his gang of brothers was naively assuaged when hearing about his removal from office and the suspension of the country's cryptic Constitution, as well as the disbanding and criminalizing of the Muslim Brotherhood as an organization. But taking a more discursive and analytical look at the current affairs in Egypt puts us face-to-face with an agonizing dilemma. How can one choose between the imperative for reclaiming the Revolution and the need to avoid a return to violence – and at what cost?

The heating up of the Egyptian political scene, as currently witnessed, is a symptom of a fundamental failure in education. Harvard Law Professor Noah Feldman denounces the events of June 2013 in Egypt "as a tragic setback for democracy, constitutionalism and the rule of law."[2] Whether or not we agree with Feldman that Egypt has fallen into "the rule of the mob," what needs to be recorded historically is that such a fatal breakdown in the democratic process is not a sudden occurrence but, rather, the result of an accumulated neglect that began more than a century ago. While ruling Egypt for twenty-four years, Lord Cromer, the British commissioner and consul-general in Egypt

[2] See Noah Feldman, "Democracy Loses in Egypt and Beyond" in *Bloomberg Review*, July 3, 2013. www.bloombergview.com/articles/2013-07-03/democracy-loses-in-egypt-and-beyond.

(1883–1907), vehemently opposed the establishment of a university, claiming that educating the Egyptians would create a class of graduates for which no jobs could be found, and would thus generate a problem of unemployment. Of course, there is more to this willful neglect of education than meets the eye.

Both the killings of peasants by the British Army of Occupation in colonial Egypt and the killings of Egyptians by the military in the post-colonial era are shameful records of barbarism. While one was practiced one hundred years ago by a colonizer, and the second by army officers, one must never lose track of the larger context of which these two events are grave symbols. As happened in the Denshawai Affair of 1906 and Egypt's military coup of 2013, official histories tend to process events, "smoothing out" the textures of pain, loss, and struggle, especially when the mapping of the new imperial world system comes into play, when the colonizer has long left the colonies and labeled them "third world," and when the colonized "Other" has inherited the baton of violence and come to terrorize and recolonize its own. I have addressed the Denshawai affair in more details elsewhere, drawing attention to the invention of Islamophobia and equation of Islam with barbarism as a legitimizing tool for colonizing Egypt.[3]

It is therefore crucial, in historicizing the turning inward of Egypt's high culture, to pose a different set of questions: Why did Egypt's culture and its dominant religion of Islam attain such dazzling crudeness just when British soldiers, politicians, engineers, and archaeologists were scheming to put together their colonial project? For the context of this study, and to extend George Steiner's salient interrogations of history's material reality outside language,[4] are there certain types or styles of language that lend themselves readily to embody this "material reality" more than others? These two questions trigger a third: Why would the novel and film art, chiefly notable for preoccupation with the individual, become the mode of choice for writing about colonized populations – about slaves, the disenfranchised, peasants – and about the rigid dogmas and madness by which these wretched populations are oppressed?

[3] See Mohammad Salama, *Islam, Orientalism and Intellectual History: Modernity and the Politics of Exclusion since Ibn Khaldun* (London: IB Tauris, 2011).

[4] George Steiner, *After Babel: Aspects of Language and Translation* (Oxford: Oxford University Press, 1975), 29.

In exploring these questions, it is important to emphasize that Egypt's heritage is not merely Islamic. The dictates of colonist and orientalist discourses have fashioned theories about the conflicts between civilizations. As a result of these essentialist theories, Islam came to be viewed as antithetical to, derivative of, or in complete denial of European influences on its cultures. A thorough history of this carefully constructed polarization between Islam and colonial modernity, and, more importantly, within a predominantly Muslim society like Egypt, is long overdue.

Take, for example, Britain's goal of creating a loyal middle class in Egypt without establishing a system of postsecondary education. Political and social institutions loosely modeled on metropolitan Britain were created in Alexandria and Cairo. The Egyptian elite were encouraged to participate in these institutions, although their design was inferior to the imperial models on which they were based. This participation, notes the political scientist Abdelslam Maghoraoui, "included defining the boundaries of the political community with the purpose of representing Egypt as the European masters wanted it to be represented: imitating Europe, but not quite European."[5] In other words, there is an inevitable and futile act of mimicry at work. "Like the Europeans who defined their 'self' against the non-European 'other,'" continues Maghoraoui, "Egyptian liberals defined their national identity in opposition to the Arabo-Islamic 'Other.' To construct a nation modeled after those in Europe, Egyptian liberals redefined the territorial, historical, racial, and cultural boundaries of the new Egyptian nation."[6] Significant writings produced in the early and mid-1920s, including 'Alī ʿAbd al-Rāziq's *al-Khilāfa wa Niẓām al-Ḥukm* (*The Caliphate and the System of Government*) and Ṭāhā Ḥusayn's *Fī al-Shiʿr al-Jāhilī* (*On Pre-Islamic Poetry*) fall within the period of Maghoraoui's study and seem to confirm his thesis by eschewing traditional Islam for the sake of a more secular and nationalist Egyptian identity. Of course, such works can easily be called political, not simply because they address political matters – e.g. when 'Abd al-Rāziq dismisses the *khilāfa* as a non-Islamic form of government, or when Ḥusayn changes the starting point for classical Arabic or Egyptian identity – but also because these works take sides in and leave memorable marks on the political

[5] Abdelslam M. Maghraoui, *Liberalism without Democracy: Nationhood and Citizenship in Egypt*, 1992–36 (Durham: Duke University Press, 2006), 69.
[6] Ibid.

confrontations and happenings in which they intervene, thus inevitably becoming part of the political discourse.

And yet intervention in colonial discourses is a double-edged sword. Once in Egypt, Britain sought hegemony over the population through coercion and suppression. The last thing the colonizer needed was an educated class that not only understood its rights but also could organize to fight for the country's independence. Cromer knew this formula quite well, as the educated elite were already causing turmoil in Egypt as well as in India. He knew that the best thing Egyptians could do – for the sake of the British Empire – was to serve as workers and as a labor force in agriculture and industry, so he fashioned his imperial policy to serve that very purpose. In this context, Cromer succeeded in the creation of an Egyptian boom and bringing order to what had otherwise been a messy financial slump since the time of Ismāʿīl.

One example of Cromer's "success" is found in enhancing the country's irrigation system and increasing the value of crops, especially cotton: he raised the crop from three million cantars in 1879 to eight million by 1907.[7] To administer an economically successful colony, Cromer needed peasants and serfs rather than teachers, lawyers, and engineers. Thus, he neglected the most fundamental and basic human right for a nation to grow organically and form a democratic government: education.[8] Cromer's intentions were clear. He asserts in *Modern Egypt*:

> Do not let us imagine that, under any circumstances, we can ever create a feeling of loyalty in the breasts of the Egyptians akin to that felt by a

[7] The cantar is an obscure measurement that has no exact equivalent, as it ranges from one cantar being equal to143–148 kg. Hence three million cantars would be around 430,000 tons. Eight million would be around 1,145,000 tons.

[8] According to the historian Joel Beinin, Egypt turned into a multinational stock house for European capital during the years of Cromer: "European capital was heavily concentrated not in industry but in loans to the government, financing cotton cultivation, and the construction of a transportation network to facilitate the import-export trade. The Suez Canal, opened in 1869, was the crowning achievement of foreign capital in Egypt. This resulted in the development of the export sector of the economy and its necessary infrastructure while other sectors were largely neglected. The earliest concentrations of wage labor in Egypt were in the transport and public utilities sectors of the economy – sectors developed by European capital to meet its needs. The only significant exception to this trend was the establishment of a large scale cigarette industry by predominantly Greek capital and labor in the years after 1875. By 1906 there were 55–60 cigarette factories in Cairo and some enterprises employed as many as 500 workers" (Joel Beinin, "Formation of the Egyptian Working Class" [*MERIP Reports*, No. 94, Feb. 1981], p. 15).

self-governing people for indigenous rulers if, besides being indigenous, they are also beneficent. Neither by the display of good sympathy, nor by good government, can we forge bonds which will be other than brittle.[9]

It is also clear, based on the record of his shrewd, pragmatic political strategy in Egypt, that Cromer sought to avoid at all costs any confrontation between the Egyptians and the Army of Occupation. If anything, Denshawai distracted Cromer from completing all the tasks of the colonial agenda that were assigned to him or that he assigned to himself. Prior to Denshawai, the major demand of the opposition was basic education and equal opportunity employment, with a view toward an improvement of the quotidian conditions for Egyptians. Local presses called for making education a right for all Egyptians and establishing a national university, an urgent need that was not fulfilled until the departure of Cromer from Egypt in 1907. Muṣṭafá Kāmil's newspaper, *al-Liwāʾ*, published numerous articles criticizing the High Commissioner for turning a blind eye to the education of the Egyptian people. *Al-Muʿayyad*, another local newspaper, denounced the practice of offering jobs to British and foreign subjects while denying them to Egyptians on the pretext that the latter were not educated enough.[10] Egyptian nationalists gained the impression that English education was not only privatized, catering to the elites as well as to the foreign minority, but also anglicized and tailored to produce submissive subjects. Clearly, educating the natives was never a part of the "civilizing mission" of British Imperialism. The point is that Cromer had a "quarter-of-a-century opportunity" to leave Egypt with a tangible promise toward self-rule, but he missed it; instead of supporting the education of Egyptians, marking his legacy by engraving his name on a public school or university, he chose instead to establish a tribunal, and marked his legacy with the blood of innocent Egyptians. But this book is about more than Cromer's Egypt; as the title suggests, it is, more precisely, about the relationship between Islam and the culture of modern Egypt. In order to introduce this relationship, the terms in the title must be explained.

[9] The Earl of Cromer, *Modern Egypt*, vol. 2 (New York: MacMillan Company, 1908), 570.

[10] See *al-Mu'ayyad* , November 13–14, 1893; November 28, December 23, 1894; January 14, February 17–19, March 17–18, June 25, 1895; January 20, March 13, October 28, 1900; February 3, June 16, 1901; March 4, October 8, 1902. See also *al-Liwā'*: January 30, February 11, 23, June 28, 1901; October 18–19, November 7, 1904.

Islam

To be a Muslim in Egypt today means living in a predominantly Sunni society, challenged by competing religiosities ranging from the conformist state-administered authority of Al-Azhar, Egypt's religious university, to politically oriented militant organizations such as the Muslim Brotherhood, *al-Jamāʿa al-Islāmiyya*, *Jamāʿat al-Takfīr wa al-Hijra*, and *Jamāʿat al-Amr bil-Maʿrūf wa al-Nahyy ʿan al-Munkar*, to pacifist and non-political groups such as *Jamāʿat al-Tablīgh wa al-Daʿwa*, and a variety of Sūfī sects. This was not the case at the outset of the twentieth century, when religious authority in Muslim Egypt was mainly represented by al-Azhar and remained so until the Muslim Brotherhood emerged as an alternative non-conformist religious establishment in the late 1920s. A situation of this sort is not unique to modern Egypt. Across time and space, Muslim societies have shifted their ideologies; specific religious or devotional practices are only understood, tolerated, fostered, or oppressed within specific historical, theological, and geographical contexts. It is difficult, if not perilous, to explore challenging insights – as acceptable as they might have been in the past – into a rigid dogma already at odds with itself, at once calcified and contested by its own intra-religious tensions. Because Islam, like all religions, maintains its very existence in the world through faith, it is unsurprising that the orthodoxy of Islamic faith, which was mostly represented by al-Azhar at the outset of the last century, would attempt to crush so-called "secularist" or enemies of Islam.[11] Secularism, a term coined in Europe in 1851,[12] was translated into Arabic in the early 1900s as *ʿIlmāniyya/ʿĀlamaniyya*, and is now hypostasized in Islamist (and public) discourse as a state of un-Godliness akin to *kufr* (disbelief). Secularism has undoubtedly influenced major transitions in decolonizing societies, including in Egypt, where a supposed "earlier cohesiveness or integrity of man's social

[11] For more on the nexus between Egypt's postcolonial despotic regimes and the reification of militant religious thought, leading to the emergence of radical Islam and the rise of dangerous and fractious epistemologies in religious thought by the likes of Sayyid Qutb and others, see Mohammad Salama and Rachel Friedman, "Locating the Secular in Sayyid Qutb," *Arab Studies Journal*, Vol. XX No. 1: 104–31.

[12] By G. J. Hoyaoke. See Eric S. Waterhouse, "Secularism" in *Encyclopedia of Religion and Ethics*, eds. James Hastings et al (Edinburgh: 1908–1921, vol. 11), 348.

and personal life," as Wilfred Cantwell Smith puts it, "once religiously expressed and religiously sanctified, has been fragmented."[13] As strong adherents found it difficult to compartmentalize their faith or to reconcile it with "worldly" aspects of societies, many proponents of the separation of mosque and state, including culture theorists and critics like 'Abd al-Rāziq and Ḥusayn, as well as secular leaders like Gamal Abdel Nasser, would immediately be targeted and labeled as enemies of Islam who must be killed or persecuted.

In the earlier decades leading to the formation of the Muslim Brotherhood and the rise of Nasserism, institutionalized religion had already created numerous challenges to independent Muslim thinkers. During the first quarter of the twentieth century, scholars with deep expertise in the culture of Islam, such as Muḥammad 'Abduh, were expelled from the academy due to its one-dimensional vision and selective use of the Islamic past. Ḥusayn, who joined al-Azhar in 1902, owes much of his intellectual development as an *'ālim* to the impressive teachings of al-Marṣafī, who was also accused of apostasy by the religious establishment for his non-traditional "scientific criticism" of pre-Islamic culture.[14] These tensions between liberal thought and traditionalism reflected a general mood on the part of the educated class in Egypt, although in today's terms 'Abduh's pleas for introducing Islamic philosophy and al-Jurjānī's work on rhetoric and Qur'ānic *I'jāz* (inimitability and apologetics discourse) into a rigid Azharite curriculum seem quite moderate; indeed, they can hardly be characterized as liberal at all. It is these interactions between persons of letters and clergymen of the letter that formed the roots of cultural *nahḍa* (renaissance/revival/awakening) in modern Egypt.

This cultural renaissance was built on institutional responses to the quotidian complexities of political and social life. The clearer the image of a modern Egypt independent from Britain was, the more Egyptian intellectuals began to disentangle Islam from the traditionalisms and mythologies accumulated throughout the centuries. In light of the fierce competition over who was best qualified to rule Egypt, there was a tremendous need for new propaganda campaigns.

13 Wilfred Cantwell Smith, *The Meaning and End of Religion* (Minneapolis: Fortress Press Edition, 1991), 124.

14 See Pierre Cachia, *Ṭāhā Ḥusayn, His Place in the Egyptian Literary Renaissance* (London: Luzac & Company Ltd., 1956). See especially Cachia's Chapter 11 on "Scientific Criticism," 143–66.

In response to the increasing intervention of foreign powers in Egyptian affairs, numerous Egyptian intellectuals began to look back to the formative moments of Islam – the roots of their own civilization – to try to recapture a sense of authenticity and legitimation for Egyptians. They also began to realize that the West has repeatedly imposed itself on Egypt in the forms of Christian or secular military campaigns and invasions. There was an overwhelming sense of the urgent need for a renaissance to resurrect a body politic that would be both Egyptian and Islamic, although the term "Egypto-Islamic" did not necessarily go unchallenged.[15]

By the beginning of the twentieth century, Britain's occupation of Egypt was becoming more and more customary and less and less of an event to the public. But for the Egyptian intelligentsia, political resistance continued in the form of nationalist resistance by figures like Muṣṭafá Kāmil, Muḥammad Farīd, and Saʿad Zaghlūl. Although Islam played a major role in their speeches and political agendas, it was not at all a dominant ideology in their ways of thinking. The educated Egyptians who grew up in the final years of the nineteenth century and imbibed secular calls for government, as well as the Islamic discussions of Jamāl al-Dīn al-Afghānī and Muḥammad ʿAbduh, reacted to those ideas in many of their writings; they included the pioneering poet Maḥmūd Sāmī al-Bārūdī and his successors, Aḥmad Shawqī and Ḥāfiẓ Ibrāhīm. While it is difficult to judge how many were influenced by these new ideas, prior to the birth of the novel in

[15] The Egyptian economist Fawzy Mansour attributes the *nahḍa* directly to local concerns among Egyptians and Arabs and to emergent nationalistic sentiments against British imperialism, and not, as commonly believed, to political reactionary responses by the Ottoman empire to gain control over its lost territories:

"It will thus be seen that the argument, now popular in fundamentalist circles that the Ottoman Empire protected 'fellow Moslem' Arab countries against the onslaught of European imperialism is false. The empire did not protect any of these countries against really determined invasion by a Western country. When such invasion took place, the empire created conditions favourable to a much more insidious attack, that of economic colonialism proceeding under the protection and privileges granted by nominal Ottoman sovereignty. Finally, when a country like Egypt attempted to secede and establish an autonomous, modern economy, the Ottoman Empire participated very actively in a consortium of European powers whose aim was to return Egypt to the fold of economic dependency and underdevelopment." Fawzy Mansour, *The Arab World: Nation, State, and Democracy* (Tokyo: United Nations University Press, 1992), 81.

Egypt, it is arguable that poetry reached an audience wider than did academic debates on religion. In any case, there is no doubt that such towering figures played an important role in shaping the Islamic tenor of the intellectual life of modern Egypt, stimulating fresh anti-establishment approaches to religion.

This new cultural perspective on religion was in every way informed by Egypt's encounter with Western Europe in the late nineteenth and early twentieth centuries, as it became apparent that, for the first time in Islamic history, the political dominion of Islam was fading and that the so-called Muslim *umma* [nation] was at the weakest that it had ever been – socially, politically, economically, and militarily. Al-Afghānī and 'Abduh strove to reposition Islam in relationship to this foreign "Other," but more importantly to itself. Metropolitan society in Egypt seemed to have featured a social hierarchy of Sunni Muslims, consisting first of Turks and Turco-Egyptians; secondly of Coptic and Jewish minorities; and thirdly of others: peasants, Bedouins, a few North Africans (Algerians and Tunisians), a few natives of India, and a considerable number of Sudanese. Both Afghānī and 'Abduh believed that the revival of the Muslim *umma* and the encouragement of national progress required a healthier sense of unity among all Egyptians and a more efficient religious institute; they therefore worked for a serious reformation of al-Azhar and its outmoded approaches to science and education. Al-Afghānī, though not an Egyptian native, had a remarkable influence on Islamic political thought in Egypt. His key position in regard to political reform consisted of a strong advocacy for Islamic foundationalism and for the reunification of all Arab and Muslim states. Al-Afghānī believed that the only way to end European colonialism and prevent Western Europe from occupying more Muslim lands was to re-empower the Islamic *caliphate*, which at this point in history was represented by the fragile Ottoman Empire, whose sovereignty over all Muslim *wilāyāt* (administrative divisions) worldwide was increasingly embattled.

'Abduh, in contrast, developed a more expansive agenda than al-Afghānī's, and took a less rigid stand toward sociopolitical and cultural reform. Unlike al-Afghānī, ʿAbduh cautioned against the return to foundationalism *per se*; instead, he called for a "neo-foundationalism," namely, a resurrection of core humanistic values in Islamic tradition. Espousing a comprehensive process that would include an *iṣlāḥ* (reform) not only of all religious institutes but also of social life, particularly in Egypt, and in the Islamic world in general, 'Abduh adopted a polity of honesty and self-criticism. He acknowledged, in a surprisingly laudatory manner, that "oriental nations have no ambition, little hope of life, and [a] willing[ness] to accept inferiority, while the Western nations have the highest and noblest of objectives."[16] In the end, neither 'Abduh's idealism nor al-Afghānī's caliphism were successful in producing well-defined and sustained political movements and parties. It is not far-fetched, however, to consider the Muslim Brotherhood as an offshoot of al-Afghānī's vision for modern Islamism.

It was not until the late 1930s that the Muslim Brotherhood became the face of Islamism in modern Egyptian politics. From that decade on, the Muslim Brotherhood has been involved in shaping the country's political course, gaining immediate popularity upon its emergence in 1928 at the hands of Ḥasan al-Bannā, perhaps in response to the abolition of the Caliphate/Ottoman Empire in 1924. *Al-Ikhwān* (the Brothers), as the Muslim Brotherhood organization called itself, gradually began to infiltrate the Egyptian cultural scene and establish centers all over Egypt. As the reign of King Fārūq (1936–52) widened the chasm between Egyptian peasants and the landed elite, the Muslim Brotherhood sympathized with the oppressed and the needy, becoming the principal home for the poor and disenfranchised majority of Egyptians seeking justice and economic sustainability in a sharply class-divided country. In the late 1930s and throughout the 1940s, the Muslim Brotherhood clashed with King Fārūq, and its founder, Ḥasan al-Bannā, became its major martyr upon his assassination in 1949. The Muslim Brotherhood continued post-Fārūq and assisted Nasser and the Free Officers in the soft, non-violent military coup of 1952 that overthrew the kingdom and established the Republic. Before long, the Muslim Brotherhood became the enemy once again when Nasser and the aspiring leader Sayyid Qutb did not see eye to eye on Islamic governance. This disagreement led to the arrest of many members of the Muslim Brotherhood as well as the imprisonment and subsequent execution of Qutb in 1966. The enmity between the Egyptian regime and the Muslim Brotherhood has continued from Fārūq all the way to Elsisi. Accruing victims/martyrs over its eighty-year existence, the Muslim Brotherhood gained legitimacy and sustainability as it continued to be the most organized and dedicated counter-government socio-political organization in Egypt.

[16] Muḥammad 'Abduh, "The Necessity of Religious Reform," in *Modernist and Fundamentalist Debates in Islam*, eds. Mansoor Moaddel and Kamran Talattof (New York: Macmillan, 2000), 48.

When the January 25, 2011 events took place, the lack of a central leadership with a clear post-Mubarak political agenda quickly led to the squandering of the hopes of the Egyptian Revolution. When the call for presidential elections was made, the only political body in Egypt prepared for leadership was the Muslim Brotherhood. Thus, it was not surprising that Egypt's new democratically elected president would be an *Ikhwānī*, nor was it at all shocking that Mohammed Morsi spent the first six months of his presidency re-delineating Egypt's "Islamic face." Until June 30, 2013, Egypt had a President-Imam who broke out in Qur'ānic recitations in the middle of his political speeches and who began surrounding himself with Muslims on the basis of their affiliation with and loyalty to the Muslim Brotherhood, rather than their professional merit or bureaucratic competence. Many Egyptians felt that, after more than eighty years as the political underdogs, the Muslim Brotherhood deserved a chance to establish the rule of law and social justice. To the revolutionaries, the ending of tyranny and autocracy was the be-all and end-all of the Tahrir Revolt, and the expectation, at that historic moment of mass revolution, was that the age of autocratic terror was over and that a new era of liberal democracy had been born.[17]

[17] As soon as he took office, Morsi began to fully Islamicize his presidential cabinet as a clever move, to his peril, to preempt any action to depose him. Seen within the context of the Egyptian political system, the Egyptian army's recent contravention of democracy/constitutionality and Abdul Fatah al-Sisi's rise to power may indeed appear to some to be the only hope for saving democracy from falling into a hopeless precipice of theocracy. Indeed, there is no democracy in theocracy, and Morsi's failure to respond to the pulse of the Egyptian street, as well as his exclusive partisanship, has ended the legacy of the Muslim Brotherhood, condemning them to a vicious yet familiar underground. Even though Morsi did Egypt a severe disservice during his short and unfinished term by continuing to solidify his Islamist base while seeking to transform the country into an obedient and compliant Islamist theocracy, we must nevertheless ask: Is a military coup or so-called "assisted removal" of a democratically elected president indeed the correct response, or, to present one alternative, should Morsi have been impeached through legal channels? While the popular upheaval of June 30, 2013 and al-Sisi's subsequent overthrow of Morsi has indeed crippled the Muslim Brotherhood's authority in future affairs for generations to come, history teaches us that military intervention is just another variation on the theme of despotic fundamentalism and an unfortunate testimony of Egypt's failure to sustain the core principles of its hard-fought revolution.

Culture

"Culture" is an ambiguous term, shot through with references and allusions that cross many disciplines. It is therefore important that I define as clearly as possible the sense in which I do and do not use "culture" in this study. I do not use it in the anthropological sense of examining patterns of human thought or behavior; nor do I do so in the sense of exploring the history of ideas, as for example in Edward William Lane's nineteenth-century *Account of the Manners and Customs of the Modern Egyptians* (New York: Dover, 1973) [1860]. I do so, rather, in the sense of a critical reflection on knowledge, in the spirit of Raymond Williams' entry on "culture" in *Keywords*. Williams concludes his entry by stressing the ambivalence of the term, which often results in outright hostility when it "involv[es] claims to superior knowledge, refinement and distinction between 'high art' (culture) and popular art and entertainment."[18] These are claims that Williams, of course, rejects. A recognition of this ambivalence is also present in the Arabic concept of *thaqāfa* (culture). Deriving from the Arabic root "ث ق ف," *thaqāfa* is etymologically related to terms for the art of sword fighting, for polishing arrows, and for the stinging taste of vinegar, as well as denoting perspicacity and sharp intelligence. The Egyptian literary critic Majdī Wahbah, in *al-Muʿjam al-Wasīṭ* of the Society of Arabic Language in Cairo, cites the following understanding of *thaqāfa* as the most commonly used definition of culture in Egyptian Arabic: "*al-thaqāfa hiya al-ʿulūm wa al-maʿārif wa al-funūn al-latī yuṭlab al-ḥadhq fīhā*" (culture constitutes all the sciences, epistemologies, and the arts that ought to be approached with critical perspicacity).[19] Wahbah's *thaqāfa* emphasizes inward receptions of and critical reflections on knowledge (especially in the context of colonial as well as comparative exchange of ideas). *Thaqāfa* can be distinguished from the work of departments of classics and archeology that aim primarily to shed light on the past, perhaps, in the process, making tenuous connections with the present. This contemporary academic focus is itself part of a

[18] Raymond Williams, *Keywords: A Vocabulary of Culture and Society* (Oxford: Oxford University Press, 1983), 92.

[19] Majdī Wahbah, "Mafhūm al-Thaqāfa" [The Meaning of Culture] in *al-Adab al-Muqāran* [*Comparative Literature*] (Giza: al-Sharika al-ʿĀlamiyya li-l-Nashr, 1991), 94.

new episteme, a post-enlightenment way of categorizing/classifying knowledge. As such, it is perhaps the dominant Foucauldian *énoncé* of our age on the historical and economic realities accompanying the production of knowledge – one which Wahbah associates more with *ḥaḍāra* (civilization), connoting historical traditions, whether classical, Islamic, pre-Islamic, or ancient Egyptian, than with *thaqāfa* (culture).

Wahbah's distinction between *thaqāfa* and *ḥaḍāra* is the main point of entry for the definition of culture in this study. Wahbah acknowledges that "*qad yaḍīq maʿaná al-thaqāfa ḥattá la yatajāwaz majālāt al-funūn wa al-ādāb wa baʿḍ jawānib al-ʿilm*" (culture could be used in a narrow sense to refer to arts and literature and some aspects of knowledge),[20] but he rejects this parochial sense. Many conflicting, narrowly focused, approaches attempted to account for the "culture" of modern Egypt. British colonialism was a nasty, brutal, and limiting reality, an imposition of Western modernity whose protracted consequences continue to be felt throughout Egypt. But it was France, not Britain, that played a major role in inspiring *les beaux arts* of modern Egypt. An intellectual current of Islamic thought, with various offshoots, also sought to position Egypt in opposition to and sometimes in symbiosis with the culture of Western Europe. An incipient Egyptianism was born out of the colonial experience in search of a national identity and a pathway for the future of culture in Egypt. Who is to say which of these components was more, or less, influential in the *thaqāfa* of modern Egypt? This book is therefore not an attempt to argue for dominant cultural ideology; it is an examination of the ontologically diverging, mutually informing, and continually ramifying currents that presented themselves in less commonly studied areas of cultural thought in modern Egypt.

Islam and the Culture of Modern Egypt thus encompasses certain cultural narratives – novelistic and cinematic – that have developed out of particular historical circumstances. Nationalism would be unthinkable without Denshawai and the denial of postsecondary education for Egyptians. Islamism would be unimaginable without the collapse of the Ottoman Empire and the official end of *al-khilāfa al-Islāmiyya* (Islamic Caliphate) in 1924. The Humanities could not be conceived outside the expatriation of Egyptian scholars, the influence of the French

[20] Ibid.

Revolution, as well as the romanticism and realism that flooded the French cultural milieu of the nineteenth and early twentieth centuries. Even existentialism, which influenced many modern Egyptian expatriates who traveled to France during and after the First World War, including Ḥusayn and al-Ḥakīm, would itself be inconceivable without both the crisis in European thought that resulted from the horrors and losses of the First World War and the growth in the academic and cultural prestige of the natural sciences *vis-à-vis* literature. Nasser's Pan-Arabism could not be envisaged outside a framework of the Second World War, the corrupt monarchy, the nationalist project, Britain's proxy colonialism, and so on. Although these connections may seem obvious, they must be re-emphasized in an age of shifting scholarly emphases, where rigorous intellectual histories are frequently demoted to "sub-cultures" in positivistic disciplines like anthropology and, more generally, in the social sciences, where cultural history is either ignored altogether or quickly dismissed as being irrelevant to a presumably dispassionate and non-essentialist historical framework.[21]

In fact, contemporary scholarship on Islam in modern Egypt has, for the most part, focused on the social sciences and the theology of the Ottoman empire, or what was left of it, rather than on the humanities, thus creating a noticeable epistemological imbalance. This unevenness has resulted in a bewildering separation between the social sciences and the humanities, raising varied questions of value, reliability, and verifiability in regard to national identity formations, the acquisition of knowledge, and historical accuracy. Even when the humanities is invoked, as I will elucidate in what follows, this invocation serves only to use "culture" to support a predetermined conclusion. The result is that most of modern Egypt's cultural heritage and its signifying documents (from archival pamphlets, to radical Islamist writings, to sermonic cassette tapes, to piety gatherings) has been surgically yet ahistorically sliced up by the so-called "deterministic sciences," falling prey to the lingering Eurocentrisms of positivistic disciplines in regard to what counts as evidence and what is to be dismissed as suspect, "singular, and unverifiable," to borrow Spivak's words.[22] A study of Islam and culture in modern Egypt – a study that

[21] Williams, *Keywords*, 92–3.

[22] I have addressed this notion of "anthropology from above" elsewhere. See e.g., Mohammad Salama, *The Qur'ān and Modern Arabic Literary Criticism: From Ṭāhā to Nasr* (London: Bloomsbury, 2018).

takes up culture not as institutional theology (whatever that entails) but as an artistic inheritance, a creator of traditions, a social practice, and as a deciding influence on questions of humanism and secularism – compels one to question common understandings of culture, to consider their implications and ramifications in a manner that expands and challenges both positivistic and structuralist approaches to Islam, especially in the matter of what constitutes verifiable historical documents for the study of Islamic cultures.

A good case in point is G. E. von Grunebaum's definition of influence and socio-religious transformations in modern Islamic societies. von Grunebaum conceives of influence as a phenomenon that is either internal or external. He defines the latter as "heterogenetic" and the former as "orthogenetic." To von Grunebaum, a heterogenetic influence is a phenomenon "noted when (a) a solution to a cultural problem, (b) a problem, or (c) both are introduced from outside into a system to which the problem and/or solution are not germane."[23] An orthogenetic influence or transformation, on the other hand, is one that emanates from within the community itself, more typically from a marginalized group that is "by no means alien to the community before the transformation sets in."[24] While von Grunebaum sees the two sides of influence as common in "the prevailing 'system'"[25] of most cultures, he contends that there is a characteristic tendency among receiving communities, and in this particular case among modern Muslim communities, to interpret heterogenetic changes as orthogenetic.[26]

This is where a rigid binary structuration of influences gets skewed. Even if we were to agree that influence could be sliced into two binary oppositional categories with such surgical and ahistorical accuracy, how is one, in a post-Orientalist age, to interpret von Grunebaum's characterization of Muslim societies as suffering from "psychological difficulties"[27]? Wouldn't a counterargument indeed be equally true, e.g. that there is a tendency in Orientalist scholarships on Muslim societies to view orthogenetic transformations as heterogenetic? While von Grunebaum acknowledges (in the margins) that

23 G. E. von Grunebaum, *Modern Islam: The Search for Cultural Identity* (New York: Vintage Books, 1964), 21.
24 Ibid., 20.
25 Ibid., 21.
26 Ibid., 20.
27 Ibid.

influence and transformation could be local and germane to their own native communities, he qualifies this definition of influence with an exteriority he deems inevitable, asserting that the "legitimate use of the word 'influence' has also been argued in cases where an outside impulse affects the intensity, or the quality, of the manifestation of an essentially native trait."[28] This approach to influence, which acknowledges yet disparages orthogenetic cultural transformations in Muslim societies, if such a term is indeed valid, and dismisses them as psychologically in denial, must be addressed and corrected before any materialist articulations of cultures can be useful.

Furthermore, in his last chapter, consciously or not, von Grunebaum uses 'cultural' instances from modern Egypt in order to advance a Eurocentric thesis. For instance, von Grunebaum characterizes Muḥammad 'Abduh as irreparably orthogenetic, that is, as denying Western contribution to the world and to Islamic cultural heritage. Von Grunebaum makes reference to a specific quote that he takes indirectly from 'Abduh's disciple, Rashīd Riḍā, in which 'Abduh early in his career is claimed to have said that, "there is nothing in books other than our own which adds anything to our heritage."[29] This is a gross mischaracterization of 'Abduh's legacy. In fact, 'Abduh's antagonism towards al-Azhar, which resulted in his final decision to resign in 1905, is predicated on al-Azhar's total dismissal of the tradition of reason and of the Western hybridization of Islamic philosophy which 'Abduh embraces and which, as he emphasizes, finds influence in Greek philosophy, notably the Aristotelian tradition. This acknowledgment is reflected in many works, including his important, but less studied, work on philosophers and Islamic *kalām*.[30]

Another example of von Grunebaum's tendentiousness is his discussion of two works by al-Ḥakīm and Ḥusayn, respectively, in which he asserts that Ḥusayn's 1938 *Adīb* (*A Man of Letters*) is superior as a work of literature to al-Ḥakīm's 1938 *'Usfūr min al-Sharq* (*Bird of the*

[28] Ibid., 21, n. 1.

[29] Muḥammad Rashīd Riḍā, *Tārīkh al-Ustādh al-Imām al-Shaykh Muḥammad 'Abduh* [*History of the Imam Shaykh Muhammad 'Abduh*], vol. 2 (2nd. ed., Cairo, 1925), 353. Quoted in von Grunebaum, *Modern Islam*, 351–2 (ft, 24).

[30] See al-Shaykh Muḥammad *'Abduh Bayna al-Falāsifa wa al-Kalāmiyyīn* [*Shaykh Muḥammd 'Abduh between Philisophers and Kalamis*], Vol. 1, ed. Sulaymān Dunyā (Cairo: Dār Iḥiyā' al-Kutub al-'Arabiyya, 1958). See especially Sulaymān's Introduction, pp. 3–64.

East) for no other reason than its protagonist's total rejection of the East and immersion in the West.[31] Based on his odd dismissal of al-Ḥakīm's text as scarcely amounting to a work of literature at all,[32] it is hard to see what theory of literary criticism or what tools of critique have allowed von Grunebaum to engage with two subtle literary texts, and to reach such conclusions other than on a superficial level of thin plot summaries where one protagonist rejects the West while the other embraces it. Indeed, his simplistic reading of both texts makes it difficult not only for the literary critic, but also for the informed reader to take seriously von Grunebaum's literary musings on al-Ḥakīm and Ḥusayn's novels. It seems that von Grunebaum's understanding of modern Islam's "search for cultural identity" – a peculiar title in its own right, conveying loss, disorientation, a stupefying predicament, and a *telos* of identity – is a scholarly project in which a version of Egypt's Islamic culture has become a product of a certain ideology if not a commodity for Western consumption. This type of academic determinism von Grunebaum employs to diminish 'Abduh's legacy and present him as a regressive anti-Western exclusivist reveals problematic orientalist biases that must be confronted by the sharp edges of historical materialism and cultural critique.

A cultural critique of Islam cannot and should not be reduced to abstract intellectual exchanges on Islam and modernity between Muḥammad 'Abduh and Renan, or to the problematic reification of theological institutions like al-Azhar and its demonization of revolutionary anti-establishment thinkers like 'Abd al-Rāziq, Ḥusayn, or Mahfouz.[33] Culture in its totality dictates that there should be as much Islam in al-Azhar *fatwá* (religious decree) or *awqāf* (endowments)

31 von Grunebaum, *Modern Islam*, 377–8.

32 Ibid., 375.

33 See Johanna Pink, "Where does Modernity Begin? Muḥammad al-Shawkānī and the Tradition of *Tafsīr*" in *Tafsīr and Islamic Intellectual History: Exploring the Boundaries of a Genre*, eds. Andreas Görke and Johanna Pink (London: Oxford University Press, 2014), 323–36. Pink's provocative and important study of the Yemeni exegete Muḥammad al-Shawkānī questions the accuracy of periodizational thought in discussing Islam (in this particular case, Qur'ānic exegesis) in relationship to modernity. Pink expertly deconstructs the modern/pre-modern dichotomy and conventional understandings of modernity/modernization as a condition that must have prompted shifts in exegetical contents as an attempt to "'catch up with' Western-dominated modernity and redefine the place of the Islamic cultural heritage with respect to a Western counterpart" (ibid., 324).

records as there is in a novel by Haykal or a film by Chahine. *Thaqāfa* includes the study of the artistic expressions of varied aspects of life and ways of understanding and living in the world under various doctrines, ideologies, or belief systems, which all are subject to the political, economic, and social realities of a given time. It is therefore crucial to conceive of a term like "culture" in all its Egyptian iterations as a concept that will allow us to rethink the history and influence of Islam on modern Egypt, especially in the aftermath of an era that seems to have forgotten how to think historically.

Modernity

Can we construct a culture of modernity as a political and artistic force free from the taint of imperialism? Can we ignore the fact that the promotion of a global economy of imperialism has always been coterminous with the denigration of nativist cultures outside of Europe? A simple and straightforward answer to these questions is "No." But this impossibility of viewing modernity apart from imperialism does not suggest that colonized cultures (always in the plural, within and among others – i.e. "culture" is never monolithic, never static, but always multiple, motive, contested) like that of Egypt would still pay homage to its own tradition and some resources in the forms and ideas of the very modernity imposed by that empire.

In the conclusion of "Modernity and Revolution," Perry Anderson writes: "Modernism as a notion is the emptiest of all cultural categories ... it designates no describable object in its own right at all: it is completely lacking in positive content ... what is concealed beneath the label modernism is ... a portmanteau concept whose only referent is the blank passage of time itself."[34] Pierre Cachia's questionable argument that there has been a "faintness of Islamic inspiration in modern Arabic literature" clearly demonstrates the limitations of this "empty notion."[35] Cachia's argument seems to find support in a

[34] Perry Anderson, "Modernity and Revolution," *Marxism and the Interpretation of Culture*, eds., Cary Nelson and Lawrence Grossberg (Urbana and Chicago: University of Illinois Press, 1988), 332.

[35] For an elaborate discussion of the complexity of modernism and modernity as definitive categories, see Richard Sheppard, "Modernism and Modernity: The Problem of Definition," *Modernism – Dada – Postmodernism* (Evanston, IL: Northwestern University Press, 2000), 1–30.

number of Egyptian writers, such as Ḥusayn, al-Ḥakīm, and Mahfouz, whose works figure as a genuinely emancipatory source for secular modernity in colonial Egypt. Take for instance Ḥusayn's provocative thesis in *fī al-Shi'r al-Jāhilī* (*On Pre-Islamic Poetry*), which attempts to prove that the Arabic poetry of the pre-Islamic era is actually not pre-Islamic but, rather, composed during and after the advent of Islam; or al-Ḥakīm's invocation of the Qur'ān to compose a play, *Ahl el-Kahf* (*The People of the Cave*), thematizing the helplessness of humans before time and the existentialist dilemma of life on earth, *à la* Sophocles. However, it is hard to argue that the writings Cachia cites do indeed stand apart from the dominant culture of Islam. In fact, all the authors cited by Cachia composed numerous texts either in response to various currents of Islamic thought – e.g. al-Ḥakīm's apologetic play *Muḥammad* (a belated yet powerful response to Voltaire's *Fanatisme ou Mahomet le prophète*, which he read in 1925), or Mahfouz's *Awlād Ḥāratinā* (*Children of the Alley*), which offers a history of God and addresses the relationship among the three Abrahimic religions – or as an attempt to correct widespread misconceptions of important events in the Islamic world, e.g. Ḥusayn's *al-Fitna al-Kubrá* (*The Great Sedition*). Although not included in Cachia's study, Ḥusayn's *'alá Hāmish al-Sīra* (*On the Margin of the Biography of the Prophet*) and 'Abbās Maḥmūd al-'Aqqād's *'Abqariyyat Muḥammad* (*The Genius of Muhammad*) are also cases in point. It is therefore parochial to claim that Islamic inspiration in modern Arabic literature is "faint," unless by "inspiration" Cachia refers to something quite arbitrary, like an attraction to fundamentalism. In any case, this attraction has infiltrated the intellectual paradigms of many modern Egyptian authors, including Aḥmad Bākathīr, Khālid Muḥammad Khālid, and Zakī Najīb Maḥmūd, most notably in Bākathīr's *al-Thā'ir al-Aḥmar* (*The Red Revolutionary*), which I discuss in Chapter 6. Islam has indeed offered modern Egyptian culture rich models for literary, cinematic, and philosophical expressions, allowing for the exploration of new levels of autonomy and transformation in the relation between God and desire, and morality and knowledge, as well as the sacred and the secular.

In order to address the history of modern Egyptian culture and its rich literary and cinematic traditions, and to raise theoretical questions about how its cultural movements are carried through space and time, it is important to examine how tenuous the demarcation lines are between the modern, the pre-modern, and the Islamic. How is a canon conceived of and perpetuated when it is based on a selective reading of its essential components and of its formative prehistory, which is at odds with historical reality? How do criticisms central to cultural representations of Islam in colonial and early postcolonial Egypt engage with the texts that both authors and scholars call modern? How do we examine this condition of the modern *vis-à-vis* Islam, colonialism, and decolonization? More importantly, if culture in its highest and lowest forms represents the degree of progress and development of a nation, how has colonial and early postcolonial Egypt experienced the dialect between Islam and the secular, between the doctrinal resolve to render the nation subservient to the purpose of God, and the urges of secular modernity to make it accountable only to itself?

Examining these questions and assessing the sway of the Islamic – in all its varied associations and stimuli – on the cultural history of modern Egypt, one must first have an understanding of the modern. It is neither fair nor correct to compare European modernity, for instance, to Egyptian, or Russian, or Latin American modernity. Time is not universal. Therefore, one must be careful of the ways that particular literary texts thrive within, through, and beyond local conditions and domestic norms that situate or displace, invoke or divorce, sacralize or vulgarize, revolt against or associate with, resurrect, cannibalize, or decisively break away from its so-called tradition.

Defining Egyptian modernity is not an easy task. Defining modernity is plagued not simply by the fact that even its artistic off-shoot, namely modernism, is a "portmanteau notion" that lacks "positive content," as Anderson puts it, but also by an almost endless proliferation and constant reproduction of definitions. Many such definitions – including those that are genre-oriented or departmental, as well as those that are historical, geographical, or both – have worked to defend or stake out territory for the modern in an ultimately stultifying manner; these definitions confuse more than they clarify. When we look closely at this proliferation of definitions, we see that each articulates claims about the essential truth of modernism, but most of these claims, particularly those that describe modernism as a category specific to Europe, are, without acknowledging the fact, responses to relatively recent historical developments. The indistinctness, multiplicity, and contingency of these definitions suggest that we have more to gain by observing how the terms "modern" and "modernist" are used, and how distinctions within them allow for a more informed understanding of their specific historical conditions, than we do by hypostatizing, and thereby universalizing, *the* "modern."

What then, one may ask, will a study of Islam and the culture of modern Egypt accomplish? Will we learn something different or "new" about Egyptian culture by way of modernity? Will we learn something about the ramifications of modernity from the perspective of a predominantly Islamic Egyptian culture? I hope I have positive answers to all these questions, but at least I aim to address them carefully. The principal objective of this study, however, is to investigate Egypt's encounter with both its own tradition(s) and those of Western Europe, and to assess the consequences of this encounter in order to re-think and to re-describe the experience of modernity in terms nuanced, neglected, and negated. I intend to do so not only from modernity's margins, but also from beyond the narrow perspectives of religious and nationalist paradigms dictated by those very margins. Overall, one cannot simply assume that the entire production of Egyptian literature and film during the colonial period remains necessarily "anti-Islamist" and anti-colonial, or that Egypt's experience of Western modernity through France and England is in all possibilities intrinsically harmful. The inherent and the monolithic are un-thinking companions. It is seriously misleading to insist that national sentiments, echoed in textual and visual narratives, are identical and indistinguishable, that the novel and film art speak for the nation, and that the nation categorically projects itself through its textual and cinematic narratives or that all "third world literature" is, in that sense, necessarily allegorical.[36]

[36] In regard to how "nation" functions here, see Benedict Anderson, *Imagined Communities: Reflections on the Origins and Spread of Nationalism* (Verso, 1991); see also George Mosse, *Nationalism and Sexuality: Middle-Class Morality and Sexual Norms in Modern Europe* (Madison: University of Wisconsin Press, 1988). In regard to so-called third-world literature, see Fredric Jameson, "Third World Literature in the Era of Multinational Capitalism" *Social Text*, 15 (Fall 1986), pp. 65–88. Jameson's article was the subject of many debates. With a situational consciousness of his own position, Aijaz Ahmad responded with a sustained critique of Jameson's claim, accusing Jameson's ideology of "dividing the world between those who make history and those who are mere objects of it." See Aijaz Ahmad, "Jameson's Rhetoric of Otherness and the National Allegory," *Social Text*, 17 (Fall 1987), p. 7.

I start, then, with the premise that modernity left modern Egypt with a moot question of identity, a typical postcolonial issue. Modernity, especially in its forceful colonial and cultural impact, is intertwined with the culture of Islamic Egypt: in the social and political life, in history, and in academic and nonacademic imaginings. Most definitions of the modern suffer from a de-anthropologizing of the term by treating it only as a distinct literary, artistic, visual, or philosophical category or movement; such definitions seek to extract something essential from it, often trying to find the common denominator of a modernism that exists within the various socio-cultural locations wherever it is encountered. But this commonality constitutes the surface and the blueprint through which we should begin to investigate "the modern" in Egypt. The industrialism of Europe's colonial modernity was felt so heavily that it propelled Egyptians to find themes and forms of expressions to reassert, question, or further explore their variegated identities. It therefore makes sense that perennial themes relating to Egypt's long history – including the pharaonic, the Mediterranean, and the Islamic – would increasingly compel authors alongside the theme of the country's encounter with colonial Europe. As I discuss literary and cinematic narratives produced by Egyptians, primarily for an Egyptian audience, the key question that invites itself and that permeates this study is the question of Egyptian, identity: What does it mean to be an Egyptian, who were the Egyptians, and who are the Egyptians now?

Yet, questions of identity are never easy to answer, precisely because of the complex and multiple ethnographic, religious, nationalist, and political ramifications surrounding the term. G. E. von Grunebaum attempted to find an answer to this question. In the opening chapter of his book, *Medieval Islam: A Study in Cultural Orientation*, he argues that the demarcation line between a medieval and modern Muslim society is simply a matter of identitarian priorities, that "throughout most of the Medieval Ages man is a Christian or Muslim first, a native of his own home district and subject of the local lord next, and only last a Frenchman, an Egyptian, or a German."[37] As the continued contestations of identity show us – contestations that, in part, constitute an identity as live, dynamic, operative – not only has such an essentialist

[37] G. E. von Grunebaum, *Medieval Islam: A Study in Cultural Orientation* (Chicago: University of Chicago Press, 1953), 1.

approach to medieval and modern Islam been exposed as incorrect in recent scholarships,[38] but the oversimplification of identity and casting it into the sacred-versus-secular debate also fails to recognize a web of intertwined religiosities, ideologies, localities, ethnicities, and nationalities that is far more complex than a hierarchical reduction to a Muslim-versus-Christian or a God-versus-the-state position can convey.

This view of continuously reshuffled human identities in response to changing priorities does not mean, however, that von Grunebaum's theory lacks a certain validity. After all, the experience of colonialism, the demise of the Ottoman Empire, the rise of nationalism, and the secularization of Egyptian legislative, judiciary, and executive authorities have changed the face of Islamic Egypt. Nonetheless, the realities one is left with is that there are considerably different historical and cultural conceptions both of what it means to be Egyptian and what it means to be Islamic.

For example, some scholars argue that modernity revived Islamic thought and compelled Muslim intellectuals to revisit and critique the tradition in which they situate themselves.[39] Another group of scholars differ on the definition of reform in relationship to modernity, and regard the Muslim scholars who engage in reforming their tradition in reaction to modernity, as missing the core understanding of Islamic reform.[40] A third group sees modernity as a pure nemesis of Islam and its cultures. Munīr Shafīq, for instance, offers a counter-enlightenment thesis on the mythologies of modernity and European progress. Shafīq argues that the term *nahḍa* (renaissance/revival) and its subsequent offshoots of *iṣlāḥ* (reform) in the modern Arab Muslim world signify an abandonment of Arab Muslim cultures and the

[38] See for instance, Muhsin al-Musawi's exposition of Orientalist periodizations in *The Medieval Islamic Republic of Letters* (Notre Dame: University of Notre Dame Press, 2015).

[39] See e.g. Albert Hourani, *Arabic Thought in the Liberal Age: 1798–1939* (Cambridge: Cambridge University Press, 1983).

[40] See for instance, Eltigani Abdulqadir Hamid, "The Concept of Reform in the Qurʾān" in *Coming to Terms with the Qur'an*, eds. Khaleel Mohammed and Andrew Rippin (New Jersey: Islamic Publications International, 2007), 3–33. While Eltigani advocates a different approach to Qur'ānic reform, notably through morphological exhaustions of terms like *fasād* and *Iṣlāḥ*, he seeks to rechannel traditional scholarly interest in associating the ideology of reform with modernity in Muslim thinkers like Muḥammad ʿAbduh and Rashīd Riḍā.

displacement of Islam with a Western culture. In other words, Shafīq considers the *Aufklärung* a project to be in "bad faith," and he sees the subsequent acculturations of Muslim societies an act of violent uprooting. To Shafīq, acculturation is tantamount to the extinction of the light of Islam, a foreclosure of its cultural networks, if not a total imperial imperative that Muslim societies comply with a new set of "ungodly cultures." Shafīq labels European modernity a threat to Muslim identities and its acculturation project as a barbaric erasure of Islam hiding under the garb of ridding Muslim societies of barbarism and bringing "civilization" to the world.[41]

In this respect, the veil is a complex and important trope for the process of acculturation by which societies subsume habits from the past and re-adapt them to new purposes. The veil has long been a traditional garb in Egypt, in the form of the *ṭarḥa* (head scarf) or other variations like the *ḥijāb*, *khimār*, or *ḥāyik* – among Copts and Jews as well as Muslims – which can be traced back to pre-Islamic times. In the present day, many Muslim women opt to wear the veil freely and willingly for genuinely faith-based reasons. However, what must be recorded historically is that the Islamic emphasis on decency and modesty of appearance for both and men and women, as equal inhabitants of the public space, has been co-opted into a patriarchal discourse that predated Islam, and the veil has become a prominent sign of gender oppression and inequality. The Western imperialists, in turn, employing a modernist discourse of liberation, pointed to the subjugation of women behind the veil of a calcified Islam as a justification for their own program of colonial subjugation. They did little, however, to liberate the veiled woman, since it was not in their interest to do so. Egyptian nationalists, in *their* turn, fell into the colonial trap of imaging and imagining the nation as a veiled woman who must be protected against the Western usurper. Women, literally and figuratively, thus became the fuel of Egyptian nationalism. The actual status of the veiled woman did not change, but the trope of the veil came to symbolize both the sacredness of the nation state and the prohibitions of a dominant patriarchal religion.

[41] Munīr Shafīq, *al-Islām fī Maʿrakat al-Ḥaḍāra* [*Islam in the War of Civilization*] (Lebanon: Dār al-Nāshir, and Tunis: Dār al-Burāq lil-Nashar, 1991), 61. See in particular Chapter 2, Section Five "Bāb fī Rafḍ al-Intiqā' iyya bayna al-Turāth wa al-Ḥadātha al-Gharbiyya" (A Section on the Rejection of the Eclectic [use of] Tradition and of Western Modernity), 81–5.

In the literary and visual culture of modern Egypt, we see how the *ḥijāb* trope changes its function according to the Islamist or Egyptian nationalist ideologies at work.[42] The Islamic *ḥijāb*, rather than the traditional Egyptian *ṭarḥa*, is markedly absent in most of the narratives selected for this study, including those by Ḥaqqī, Haykal, al-Ḥakīm, Idrīs, and even Chahine. In Ḥaqqī and Haykal, the veil trope does not appear literally: if there is a veil, it is a figurative one, the veil of ignorance and bias which blinds the nation to social justice and the restoration of reason, until it can triumph over stifling and antiquated tradition. Ḥaqqī's peasants in the *Virgin of Denshawai* are metaphorically veiled; they are the victims left in the dark, whose credulity, as depicted in the trial scene of the novel's eighth chapter, is revealed in order both to produce laughter and to deepen the reader's sense of the barbarism of the occupation as it finds ways to justify the killing of naïve and innocent civilians. Think of a deceptive killer leading blindfolded and trusting victims to their death.

Unlike Ḥaqqī, Haykal opts to face the veil of traditionalism openly. That is, Haykal chooses direct confrontation over subtle allegory, and self-critique over tongue-in-cheek satirizing of the barbarity and vulgarity of the dominating "Other." In Haykal, the entirety of Egypt is veiled in unhealthy traditionalism, making the trope an urgent call for Egypt to cast of the veil of ignorance and customs in an act of rebirth and liberation.

These varied critiques of the veil from within a predominantly Muslim society are quite ironic when compared to the enormous body of Western writings on Islam, from Lord Cromer to Stephen Harper, where the *ḥijāb* becomes a prominent symbol of the East–West divide and a metonym for oriental repression versus Western liberalism.[43] In further irony, the veil would loom large on the Arab/Muslim colonial scene mid-century when Frantz Fanon discusses the unveiling of

[42] This metonymy has also been discussed in various colonial and postcolonial discourses. See for instance, Partha Chatterjee, *The Nation and Its Fragments* (Princeton: Princeton University Press, 1993), 23.

[43] See Cromer *Modern Egypt*; see also *Leila Ahmed, Women and Gender in Islam* (New Haven: Yale University Press, 1992), 153. See also Katherine Bullock's chapter "The Veil in Colonial Times" in *Rethinking Muslim Women and the Veil: Challenging Historical and Modern Stereotypes* (London: The International Institute of Islamic Thought, 2002). See Mohammad Salama, "It's the Niqab Again: Stephen Harper and the Barbarism of Politics" (Stanford: Arcade Blog, October 19, 2015).

Algeria in *A Dying Colonialism*, an unveiling that receives yet another nationalist twist in the dramatic secularization the viewer witnesses in Chahine's film on the Algerian war of independence.

Modernism

In cultural terms, Egyptian modernism is among those "other" non-European modernisms that have often been studied not as a mirror or a reflection of a Western ideal, but tangentially and epiphenomenally. Due to the domination of this view of modernism in the Arab world, the term "modernism" in modern Arabic criticism has acquired more stability than it has in the West, a reification that leads many critics to take the term for granted.[44] For instance, a study of modern Arabic poetry by Ṣalāḥ Faḍl refers to *al-ḥadātha* (literary modernism) as a flood that has almost drowned the essential qualities and uniqueness of Arabic literature. The monstrosity of Arabic poetic modernism, according to Faḍl, consists mainly of a variety of factors that have caused inordinately rapid and inappropriate changes to the field of Arabic literature, both thematically and stylistically. To present this case thoroughly, I quote Faḍl's summary at length:

> The first factor is the eruption of many schools of poetry in a short historical span, beginning with the resurrection school at the hands of al-Bārūdī, which continued with Shawqī, Ḥāfiẓ, al-Zahāwī, and al-Raṣṣāfī throughout the first decades of the century… But before this movement even came to end three other schools of poetry emerged, representing the so-called 'broken wings of romanticism', to borrow Jibrān's catchy image: (1) the immigrant-school with its prophets and disciples who range from Jibrān to Mīkhā'īl Nuʿayma to Īlīyā Abū Māḍī, and others; (2) the Dīwān School in Egypt, with the leadership of poets like al-ʿSchoo, Shukrī, and al-Māzinī who used the Romantic theory of English literature to critique the school of al-Iḥyā', but ending up producing a different and non-popular style of poetic composition; (3) the Apollo school, which was founded by Aḥmad Zakī

[44] See for instance Aḥmad Haykal, *Taṭawwūr al-Adab al-Ḥadīth fī Miṣr* [*The Development of Modern Literature in Egypt*] (Cairo: Dār al-Ma'ārif, 1971); Anas Dāwūd, *Usif, fī al-Shi'r al-'Arabī al-ture i* [*Myth in Modern Arabic Poetry*] (Cairo: Maktabat ʿAyn Shams, 1975); Shawqī Ḍayf, *Dirāsāt fī al-Shi'r al-'Arabī al-Mu'āṣir* [*Studies in Contemporary Arabic Poetry*] (Cairo: Dār al-Ma'ārif, 1959). See also Alī 'Ashrī Zāyid, 'An Binā' al-Qaṣīda al-'Arabiyya al-Ḥadītha [*On the Structure of the Modern Arabic Poem*] (Cairo: Maktabat Dār al-'Ulūm, 1979).

Abū Shādī and chaired by Shawqī. The third wing represents the eruption of *Shi'r al-Taf'īla* [Free Verse] and its concomitance with the rise of nationalism in Iraq, Lebanon, Syria, and Egypt. This school shattered the Arabic poetic tradition, changed poetic forms, and took up Arab socialist, ideological, and nationalist themes. The prominent figures of this school include al-Sayyāb, Nāzik al-Malā'ika, al-Bayatī, Nizār Qabbānī, 'Abd al-Ṣabūr, Ḥijāzī, Khalīl Ḥāwī, and many others.

The second factor is the inability of educational institutions to catch up with the speed of these movements; most of them dwelled too much on the resurrection phase while quickly dismissing the romantic school. Add to this, the slow and uninformed journalistic criticism which failed miserably to comprehend or assess the magnitude of change in modern Arabic poetry.

The third factor lies in creating foreignness and defamiliarization in Arabic poetry, which confused poetry readers and deprived them of the straightforward and direct message of the traditional poetry they were used to, to the extent that some recent poetic productions appear as if they are pale translations of texts that belong to other continents and other alien cultures.[45]

Faḍl's approach to the loss of traditional poetry is nostalgic and yearns for a time when poetry was the "musical voice of the political and social life," when it was "front-paged on daily papers" because to him, the traditional *qaṣīda* better reflected the pulse of "the political, social, and economic events."[46] According to Faḍl, modernism happened "too quickly and too soon" for Arabic literature, creating a gulf between readers and texts and alienating art by embracing difficulty and abstraction. Poetic Modernism in Faḍl's eyes is "haughty," "irresponsible," and "at risk" of losing both the music and the deep significations that characterize the traditional *qaṣīda*:

Modernism is a movement of speed, one that alienated the reader and rushed the Arabic language into losing its organic genuineness without allowing the opportunity for steady development so it could pull forward the heavy train of Arabic culture and not just one compartment at the expense of all others.[47]

45 Ṣalāḥ Faḍl, *Taḥawwulāt al-Shi'riyya al-'Arabiyya* [*Transformations of Arabic Poetics*] (Al-Hay'a al-Mis of A al-'Āmma lil-Kitāb, 2002), 8–10.

46 Ibid., 11.

47 Ibid.,16. Faḍl's criticism of modernism as "too fast, too soon" is indeed part of a defense of an orthodoxy that likes to believe that the end of classicism is the also the end of art. Hence Faḍl's persistent concern that the transformations brought by *al-ḥadātha* have deformed the so-called integral and unified body of the Arabic *qaṣīda*. It is evident from Faḍl's criticism of what he perceives as the negative effects of literary modernity on Arabic literature that there is a remarkable tension between literature and literary criticism.

Faḍl does not address various understandings, but he chooses instead to emphasize the invasive implications of a modernism expanding beyond the Western paradigm. Instead of seeing modernity as a foreign invasion, it would have been more effective to search for the possible existence of a new kind of reality in the text of an "Other" literary tradition. Criticism indeed benefits from discovering a new literary constellation, a space and time between coherently related differences in European and Egyptian modernisms, and to limn therein a set of possibilities that allows what we call modern Egyptian literary and visual culture to respond to shared aspects of various historical and socio-political contexts. Even if Egypt's cultural modernity is, because of colonial imposition and absorption, only thinkable in relation to the West, the emergence of the modern does not concern the West alone. What remains at stake is the possibility of arriving at a far-reaching understanding of the modern, one that cannot and will not happen without transcending the geopolitical confines of European modernity. Modernity both led and followed European troops; when the troops returned home, modernity lingered behind. If there is to be a more historically and aesthetically informed understanding of what defines the modern, this understanding is not to be found only where the ball was kicked when the project of modernity was "launched," but also where that ball landed and on the new grounds that received it.

It is therefore crucial to address some specific issues. The first is the necessity of reading literary and visual culture not merely as a conglomerate of socially representative texts, but also as "textual events" in themselves. This reading enables us to see in modern Egypt at times a clarion tension, and at others, a reconciliation between Islam and modernity. From this point of view, a broader comparison between Europe's culture of modernism and Egypt's is not entirely far-fetched. Nor is Faḍl's characterization of the unnatural speed with which it shattered the tradition of the Arabic *qaṣīda* any less of a "catastrophe" than what Frederic Jameson sees in Western modernism.[48] What he has said of European modernism – that it "dashes … traditional structures and life ways to pieces, sweeps away the sacred, undermines immemorial habits and inherited languages" – is true of

[48] Fredric Jameson, *Seeds of Time: Utopia, Modernism, Death* (New York: Columbia University Press, 1994), 84.

Egyptian modernism as well. Much like Percy Bysshe Shelley's quibble with conservative theology, although he is hardly a modernist, which led to his dismissal from Oxford in 1811, Ḥusayn's philological project on pre-Islamic poetry, where he separates scriptural from historical narratives, led to his dismissal from the university in 1932, a punishment for the launch of cultural critique in modern Egypt.

Other examples of this Jamesonian shattering abound in the high art of modern Egypt; like Goethe's Faust, al-Ḥakīm's Qur'ānic protagonists lose their faith and surrender to the absurdity of human existence. In *Hams al-Junūn* (*The Whisper of Madness*) Mahfouz's madman brings the reader back to a Degree Zero of minimal reason only to take this reason away altogether and surrender to a universe of disorder and insanity, where neither God nor humanism can save the world from its own recessive genes of self-destructiveness. The text preoccupies itself with the question of insanity and its mysterious causes. However, unlike Foucault's *Madness and Civilization*, which critiques the history of reason in the Age of Reason by offering a history of its opposition, namely, madness, Mahfouz's short story invites the reader to wonder how writing about madness is even possible in the first place. Thus, the specifically modernist features that mock conventional structures and de-auratize the sacred, in the Benjaminian sense of the modern function of art in a technological age of reproducibility, are clearly reflected in Egyptian narratives of the first half of the twentieth century. The characters in both al-Ḥakīm's and Mahfouz represent not only the disdainful antithesis of the most venerated pillars of holiness (reason and/versus faith), but also, and quite sardonically, the complete farcicality of human existence. The catastrophic breakdown of these protagonists is tantamount to total nihilism. Narrative burns the bridges between God and humanity, puts humankind face-to-face with a wasted earth, and tears asunder the divine contract of a promised Elysium.

Like Mahfouz's "The Whisper of Madness" and al-Ḥakīm's *The People of the Cave*, Yūsuf Idrīs's novella *Jumhūriyya-t-Faraḥāt* (*Farahat's Republic*) is a variation on the theme of the loss of faith, except this time it represents disillusionment with Nasser's socialist utopia. The text cleverly satirizes Nasserism through the character of a powerful yet uneducated police sergeant. The writing of *Farahat's Republic* coincides with a time in Egypt when Nasser's attempts to develop a welfare state had come to a critical impasse. With the birth of the so-called "third world," social harmony did not seem far from possible, a "happy" republic (to invoke the literal Arabic meaning of Idrīs's hero, Faraḥāṭ) appeared achievable, and the Utopia the Egyptians have been dreaming of almost became a reality. Idrīs's novella dispels this utopian myth through one of the darkest satires in modern Egyptian narrative.

Such disillusionment did not, however, take place in the Egyptian film industry of the 1950s. Given the influence of the West on contemporary film, since its inception, film art has not been particularly welcome on Egyptian soil by various groups of Islamists. Even before the Muslim Brotherhood was established, numerous fundamentalist circles opposed the film industry altogether. This opposition grew out of a belief that film was anti-Islamic and damaging to Muslim sensibilities and the morality of the masses. Opposition extended to other performative arts, including theater, acting, dancing, ballet, and all art forms involving personification and characterization, especially of historical events and figures of the Islamic past. Because of the popularity of its visual representation and its clever approximation of "reality," but, more importantly because of, as Jameson puts it bluntly, the fact that film is "essentially pornographic," Islamists paid film their special attention.[49] Between 1926 and 1927, religious authorities of al-Azhar opposed the establishment of a film industry in Cairo, registering their grave concerns over the possibility of any disrespectful representations on the screen of the Prophet Muhammad or the companions of the first Muslim community.[50] In 1930, and only three years following its establishment in Cairo, *Jam'iyyat al-Shubbān al-Muslimīn* (Association of Muslim Youth) submitted an official grievance to Egypt's Prime Minister, which it also leaked to the media, objecting to a foreign film industry's plans to use Egypt as a setting for the story of the life of the Prophet

[49] In his exploration of the film industry and its surrounding culture, Fredric Jameson examines the relationship between the imaginary world of the film and the external world unto which it screened. Jameson starts his work with the powerful statement that "[T]he visual is essentially pornographic" and that "films ask us to stare at the world as though it were a naked body." Fredric Jameson, *Signatures of the Visible* (New York: Routledge, 1992), p. 1.

[50] See J. Swanson, *Mudhakkarāt Mu'assis Ṣinā'at al-Sinimā fī Miṣr (Memoirs of the Founder of Film Industry in Egypt)*, a collection of articles in *Dunyā al-Kawākib*, 1953–1954 (*Dunyā al-Kawākib*, Jan. 12, 1954), pp. 26–7. See also *Al-Ahrām* (Daily), Dec. 4, 1951, p. 6, and *Aakhir Sā'a*, Dec. 29, 1954, p. 16.

Muhammad and his companions.[51] Following a series of complaints, Islamic authorities in Egypt asked for stricter parliamentarian rules to censor cinematic productions and screenings of romantic films.[52] The Egyptian government was careful to censor film in order not to yield to complaints by Islamists, which would give them a say in dictating cinematic taste. But there were few occasions when the Egyptian government actually succumbed to the Muslim Brotherhood's demands to ban certain films. For instance, the short sketch *Bint al-Jirān* (*The Neighbors' Daughter*) was banned on account of using sexually suggestive language and a girl's private bedroom as the film's *mise en scène*.[53] This very tension squarely situates film at the very heart of the conflict between the sacred and the secular, and makes film a powerful vehicle of the critique of the culture of modern Egypt.

With Nasserism, Egyptian film became the object of a new form of power capable of manufacturing a whole cluster of practices and forms of knowledge under the rubric of nationalism. Chahine's eponymous film on the Algerian case of Djamila Bouhired is manipulated by a socialist regime to inculcate its message to the masses, which is itself a modern phenomenon. This visual propaganda helps define Egyptian nationalism in the 1950s through a basic reformulation of film art into a tool for the nationalist discourse. This is where a critique of visual culture narratives becomes necessary in order to situate events in the context of a larger statement of sociological, political, educational, and cultural sensibilities. Such institutional recruitment of an entire film industry in the service of the regime confirms the Foucauldian formula that history is not the result of individual ideas; it is, rather, based on discursive structures beyond subjects. This is what allows us to reconsider not only the place of visual and literary representations in relationship to Islam in modern Egypt, but also the place of Islam itself in relationship to those very representations.

While the chapters in this book juxtapose Islam to the question of modernity and modernism in Egyptian culture, the task is not to

[51] See *Majallat al-Shubbān al-Muslimīn*, Ramadān 1348 (Feb. 1930), pp. 356–7.

[52] See al-Balāgh, July 18, 1936. See L.V.V.'s summary of this demand in *Oriente Moderno* (Monthly, Rome), Vol. XVI, Sept. 1936, p. 531.

[53] See Al-Akhbār al-Jadīda, July14, 1952, p. 8. The incident was also reported in al-Miy14 (daily), July 14, p. 10. Similarly, an Egyptian documentary on the Sudan was banned after a week of screening in Cairo because it included naked scenes of local Sudanese men. See *Jérusalem Post*, Mar. 22, 1954.

argue that the culture of modern Egypt represents one particular configuration of Islam, modernity, film, fiction, and postcolonial ideologies. Indeed, investigating this complex interweaving or, to use a more accurate metaphor, this abrupt clashing of Egypt's local Islamic tradition with modernity, is a challenging project for two important reasons. First, there are controversial views on whether or not the Egyptian cultural scene assimilated or resisted the onslaught of European modernity; these contestations both inform my resistance to any monolithic Egyptian "scene" in the singular and influence my turn to diverse expressions, such as the novels and films I discuss below. The fact that all of these texts offer versions of Islam provides an important opportunity for insight into what one might call the cultural expressions of Islam in modern Egypt in the era of imperialist modernity.

The second reason, based on the first, but not entirely dependent upon it, takes us back to the question: What is an Islamic culture? How should we live (with) it? Can it be progressive and liberal, or must it be regressive and fundamentalist? Might this question itself, especially in regard to Islam, reflect a modern project based on linearity, (differential) freedom, and binary logic? When we speak, say, of the enlightened thought of Muḥammad 'Abduh, the increasing influence of the Muslim Brotherhood, the polemical reification of Nasserism, the intellectual acuity of Ṭāhā Ḥusayn, the novelistic genius of Naguib Mahfouz, the cinematic shrewdness of Youssef Chahine, the vocal charm of Umm Kulthūm, the political assassination of Ḥasan al-Bannā, or the radicalization of Sayyid Qutb, we are framing the discourse in a way that seems, implicitly, to refer to major events that are unique to modern Egypt. Is this uniqueness, then, a "common" trait, ironic as it seems, that could necessarily teach us something about modern Islam as an event and a postcolonial condition?

The word "event," whose Arabic equivalent "*ḥadath*" shares the same root as "modern" and "new," reminds us of yet another event: the emergence of the novel and film as new literary and visual narratives alongside the long-established genre of classical poetry. What does this supplement of *ḥadath* signify at this particular juncture in modern Egypt? There is no single, straightforward answer to this question. However, if the most important aspect of the work of art as a cultural production is "what it does not say," as Pierre Macherey contends, then a juxtaposition of these texts, in light of both their local Islamic characteristics and their broader interactions with colonial modernity, is of critical significance for a more informed understanding of Islam and the culture of modern Egypt.[54] A reductionist probing for signs of Islam and modernism by a "faithful" examination of texts in isolation can only result in a myopic assessment, on the one hand, of the structure and value of the texts themselves and, on the other, of the importance of the arts in general for a cultural and historical understanding of the *thaqāfa* of Islam and the culture of modern Egypt.

[54] The French text reads as follows: "*ce equi est important dans une oeuvre, c'est ce qu'elle ne dit pas. Ce n'est pas la notation rapide: ce qu'elle refuse de dire.*" Pierre Macherey, *Pour Une Théorie de la Production Littérature* (François Maspero, Paris, 1966). See also Pierre Macherey, *A Theory of Literary Production*, trans. Geoffrey Wall (London: Routledge and Kegan Paul, 1978), 87.

1 *History Matters*

But then some strange event happened to Egypt during those times. This nation, which many thought had surrendered to its fate and had become an invalid, suddenly rose in the year 1919 supporting its leader Saʿd Zaghlūl and demanding its right to life and its right to independence. National feelings boiled over the entire populace and many people lost their lives. It was in the heart of this revolution that the music of Sayyid Darwīsh and the modern school of literature emerged. Both came as a result of a dire need for a new popular art with genuine expressions, one that is free from imitations and borrowed tropes.[1]

Yaḥyá Ḥaqqī

History teems with markers that invite us to decipher its many codes and categorize events as crises of one sort or another: wars, liberations, occupations, migrations. History is 1492, 1616, 1776, 1789, 1882, 1924, and 1952. History is also the Scramble to Africa, the First and Second World Wars, Hiroshima, and Apartheid. In today's Western academia, however, history has acquired a different materiality and has become a discourse of selectivity and intellectual bias, one whose very composition is dictated by the politics of the present. Fredric Jameson has repeatedly reminded us that history cannot be reduced to text, yet it is only made available to us through text. History is text, then, plain and simple: an incomplete act of language, incomplete because history is more than just the semantic arrangement of words on a page and because language itself – as a communicative system of signs – will always be lacking the evidentiary "referent" to support the veracity of the (hi)stories we tell. What counts as a document of history, then? What gets emphasized, glorified, and celebrated when we choose to write history, and what remains left out, entombed, silenced, or repressed? Is it far-fetched to argue that in language there is no such thing as history, that the only

[1] Yaḥyá Ḥaqqī, *Fajr al-Qiṣṣa al-Miṣriyya* [*Dawn of Egyptian Narrative*] (Cairo: n.p., 1960), 75–6.

history there is a series of impressions, a history that always calls itself into question? This questioning brings us face-to-face with the inadequacy, suspect nature, and susceptibility to manipulation not just of the so-called official documents of history, but of all systems of representation when it comes to genuine understandings of history.

One of those systems of representation is historical biography. While biographies are one of the most intriguing ways to engage with history, they are seldom written with attention to the larger contexts. This is not the case, however, with Roger Owen's *Lord Cromer: Victorian Imperialist, Edwardian Proconsul.*[2] The book's title and overall composition cleverly position us within the epistemological complexities of the life of one of colonial England's most prominent figures. An eminent historian of the modern Middle East, and especially of its economic histories, Owen delivers the most exhaustive and comprehensive study of Lord Cromer's life to date. Owen's thesis is abundantly clear: Cromer possessed an impressive and under-appreciated financial talent. Cromer's successful efforts to solve Egypt's complex economic crisis and navigate her out of debt must be understood, and appreciated, within the framework of "economic globalization, rather than empire per se."[3] In his book, Owen shows mastery in capturing and detailing the circumstances (that he was able to find) of Cromer's life, which shaped his mastery of economics. Owen thus sheds a new light on Cromer. While admitting to certain shortcomings, such as arrogance and lack of political savvy, Cromer, Owen argues, is "better seen as an energizer, a coordinator, an implementer, a problem-solver, and an apologist" – he urges the reader against subsuming Cromer's legacy under nationalist metanarratives and dismissing his rescue of Egypt from financial ruin and his genuine care for Egyptians.[4] This care manifested itself in Cromer's insistence, as Owen writes, on "the importance of low taxation," "listening carefully to the uncensored views to be found in the vernacular newspapers," and "sympathy with the peasant population."[5]

While many historians of colonialism and Islam in modern Egypt might find Owen's "care" argument unconvincing, especially Cromer's alleged "sympathy with the peasant population," it is not the intention

[2] See Roger Owen, *Lord Cromer: Victorian Imperialist, Edwardian Proconsul* (Oxford: Oxford University Press, 2004).
[3] Ibid., 400.
[4] Ibid., ix.
[5] Ibid., 86.

of this study to examine in detail Owen's premises. Other writers, notably Daniel Gorman, John Fisher, Saul Kelly, and M. E. Yapp have already reviewed Owen's book and critiqued its main tenets, and many, including Edward Said, Timothy Mitchel, Zachary Lockman, and Leila Ahmed, have exposed the Orientalist underpinnings of Cromer's imperial discourse. But since Cromer's commission in Egypt serves as the prehistory of this study, Cromer's legacy invites a different set of questions relevant to Islam and modernity in Egypt: What makes a political master of Late-Victorian and Edwardian imperialism a hero or a villain in the consideration of modern Egypt? More broadly, what historical narratives, tools, and vocabularies guide our visions in understanding the antipathy of modern Europe toward Islam, and what academic goals channel our thoughts in writing such narratives? For whom do we write them? Why, and especially, why *now*?

Dwelling on the life and achievements of a Victorian imperialist who spent twenty-four years ruling a foreign country in devotion to the colonial enterprise of his own country is never just one economic historian's task alone. Surely a broader perspective than economic history is essential for a fuller assessment of Egypt's colonial experience. Even in an important field like Owen's, the task is so complicated that it would require a cluster of economic historians to examine it adequately. Imperialism "over there" is also a disaster at home. If we take the date of 1882 – the year England defeated 'Urabī, destabilized France's colonial scheme in Egypt, and exhibited its military power – as the establishment of a new imperialist system in Egypt, if not the whole of Africa, then a variety of social, political, and cultural events would come to mind. It is historically legitimate, no doubt, to approach a personal biography using certain theories of imperialism whose political focus is exclusively on "globalization," "world market investment," and "economic crisis" as the pre-context for governance in the colonies (in however revisionist a fashion this might be). But the stakes in colonial history are much higher than those in personal biographies. To act on an assumption of impartiality and ethics underlying the motivation of imperialism, regardless of the imperial actor in question, would indicate that we have learned nothing from the experience of colonialism. To do so faces the risk of dissolving one historical context in another, of losing sight of the historical specificity of the colonial encounter, and of dispersing the event of imperialism – the event that *is* imperialism itself – in a fashionable array of specialized political theories.

The very obvious point that imperialism has a systematic way of crippling the resources and economies of the nations colonized is absent in Owen's study. Where do we find in this biography the critique of the lust for power and domination? In the specific context of Egypt, how does Cromer's personal life or personal code help him understand or govern the natives and their different culture? How does he understand Muslims and Islam? Owen's concluding chapter provides passing reference to climactic events in the last two years of Cromer's rule in Egypt, events that have changed the color of his legacy until today. It is no secret that Cromer harbored a profound distaste for Islam. In *Modern Egypt* he justifies the British "civilizing mission" in Egypt by emphasizing the inadequacy of Islam as a social system, dismissing the possibility of Egyptians' ability to exercise self-rule, pitting Islam against Christianity, and contending that the high moral values of the latter would allow the British Empire to last and to avoid the shortcomings that brought the Roman Empire to ruin.[6]

Like the writing of history, the writing of biography is not an empirically verifiable undertaking; it remains in essence a historiographic choice. Handling the epistemological baggage that comes with this choice may result in a historical narrative of daunting complexity. The usefulness of this complexity, however, remains suspect and makes one wonder if the employment of superficially impressive adjectives like "complex" and "controversial" is itself a clever narrative tool that obfuscates rather than clarifies, that defers rather than addresses, what is already an unequivocal matter, especially when alternative "histories" on Cromer's life and achievements in Egypt are not at all scarce, but can be found in virtually all studies of England's colonial and imperial history and are available in both English and French, as well as other important languages, including Hindi, Urdu, Turkish, and Arabic. This verdict is most brilliantly ironized as it is stuttered by a Salman Rushdie character, Whisky Sisodia, in *The Satanic Verses*: "[T]he trouble with the English is that their their hiss hiss history happened overseas, so they do do don't know what it means."[7]

One of the incidents that Cromer ignores in his sanitized account of history in *Modern Egypt* is the Denshawai Affair. The scene is 1906 Egypt on a hot day in June. What is historically recorded of this

6 See The Earl of Cromer (Evelyn Baring), *Modern Egypt*, vol. 2 (New York, NY: MacMillan Company, 1908). See also Cromer, "The Government of Subject Races," *Edinburgh Review* 207 (January 1908), 1–27.

7 Salman Rushdie, *The Satanic Verses* (London: Viking, 1988), 343.

gruesome event is that it involved a clash between British officers and Egyptian peasants. A group of British officers went pigeon hunting in Denshawai, an Egyptian village in the mid-Delta region, with the result being an accidental shooting of a village woman and setting fire to a threshing floor. In the subsequent confusion, one of the British officers was killed. Offended by the death of an officer in the Occupation Army, Cromer decided to teach the Egyptian peasants a lesson. A tribunal was held in Shibīn al-Kūm, a district close to Denshawai, where the incident is said to have taken place. Four Egyptians were sentenced to death and fifty to flogging and imprisonment. The condemned were hanged and whipped in front of their families in their own village.[8,9]

[8] See Ḥāfiz Ibrāhīm's poem "The Denshawai Event" (1906); Ahmad Shawqī's poem "Denshawai's Anniversary" (1907); and Bernard Shaw's "Preface for Politicians" in *John Bull's Other Island* (1907). One of the most chronic and intransigent malaises of historiography has been that of the unreliability of literature as a document of history. None of these long-held beliefs should strike us as convincing or reasonable anymore. Colonial violence has affected all aspects of life in the colonies, and in many instances literature served as the only witness to the atrocities of the colonizer in times of political censorship. Colonial violence remained present in public, not only in Egypt, but also throughout every colony in Africa, until the second half of the twentieth century. It is also crucial for this article to emphasize that long after gibbeting and public hanging in chains were condemned as "barbaric" and for that reason abolished in England (in 1832 and 1834, respectively), both were still practiced in the colonies of the Empire.

[9] For an elaborate discussion of various versions of the Denshawai event, see Muḥammad Ali Al-Masaddī, *Denshawai* (Cairo: al-Hay'a al-Miṣryyia al-'Āmma lil-Kitāb, 1974). Another version is given by Jacques Berque in *Egypt: Imperialism & Revolution*, trans. Jean Stewart (London: Faber and Faber, 1972), 237–8. Berque's version reads:

Some officers out pigeon-shooting set fire to a threshing-floor. In the ensuing affray, one of them was killed. The facts are uncertain, the incident itself not of the first importance. But Cromer exaggerated it. "He seems," wrote one diplomat, "to have been influenced by those who demand excessive reprisals." He wanted to make an example. An extraordinary tribunal was immediately convened at Shbin al-Kumm. The sentence was carried out under conditions that combined the cruelty of Eastern justice and the unpleasantness of colonial justice; the condemned men were flogged and hanged in their own village, while their families, gathered in the terraces, looked on. The chairman of the court was Butrus Ghāli; Fathi Zaghlūl, speaking for the prosecution, praised the magnanimity of these officers, "famed for their heroism, who might well have shot down their aggressors instead of pigeons!" The incident aroused terrible emotions. The poets of the time, led by Shawqī, poured forth odes of vengeance. The peasants became martyrs. A violent controversy broke out between liberal and governmental newspapers. The Mu'aiyad passionately challenged the Egyptian Gazette, which described the fellahs as "African savages". Jāwīsh, in al-Liwā', attacked the Egyptian magistrates: they had contributed to the judgment which "tore these innocent souls from their bodies, as threads of silk are torn off a thorn bush.

Cromer served British colonialism and did not consider Denshawai worthy of mention in his two-volume work on *Modern Egypt*. Written from the perspective of a specialist in the economic history of the Middle East, Owen's biographical study acts like an appendix to Cromer's own *Modern Egypt*; it celebrates Cromer's economic genius and his extraordinary reforms, financial and otherwise, during his twenty-four years of rule as High Commissioner in Egypt. In pursuit of this aim Owen sheds new light on Cromer's personality, especially with reference to his childhood days and to his army career, which the former describes in exquisite detail. From an economic-historical viewpoint, Denshawai, which Egyptian and Irish nationalists regard as an embodiment of barbarism at its worst, does not have any material importance to Owen's study. In the end, Denshawai has become a textual event, as has Cromer himself. It is up to the reader to remember/historicize him either as the unruly little boy chasing his German governess with a burning poker, or as the malicious colonizer who left innocent men swinging from the gallows in front of their friends, parents, wives, and children.

The Egyptian novel began as "other than" what is silenced and entombed in histories like Cromer's *Modern Egypt* and the works of his orientalist cronies, as a modern vehicle for writing history against the grain and for offering alternatives to colonial violence. The loss of immediate meaning and of home in its traditional sense are the preconditions that caused the emergence of the European novel as a necessarily modern genre. A latecomer to Egyptian literary tradition, the novel became a medium for writing that was both reflective of various contemporaneous cultural and ideological currents, and consistent with a self-consciousness of a "modern" Egypt that regards Islam as part of its identity, though not necessarily as the center. The result comprises nuanced narratives, at once documenting the colonial experience and reflecting various contemporaneous cultural and ideological currents consistent with a self-consciousness of alternative pathways to modernity. Debates on the beginnings of the modern Arabic novel are far from conclusive.[10] Yet the condition of what contemporary Egyptian critics loosely term *Tajriba-t-al-Ḥadātha*

[10] See e.g. Raḍwá ʿĀshūr, *Al-Ḥadātha al-Mumkina: al-Shidyāq wa al-Sāq ʿalá al-Sāq al-Riwāya al-ʿArabiyya al-ūlá fī al-Adab al-ʿArabī al-Ḥadīth* [*Possible Modernity: al-Shidyāq and the Leg Over Leg (Being) The First Novel in Modern Arabic Literature*] (Cairo: Dār al-Shurūq, 2009).

(The Experience of Modernity)[11] necessitates a radical contextualization and a close scrutiny of certain ideologies and currents of thought dominating the Egyptian intellectual scene from al-Jabartī to Haykal.

Maḥmūd Ṭāhir Ḥaqqī's novella, *ʿAdhrāʾ Denshawāi* (*The Virgin of Denshawai*) (1906), cannot be fully understood without reference to socio-economic determinants that range from the postsecondary French education of its author to the corruption of the Khedive, and from the barbarity of the colonial event to the cold-blooded collaboration of Egypto-Turkish officials with Lord Cromer and his Army of Occupation. These are precisely the kinds of issues of social and political life with which Owen's *Lord Cromer: Victorian Imperialist, Edwardian Proconsul* refuses to engage.

In every way, *ʿAdhrāʾ Denshawāi* is a shocking work of art: a subtle satire of ruthless colonial victimization of Egyptian country folk that is comic, yet deeply historical and psychological. The novel portrays an innocent and idealized image of Egyptian *fallāḥīn* (peasants/farmers) unaware of the imposed political circumstances surrounding them or of the brutal colonial law condemning them. In a style of writing relatively new to Egyptian readership, Ḥaqqī treats the events of his historical novel with a degree of subtlety, unmistakably drawing on the French narrative tradition, particularly the work of the seventeenth-century fabulist Jean de La Fontaine. For instance, Ḥaqqī cleverly fuses fact with fiction and employs the technique of interior monologue for one of the characters, al-Hilbāwī, to show this character's dividedness between national and colonial interests. This neither arose from an existing local literary tradition nor did it mimic the stance of unquestioned realism typical of the beginnings of the European novel. It jumped, rather, to a level of

[11] For more on the question of Arab and Egyptian literary modernity, see: Ḥaqqī, *Fajar al-Qiṣṣa al-Miṣrīyya*; Aḥmad Haykal, *Taṭawwur al-Adab al-Ḥadīth fī Miṣr* [*The Development of Modern Literature in Egypt*] (Cairo: Dār al-Maʿārif, 1978); Muḥammad Dakrūb, *Tasāʾulāt Amāma 'al-ḥadātha' wa 'al-wāqiʿiyya' fī al-Naqd al-ʿArabī al-Ḥadīth* [*Questions of 'Modernism' and 'Realism' in Modern Arabic Criticism*] (Damascus: Dār al-Madá, 2001); Riyāḍ Najīb al-Sayyid ed. "Miḥnat al-Shiʿr al-ʿArabī al-Ḥadīth: A Public Discussion Among Seven Poets and Critics" Majalla-t-al-Nāqid *Al-Nāqid Periodical* (August 1988); Ghālī Shukrī, *Burj Bābil: al-Naqd wa al-Ḥadātha al-Sharīda* [*Babel Tower: Criticism and the Wretched Modernism*] (Cairo: Dār Naguib al-Rayyis, 1989) and Ghālī Shukrī *Adab al Muqāwama* [*Resistance Literature*] (Beirut: Dār al-Āfāq, 1979).

sociopolitical satire when both the idea of the "novel" and its content were new to the Egyptian readership. *Adhrāʾ Denshawāi* is a fatherless novel written by an Egyptian to a limited audience, namely those with cultural literacy in both French and Arabic. It is not surprising that the novel would posthumously fall prey to traditional methods of critical literary discourse in Egypt, methods unable to fully grasp the profundity of its black comedy effects as well as its counter-historical potency.[12]

Overall, one cannot simply assume that the entire production of Egyptian literature during the colonial period remains necessarily resistant and anti-colonial, or that Egypt's experience of Western modernity, first through France and then through Britain, is in all possibilities intrinsically harmful. It is not enough to insist that national sentiments and novel writing are identical and indistinguishable, that the novel speaks to the nation and that the nation projects itself through the novel, as Benedict Anderson has argued for instance.[13] The place of so-called Third World literature in literary theory has been the subject of heated debates in Europe and North America since the 1980s. Fredric Jameson sparked this debate when he argued in his 1986 essay that "third-world texts necessarily project a political dimension in the form of national allegory," thus triggering an avalanche of critical responses. This provocative thesis triggered responses from various critics, including Aijaz Ahmad, who takes issue with Jameson's critique and counter-argues that "it is in the metropolitan country ... that a literary text is first designated a Third World text."[14] The Jameson–Ahmad debate thus serves as a point of

[12] See e.g. Ṭāhā Wadī, *Madkhal ʾilá Tārīkh al-Riwāya al-Miṣriyya min 1905–1952* [*An Introduction to the History of the Egyptian Novel from 1905–1952*] (Cairo: Maktabat al-Nahḍa, 1972); Yūsuf Nūfal, *al-Qiṣṣa wa al-Riwāya bayn Jīl Ṭāhā Ḥusayn wa Jīl Najīb Maḥfouẓ* [*Narrative and the Novel between the Generation of Ṭāhā Ḥusyan and the Generation of Naguib Mahfouz*] (Cairo: Dār al-Nahḍa al-ʿArabīyya, 1977). I have addressed this level of complexity in Ḥaqqī's novel elsewhere. See Mohammad Salama, "Disciplining Islam: Colonial Egypt, a Case Study," in *Islam, Orientalism and Intellectual History: Modernity and the Politics of Exclusion since Ibn Khaldūn* (London: I.B. Tauris, 2011), 147–88.

[13] See Benedict Anderson, *Imagined Communities: Reflections on the Origin and Spread of Nationalism* (London: Verso, 1991).

[14] See Fredric Jameson, "Third World Literature in the Era of Multinational Capitalism," *Social Text*, 15 (Fall 1986), 65–88. See also "Jameson's Rhetoric of Otherness and the National Allegory," *Social Text*, 17 (Fall 1987), 3–25.

entry into modern Egypt's cultural scene, allowing for an interrogation not just of the validity of trendy critical theorization from above, but more importantly of the intellectual framework in which a Muslim society conceives of its own cultural production at a certain historical period and outside the context of ostentatious, immaterial wholesale Western theoretical forays.

In this particular context, the culture of modern Egypt demands an explicit and rigorous reexamination not only of the question of "Third World literature," but also, and more pertinently, of the very idea of thinking and categorizing literature. Many Arab critics see the aesthetics of modern Arabic literature as an important alternative, as filling a gap in traditional cultural narratives. This alternative has begun to present itself gradually as both revolutionary and secular. Muhsin al-Musawi, for instance, has attempted to link the rise of revolutionary thought to the rise of the Arabic novel. Al-Musawi emphasizes that "while literature springs out of and at the same time creates resistance against all that is pernicious and false in our societies, it does not have the same terminality revolution does. Literature does not simply vanish at the moment it triggers a revolution. On the contrary, resistance in literature is never an end in itself, but a continuity, which makes it more revolutionary than revolutions themselves."[15]

In his seminal 1934 essay "The Author as Producer," Walter Benjamin revisits the traditional question of the work of art in relationship to history.[16] He argues that while it is true that a literary text is bound by certain techniques as well as by generic and subgeneric articulations, such techniques become part of the productive forces of art capable of effecting an *Umfunktionierung* (functional transformation),[17] a term he borrows from Brecht, which entails a set of social relations between the author or the intelligentsia producing the text and the class struggle of the audience receiving it.

Benjamin draws special attention to certain types of writers: revolutionary authors who are not simply content with existing forces of

15 Muhsin Al-Musawi, *Al-Mawqif al-Thawrī fī al-Riwāya al-ʿArabiyya al-Muʿāṣira* [*The Revolutionary Position in the Contemporary Arabic Novel*] (Baghdad: Manshurāt Wazārat al-Iʿlām al-ʿIrāqiyya, 1975), 147. My translation.

16 See Walter Benjamin, "The Author as Producer," in *Understanding Brecht*, trans. Anna Bostock (New York, NY: Verso, 1973), 85–103.

17 Benjamin, "The Author as Producer," 93.

artistic production, and who strive to subvert and challenge such forces. The result is a new set of social relations between author and audience. The originality of this theory lies in transcending the conventional Marxian paradigm, which treats authors as passive cogs in the wheel of social production. Literature is revolution, and revolutionary authors not only write against the mainstream forces of production, but also create oppositional streams as they partake in revolutionizing the very forces set to contain them. Revolutionary authors are not content with using art to convey radical messages; their real contributions lie in revolutionizing not only their own societies, but also the medium of art itself.

Notably, Benjamin defines revolutionary literature in terms of historical commitment. He describes this commitment as "more than just the matter of presenting correct political opinions on one's art; it reveals itself in how far the artist reconstructs the artistic forms at his disposal, turning authors, readers and spectators into collaborators."[18] Literature as "more revolutionary than revolutions" and the author as revolutionary, what the Italian Marxist Antonio Gramsci refers to as a "permanent persuader" and not just a simple orator, present a fresh understanding of the role of literature in society: not as a "reflection or mimesis of a fixed reality out there, but as a negotiation of how events, characters and ideas are conditioned, whether socially, politically, economically, etc., how they could have been, and still can be different."[19]

Adab al-Iltizām (Literature of Commitment) as it is known in modern Egypt, is a term with a long history that accords with Benjamin's reflections on the revolutionary author. Although the term itself appeared in the late 1940s, committed fiction began in Egypt with the inception of the novel itself as a genre, as it offered its first critique of colonialism which it continued to pursue throughout decolonization. From Ḥaqqī to Yūsuf Idrīs, in the time frame of this study, passing through Haykal, Mahfouz, Bākathīr, and al-Ḥakīm, the works of such revolutionary authors reveal how their texts are not just a reflection *of*, but rather a reflection *on* the Islamo-social as well Islamo-political realities in Egypt's tumultuous passage, in the span of

[18] Ibid.

[19] Antonio Gramsci, *Selections from the Prison Notebooks of Antonio Gramsci*, eds. and trans. Quintin Hoare and Geoffrey Nowell Smith (London: Lawrence & Wishart, 1971), 9–10.

fifty years, from colonial rule to colonial tyranny to postcolonial despotism.

The Arab intellectual historian and literary critic Fayṣal Darrāj rightly argues that "the Arabic novel emerged at a time when there was no reliable history writing, and that it was the only history we have."[20] Darrāj's important study invite us to interrogate the significance that the colonial period and its consequences would acquire within this logic, with particular reference to a historical redefinition of European literary modernity and its peripheral offshoots in the colonies.[21] Precisely because of its exposure to Europe's colonial modernity, late nineteenth-century Egyptian narrative was caught in the middle of two currents by which it was influenced, and to which it responded: the Western novel and the tradition of classical Arabic literature. Egypt was also composed of a multiplicity of races, religions, and political affiliations at odds with each other. It followed that the question "What is an Egyptian?" would become the new genre's key motif in the works included in this study.

After Haykal, Egyptian narrative underwent numerous phases before it reached a sustained level of growth in the 1940s and 1950s, exemplified by writers such as Naguib Maḥfouz and Yūsuf Idrīs. Across five decades of narrativity in Egypt, and coupled with ebbs and flows in religious sensibilities as well as an expanding sense of nationalism that culminated in the 1950s, some writers experimented with autobiographical and personal narratives, refusing to engage with the totality of the various relations structuring their social and political life. Others opted to project the partiality and fragmentation of their own personal narratives onto the nation's collective experience. But even the most singular of experiences could still add up to a picture of totality. In this particular case, a key question would be whether or not Egyptian narrative allowed the integration of the singularity of personal experience with the totality of national and/or

20 Fayṣal Darrāj, *Al-Riwāya wa Ta'wil al-Tārīkh [The Novel and the Interpretation of History]* (Casablanca: al-Markaz al-Thaqāfī al-ʿArabī, 2004), 89–163.

21 See Jābir ʿUṣfūr, *ʿAṣr al-Riwāya* [*The Age of the Novel*] (Cairo: Al-Hay'a al-Miṣriyya al-ʿĀmma lil-Kitāb, 1986). See also Jābir ʿUṣfūr, *Zaman al-Riwāya* [*The Time of the Novel*] (Damascus: Dār al-Madá, 1999); ʿAbd al-Muḥsin Ṭāhā Badr, *Taṭawwur al-Riwāya al-Hadītha fī Miṣr* [*The Development of the Modern Novel in Egypt*] (Cairo: Dār al-Maʿārif, n.d.).

religious consciousness, and whether or not the tension between Islam and the secular is just one modality of the variegated cultures of modern Egypt.

In his essay, "Arabic Prose and Prose Fiction After 1948," Edward Said presents a semi-Marxian theory of the novel, arguing that novel-writing in general is reflective of the spirit of its time, no matter how "imaginative or trans-historical the novelist may be." Indeed, Said continues, "narrative, in short, is the historical mode as it is most traditionally understood."[22] Said's statement resonates with the situation of modern Egyptian narrative. Like Jameson, Said regards novel-writing in general as socially symbolic. Said's reflections on Arabic fiction is highly informed by, and in many ways recapitulates, Georg Lukács's 1916 Theory of the Novel. Both Said's essay and, to some extent, Lukács's theory, serve as an excellent preamble to a sustained re-examination and analysis of modern Egypt's novelistic productions. Lukács's work in particular offers insights into the genre by relating it to three concepts: totality, secularity, and utopia. In Lukács we learn that the art of the novel opens our eyes to a better understanding of the relationship between imperialism and culture. To Lukács, the novel as a genre is born out of the shattering experience of modernity, its divisiveness and destruction of home and God; it is the "epic of a world that has been abandoned by God."[23] Thus the world is saturated with meaning *per se*, and hence, "home" in its valence of comfort, belonging, and identity falls away. What emerges in this situation of loss – what strikes the individual as "new" in the innovative spirit of modernity – is the genre of the novel. This is particularly true of the novel in Egypt, which became a medium for writing that was both reflective of various contemporaneous cultural and ideological currents and consistent with a self-consciousness of a "modern" Egypt that regards Islam as part of its identity and not necessarily as the center.

In the spirit of historical materialism, it could be argued that neither Ḥaqqī nor Haykal could have written their novels at different times, not because of their subject matter, but because the two works

[22] Edward Said, *Reflections on Exile and Other Essays* (Cambridge: Harvard University Press, 2000), 42–3.

[23] Georg Lukács, *The Theory of the Novel: A Historico-philosophical Essay on the Forms of Great Epic Literature*, trans. Anna Bostock (Cambridge: MIT Press, 1971), 88.

reflect a specific historical framework, a particular geographical space, and a community of subjects that – far from being "imagined" – could only be Egyptian and nothing else. In their lucid expressions of a people aspiring to be a nation, Ḥaqqī and Haykal chose a non-Islamic, non-Arabic form to address exclusively secular themes that exemplify Egypt's oscillation between foreign and local powers on the one hand and traditional and modern values on the other. For Ḥaqqī and Haykal, modernity, however, does not seem to separate home and God (at least not directly) or to shatter them altogether; it seeks to rearrange the religious-secular cultural cards in a manner that corresponds to the dictates of the political moment.

Even if we agree with Lukács that the rise of the European novel as an expression of "transcendental homelessness" is built around a "separation between interiority and adventure, and abandonment by the Divine," the circumstances leading to the emergence and growth of the novel in colonial Egypt require a reconsideration of some of the postulates of Lukács's theory.[24] Egypt's modern cultural history did not indulge in the prolific novelistic productions of single authors like Richardson, Proust, Flaubert, Defoe, or Dickens – at least not before Ṭāhā Ḥusayn or Naguib Maḥfouz. If anything, there was a "genre war," as it were, among leading Egyptian authors in the late 1930s and early 1940s: namely, that acrimonious debate between Maḥfouz and al-'Aqqād on the supremacy of poetry over the novel, or vice-versa.[25]

The novel gradually became the archetypal art form of twentieth-century Egyptian culture, perfectly expressing the country's preoccupation with conceptions of nationalism and modernity. It is difficult to argue that the Egyptian novel did not in some ways replicate European themes in its early stages, a characteristic that certainly applies to Haykal's *Zaynab*, but it at least assumed different connections to artistic representations than in France. The Egyptian novel was not simply a form of art with which only sophisticated and learned people could engage seriously, although at that time, only the sophisticated and literate had access to it, given low literacy levels. Nevertheless, the novel was meant to reach the entire population of Egypt, especially its peasants and working class, since its formative

[24] Ibid.
[25] See 'Usfūr, *Zaman al-Riwāya*, 153–64.

material is the Egyptian peasant, or "the most commonplace, the deadest among the living, [who] may play a part in a great drama,"[26] to borrow James Joyce's forceful words. What animated the first historical Egyptian novel as a genre of modernity is something wholly missing in Europe: the desire for a kind of nativist, heroic, anti-colonial writing predicated on asserting identities in the face of a usurping other.

Ḥaqqī's *'Adhrā' Denshawāi* and Haykal's *Zaynab* confirm that colonial Egyptian narrative at its very early stages is not simply nationalistic or anti-imperialistic, but also secular in its reflection, consciously so, of key cultural and socio-theological issues in the Egyptian society. A crucial observation is that the setting of the two novels lies beyond the metropolis. This suburbanization means that the translation of the colonial experience into a sequential plot that people could read and follow is located elsewhere: in the countryside. The act of positioning the colonial experience outside Cairo, the city where the two writers lived and worked, redefines the center of the occupied city by its peripheries, thus implying the ramifications of the city. This involves the paradox of, on the one hand, centralizing what is geographically, economically, politically, and intellectually de-centered, and, on the other, of making of the Egyptian countryside a periphery of the periphery, doubly isolated from the colonial center exemplified in England.

In the aftermath of the British occupation of Egypt, a school of important and challenging novels arose. Generally, one can distinguish two novelistic waves. The earlier is pioneered by Ḥāfiẓ Ibrāhīm, Maḥmūd Ṭāhir Ḥaqqī, Muḥammad Ḥusayn Haykal, Ṭāhā Ḥusayn, and Yaḥya Ḥaqqī. The second, more internationally recognized and more "translated" wave, is led by Naguib Maḥfouẓ, Tawfīq al-Ḥakīm, and Yūsuf Idrīs. All these writers differ greatly from one another in intention and achievement. What they may have in common is a rejection of the idea that the novel's task is to tell a story and delineate a character according to European novelistic conventions. For these novelists, writing a novel meant writing a history, as if each writer signed a contract of social and political commitment to

26 James Joyce, "Drama and Life," in *James Joyce, Occasional, Critical, and Political Writings*, ed. Kevin Barry (Oxford: Oxford World Classics, 2000), 26.

the nation. A major function of early twentieth-century Egyptian literature lies in its attempt to reconstruct religious and national notions of identity rendered problematic during colonialism.

In the few years that followed the Denshawai Affair, Egyptian literature became explicitly and unabashedly political: poets continued to compose verse criticizing both the British and the Khedives, a role readers and listeners grew to expect from them. The release of the Denshawai prisoners in September of 1907, followed by the premature death of Muṣṭafá Kāmil in 1908, inflamed national feelings among Egypt's intelligentsia and triggered a realization among Egypt's working and middle classes that they should unify against colonial rule. The press continued its sharply critical attitude: publications often took a nationalistic tone and subordinated all other concerns to the question of Egypt's political destiny.

The novel thus allowed writers to reflect on and to narrate the political and socio-economic conditions of the Egyptian community, to elaborate, through narrative, on its implications, and to consider the roots and consequences of its customs. As a genre new to Egypt, the novel helped redraw the country's geo-political map and soon became fundamental in representing social as well as political contentions in line with the shifting sentiments of anti-colonial nationalism, Islamism, and secularism. Although Egypt's first novelistic attempts gave voice to elaborate expressions of colonial discontent, as we have seen in the example of Ḥaqqī's *'Adhrā' Denshawāi*, the use of the novel to address, critique, and reform the native culture of colonial and postcolonial Egypt would become invaluable in a country whose high culture had so far been mainly concerned with serving a national cause and addressing political, rather than social and domestic, issues.

One of the main factors that led to the emergence and development of the novel in Egypt is the shift in intellectual thinking and social structure. Precolonial nineteenth-century Egypt was an agricultural Ottoman state ruled exclusively by a self-centered dynasty. The feudal economy created a vast gulf between classes. All social units in Egypt were basically estates and counties; cities were still emerging, but as the exception, not the rule. Only land-owning and ruling classes had access to education. But interest in science and foreign education was not extensive among the aristocracy, who, in all aspects of life, adhered to traditionalism, creationism, and conservatism, as represented by al-Azhar's conservative theology.

Al-Jāmiʿa al-Miṣriyya (the Egyptian University as it was first called) was founded in 1908, on a European-inspired civil model "to fill the gap in the official system of education."[27] Its aim was to enable the Egyptian bourgeoisie to fashion a distinct ideological space: one contrary to the arbitrary powers of both the Khedive and the English, and it was strongly supported by many prominent members of the Egyptian community who "contributed to the funds of the proposed university with enthusiasm, and ... gave devoted services to the scheme."[28] The philosophical and intellectual currents of the time echoed a general state of contradictions: sociopolitical relativism clashed with stagnant absolutism while Islamic fundamentalism, represented in al-Azhar's conservative theology, conflicted with the purported liberalism of a secular university. It is in this context that the Egyptian novel began as a form of social criticism; and it is in this context as well that, subscribing to a linear view of history, a shared land, a mutual enemy, and common political goals, it embodied the same state of contradictions.

In Egypt, as in Europe, the rise of the novel accompanied the rise of the middle class; though in Egypt this was in the context of the feudal system that characterized the Ali dynasty.[29] The Egyptian novel soon became instrumental in disseminating the ideas and ideals of the middle class, over and against the aristocratic hierarchies imposed by the Ali dynasty's political system and sustained by Britain's occupational bureaucracy. With the novel's emergence as a dominant genre alongside the well-established and powerful genre of poetry, Egyptian literature turned into an arena of political discussions. Following

[27] Jamal Mohammed Ahmed, *Intellectual Origins of Egyptian Nationalism* (London: Oxford University Press, 1960), 56.

[28] Ibid.

[29] Although crucial to the rise and development of modern Egyptian literary thought, the pre-colonial and colonial conditions that led to the rise of feudal capitalism in Egypt are outside the scope of this book. For sociopolitical and historical perspectives on economic changes in Egypt, see Maḥmūd Mutawallī, *al-Uṣūl al-Tārīkhiyya lil-Raʾsmāliyya al-Miṣriyya* (Cairo: al-Hayʾa al-Miṣriyya al-ʿĀmma lil-Kitāb, 1974); Anouar Abdel-Malek, *Egypt: Military Society; the Army Regime, the Left, and Social Change under Nasser*, trans. Charles Lam Markmann (New York, NY: Random House, 1968); Robert L. Tignor, *State, Private Enterprise, and Economic Change in Egypt: 1918–1952* (Princeton, NJ: Princeton University Press, 1984). For more recent studies, see Timothy Mitchell, *Rule of Experts: Egypt, Techno-Politics, Modernity* (Berkeley, CA: University of California Berkeley, 2002); Roger Owen, *State, Power, and Politics in the Making of the Modern Middle East* (London: Routledge, 1992).

Ḥaqqī's Denshawai-triggered politicization of Egyptian narrative at the outset of the twentieth century, a new cultural form began to impose itself on the traditional power structure of Egyptian society, culminating in the 1919 Revolution.

Therefore, the novel signals a major shift in modern Egyptian cultural thought. In investigating the origins of the Egyptian novel and its communal affiliations, however, it is not enough to look at the social milieu or educational background of its pioneers. We must also situate them within the tumultuous dynamics of a colonially controlled Egyptian politics, especially in the anti-imperialist stages at the end of the nineteenth century and the beginning of the twentieth.

The moral ambiguity of some fictionalized historical figures, e.g. al-Hilbāwī in Maḥmūd Ṭāhir Ḥaqqī's *ʿAdhrāʾ Denshawāi*, showcases the corruption of the country's upperclass in collaborating with the Occupation Army against their own countrymen. But the literature of that age also evinces an affiliation with a European ideal, in contrast to a European reality that belies its own dicta of political freedom and self-determination through colonialism. Ironically enough, it is mainly ideas of freedom and equality promoted by European philosophy, literature, and the arts that inspires the Egyptian intelligentsia after al-Afghānī's nostalgic call for Islamic unity failed to unite all Egyptians and the Arabs against the English occupation.[30] This explains why Muṣṭafá Kāmil's (1874–1908) Denshawai-inspired campaigns in England and France helped gain support against the "civilization" of Cromer and his army. Kāmil was aware that the British Commissioner's practices in Egypt violated principles of justice and civil rights supposedly respected by the English and French in their own countries. This complex contradiction between Cromer's actions and his supposed principles and between the nationalist's admiration

[30] See Israel Gershoni and James P. Jankowski's discussion of Muḥammad Rashīd Riḍā's attempts to resurrect the Caliphate post-1924 in *Egypt, Islam, and the Arabs: The Search for Egyptian Nationhood, 1900–1930* (Oxford: Oxford University Press, 1986), 265–7. See also Albert Hourani, *A History of the Arab Peoples* (New York, NY: Warner Books, 1991), 307–14. Hourani positions Jamāl al-Dīn al-Afghānī, ʿAbduh, and Riḍā as proponents of a reformed Islam rid of imitation and true to its core values as a religion that encourages the acquisition of knowledge and the fulfillment of God's wisdom on Earth. Hourani also elaborates on al-Afghānī's influence on Islamic thought and "the Eastern Crisis of 1875–1878" in his earlier book *Arabic Thought in the Liberal Age 1798–1939* (London: Oxford University Press, 1962), 103–29.

for Europe and their hostility to it at the same time, was transmitted to Egypt's nationalist project as the country's intelligentsia strove to fashion a collective movement to withstand Britain's colonial modernity.

One of the paradoxes of Egyptian nationalism is its emergence from what could be roughly called a dialectic of negation and affirmation. That is, it desired to establish and renew itself as the only hope for political democracy and social stability in the face of a tyrannical "Other," yet it used the same principles that defined the nationalism of that very "Other." This dialectic I take to constitute a condition of uncritical mimicry in Egypt's protracted move toward decolonization. This nationalist mimicry reveals itself not only in political and social movements, but in literature as well, especially in the novel in at least the first two decades of the twentieth century.[31]

Although not every writer was able to grasp and represent the complex relationships between social and political life – indeed, some confused the partiality and fragmentation of their own experience for a collective one and exaggerated their responses to sociopolitical conditions – the mass of modern Egyptian novels, taken as a whole, add up to a totality of Egyptian life.[32] A key recognition that dominated the Egyptian social sphere was twofold: that Egyptian literature

[31] In some ways, my definition of mimicry is an extension of Homi Bhabha's. I agree with Bhabha that mimicry in the colonial discourse is "a form of resemblance" resulting from "subjection," that it is "the process of the fixation of the colonial as a form of cross-classificatory, discriminatory knowledge within an interdictory discourse." But the Lacanian framework which informs Bhabha's theory anchors it in a psychoanalytical plateau that overlooks cultural and sociological elements as well as historical specificities vital for a better assessment of the role of mimicry in colonial discourses. Egypt, while militarily and politically occupied by England, was culturally and linguistically occupied by France. This cultural occupation manifests itself in legal and other institutional fields throughout the nineteenth century and served as a model for education and an instrument of national resistance against the English. See Homi Bhabha, *The Location of Culture* (London: Routledge, 1994), 85–92.

[32] I refer here to al-Ṭahṭāwī's personal conflict with Ismāʿīl and his use of literature to critique his rule. A feud is said to have taken place between ʿAbbās I and al-Ṭahṭāwī in which the former shut down the al-Alsun school and the latter was relieved of his duties and banished to Sudan between 1849 and 1858. It was in Sudan that al-Ṭahṭāwī decided to write *Mawāqiʿ al-Aflāk fī Waqāʾiʿ Tilīmāk*, mostly as a critique of ʿAbbās I's harsh treatment of him. See ʿAbd Allāh Ibrāhīm, *al-Sardiyya al-ʿArabiyya al-Ḥadītha: Tafkīk al-Khiṭāb al-Istiʿmārī wa Iʿādat Tafsīr al-Nashʾa* [*Modern Arabic Narratology: The Deconstructing of Colonial Discourse and Reinterpretation of Beginnings*], vol. 1 (Beirut: al-Muʾassasa al-ʿArabiyya lil-Dirāsāt wa al-Nashr, 2013), 121–8.

should create a sense of national unity by incorporating dialect, and that it is simply part of a larger national uprising.

While various aspects of narrative had existed in Egyptian literature long before its encounter with the West, early twentieth-century Egyptian novelists acknowledge that the novel was imported from Europe.[33] In broader terms, one can distinguish three major phases that modern Egyptian fiction underwent in its encounter with European literature from the mid-nineteenth century until the beginning of the twentieth century: mimicry (Arabization), resistance, and independence. The last phase did not materialize until the beginning of the twentieth century, when Egyptian authors in Haykal's generation began to produce literary works infused with local color and realistic characters.

The first phase is generally characterized by eclectic adoptions, unfaithful translations, and partial understandings of the significance of the European novel. Some Arab critics, notably Muḥammad Ghunīmī Hilāl, describe this condition as an attempt to break away from classical Arabic tradition, marked by an increasing reliance on mature novelistic examples from the Western tradition.[34] In the beginning of that first phase, a writer would reproduce a text, guided by the European original, while taking the liberty to fashion it in a manner suitable for Arabic taste. A good example of this category is best represented by Rifāʿa Rāfiʿal-Ṭahṭāwī, who Arabized Fénelon's didactic seventeenth-century novel *Aventures de*

[33] The earliest narrative in Arabic goes back to the famous seven pre-Islamic *muʿallaqāt* (translation), which tell of the exploits of famous heroes like ʿAntara Ibn Shaddād al-ʿAbsī and his beloved ʿAbla. With the advent of Islam, narrative continued to exist in the form of qaṣas (stories) of the Holy Qurʾān and the Sīrā (biography and achievements of Prophet Muḥammad). History writings in the hands of early Muslim scholars like al-Ṭabarī and al-Masʿūdī also produced a kind of narrative and story-telling based on the Islamic method of *al-Isnād* (a concatenation of trusted verbal sources). From the twelfth to the fourteenth centuries, other Egyptian folkloric *Ḥikāyāt* (tales) of heroism appeared; famous among them are tales of Abū Zayd al-Hilālī, Sayf Ibn Dhī Yazan, and al-Dhāhir Bībars.

[34] Muḥammad Ghunīmī Hilāl, *Al-Adab Al-Muqāran [Comparative Literature]* (Beirut: Dār al-ʿAwada wa Dār al-Thaqāfa, 1962), 245. Another famous example of this phase is Muṣṭafá Luṭfī al-Manfalūṭī (d. 1924), who translated "Paul and Verjeaniny" into an Arabic story called *al-Faḍīla* (Virtue), and changed "Serrano De Jiraq," a play by the French poet Edmond Roustan, into the story *al-Shāʿir* (*The Poet*).

Télémaque and gave it the Arabic title *Mawāqiʿ al-Aflāk fī Waqāʾiʿ Tilīmāk*.[35]

The second phase, resistance, took place when Egyptian narrative felt the need to reassert itself against the onslaught of European cultural modernity. This desire for nativist narrative capable of restoring the past to offer alternative commentaries on the present is clearly exemplified in Muḥammad al-Mūwayliḥī's *Ḥadīth ʿĪsá ibn Hishām*. Al-Mūwayliḥī's text is a modern variation on the traditional aspects of the Arabic *maqāmāt* genre, written entirely in traditional rhymed narrative form, where there is a hero, a narrator of that hero's exploits, and a succession of tales connected only by the character of the hero, with extensive attention to *sajʿ* (rhymed prose). Western influence could be found in the change of scenes, the nature of the adventures of ʿĪsá ibn Ḥishām, the psychological analysis of characters in their struggles, and in the social critique that the text provides for a new era of conflict between traditional values and an emerging social consciousness.[36] Al-Mūwayliḥī often ends with an attempt to strike a balance between the best in the Arabic-Islamic tradition and the Western one.[37]

35 For more on this intricate phase of Arabization/translation, see Shaden M. Tageldin, *Disarming Words: Empire and the Seductions of Translation in Egypt* (Berkeley, CA: University of California Press, 2011), especially the third chapter, "Suspect Kinships: al-Tahtawi and the Theory of French-Arabic Equivalence, 1827–1834," 108–51. For a thorough understanding of the question of *taʿrīb* and particularly of al-Ṭahṭāwī's pioneering role of "Arabization," see ʿAbd Allāh Ibrāhīm, *al-Sardiyya al-ʿArabiyya al-Ḥadītha*, especially the third chapter on al-Ṭahṭāwī, "al-Taʿrīb wa Muḥākat al-Marwīyāt al-Sardiyya" ["Arabization and the Parody of Prose Narratives"], 109–61. See also Lūwīs ʿAwaḍ, *Tārīkh al-Fikr al-Miṣrī al-Ḥadīth* [*The History of Modern Egyptian Thought*] (Cairo: Dār al-Hilāl, 1969); Jamāl al-Dīn al-Shayyāl, *Tārīkh al-Tarjama wa al-Ḥaraka al-Thaqāfiyya fī ʿAṣr Muḥammad ʿAlī* [*History of Translations and Cultural Movements in the Era of Muḥammad ʿAlī*] (Cairo: Maktabat al-Thaqāfa al-Dīniyya, 2000); Pierre Cachia "Translation and Adapation 1834–1914" in *The Cambridge History of Arabic Literature: Modern Arabic Literature*, ed. M. M. Badawi (Cambridge: Cambridge University Press, 1992), 23–35; ʿAbd al-Raḥmān, *al-Rāfiʿī ʿAṣr Ismāʿīl* [*The Age of Ismāʿīl*], vol. 1 (Cairo: Dār al-Maʿārif, 1987).

36 See Roger Allen's scintillating analysis of Ḥadīth ʿĪsá ibn Ḥishām in "The Beginning of the Arabic Novel" in *The Cambridge History of Arabic Literature: Modern Arabic Literature*, ed. M. M. Badawi (Cambridge: Cambridge University Press, 1992), 184–7.

37 Hilāl, *Al-Adab Al-*, 243. See also ʿAbd al-Muḥsin Ṭāhā Badr, *Taṭawwur al-Riwāya al-ʿArabiyya al-Ḥadītha fī Miṣr 1870–1938* (Cairo: Dār al-Maʿārif, 1983).

The third phase can be described as the "nationalization" or the "internalization" of the foreign. It consists mainly of replacing the events of an existing text with local ones while keeping the main structure of the plot and spirit of the original text intact, as seen in Haykal's *Zaynab*. The writer has to re-create the local color in order to address social, cultural, and specifically national issues. As a genre, the Egyptian novel emerged, then, as a result of an intellectual struggle between foreign and traditional forces, one that left remarkable imprints on its formative stages. This is particularly true of the subject of the next chapter, Haykal's *Zaynab*, a work of "authentic temporal and spatial context" that seeks to "explore some of the pressing social issues of its day,"[38] as Roger Allen brilliantly puts it, and by so doing raises many questions about the politics of Egyptian identity in the 1910s, making the text itself a sign of the repressed colonial tensions and histories that produced it.

[38] Allen, "The Beginning of the Arabic Novel," 191.

2 Nahḍa-t Miṣr: Zaynab *and the Cultural Renaissance of Modern Egypt (1912–1913)*

The world is the external, the domain of the material; the home represents our inner material self, or true identity. The world is a treacherous terrain of the pursuit of material interests, where practical considerations reign supreme. It is also typically the domain of the male. The home in its essence must remain unaffected by the profane activities of the outside world and woman is its supreme representation.

Partha Chatterjee, "The Nationalist Resolution of the Women's Question"

Confronting the Egyptian novel in its nascent stage was a central issue: To what extent is it possible for Egyptian novelists to tell a story exposing the malaise of their own society without falling into the trap of anti-nationalist, European assimilation? That is, to become an Egyptian novelist capable of recasting the genre in the context of an occupied country required not only a deep understanding of Egypt's Islamic tradition and cultural past but also an awareness of the genre's permutations in other nations' literatures and, more broadly, a modern European education (including reading knowledge of French and English) and extensive travel. Only members of the upper-middle class with close connections to the ruling class were equipped with such privileges. It is in this context that one can legitimately raise the question of whether *Zaynab*, the radically anti-traditionalist, counter-hegemonic novel by Muhammad Ḥusayn Haykal, was European, Egyptian, or both. To answer the question, one needs to emphasize both the novelty of the novel genre in Egypt and the class of "entrepreneurs" engaged in tailoring it to the Egyptian literary sphere.

The 1910s were a time of real possibilities for significant change and new politics in Egypt. In 1914, England declared Egypt a British Protectorate, thus severing it completely from Istanbul. With this political maneuver, the question of Egypt's national destiny and political identity began to crystallize even more sharply among Egyptians. In the 1919 Revolution, which represented a tremendous investment by educated Egyptians and an engagement of intellectuals of all kinds, writers rose to prominence by staking out what appeared to be a new collective movement toward the meaning of Egyptianness.

At this point in history, Egypt was caught between a longstanding love–hate relationship with Istanbul and an instinctive distrust of the alien English invader. The 1914 liberation from Turkey only served to emphasize the grim reality of English colonialism. Paradoxically, though, for Egyptian intellectuals the European idea of nationalism sparked the desire to forge their own nation, free of European domination. De-Ottomanized and de-Khedivized (at least politically) in 1914, Egypt had to face the inevitable question of self-definition and identity. "What is an Egyptian?" was the most pressing question asked by many Egyptians in the second decade of the twentieth century. But this ontological question, with its implications of essentialism, triggered yet another question, which threw the essential nature of Egyptianness in doubt: "What is the status of Egyptian minorities?" These minorities included Coptic Egyptians who, while still proud to be Egyptians and staunch supporters of Egypt's independence from Britain, could not, understandably, bring themselves to subscribe to the pan-Islamic ideal of *nahḍa* outlined by Muslim intellectuals like al-Afghānī and ʿAbdūh at the outset of the century and continued in the rhetoric of Islamists like Rashīd Riḍā and the Muslim Brotherhood.

In short, Egypt needed a new definition of itself, one that would transcend its multiple religiosities and ethnicities and bring all Egyptians under a single narrative that would inspire political confidence and lead, eventually, to self-rule. In order to achieve self-rule, Egypt had to prove, to itself and to Britain, that it had the ability to fashion its own political destiny. The tension caused by the First World War, arising from both the behavior of the British and the sacrifice of many Egyptians, only intensified the spirit of Egyptian nationalism, and a new attitude toward the national past began to arise. To construct a national identity, Egypt needed to shape its past in a way that would make it possible to establish a single-minded history of glory and heroism that would be a source of pride. Only then could the colonized community of Egypt understand its present historically, as well as demonstrate a modern, coherent national vision to and against Britain. But given that political pluralism is itself a sign of modernity, one of the main challenges of Egyptian nationalism was to acknowledge its multiple religiosities and ethnicities, rather than just deny them.

After Denshawai, the question that engaged many Egyptian thinkers was how best to represent the politics of patriotism to the public. In other words, how is a true national consciousness to be articulated? And, more specifically, what does it mean for this articulation to take a gendered form? Following Ḥaqqī's *ʿAdhrāʾ Denshawāi*, the articulation and politicization of a symbolic category for nationalism took significant strides toward feminization. This intersection of the question of women with nationalism brought a new dimension to the issue of Egyptian identity. In a grammatically gender-based language like Arabic, where almost all names of countries and cities are feminine, the word *umma* [nation] in particular derives directly from *umm* [mother]. With a feminine suffix added to what is already coded feminine, the Egyptian sense of nation as mother is doubly ingrained in its language.

Egyptian nationalism, like all nationalisms, must be understood in its historical specificity. Western theorists like Hobsbawm, Anderson, and Gellner acknowledged, in principle, the historical specificities that govern national movements, including language, religion, regional economies, and the spread of print and visual cultures. But in practice their analyses of the rhetoric of nationalism tended to rely on an unconsciously Eurocentric account of tropes such as nativism, the common enemy, the sacredness of the land, etc. This is especially true with regard to one trope with particular relevance to the Egyptian nationalism, namely, the trope of the nation as woman. In European nationalisms the alignment of the nation with the woman predates the sociopolitical rise of the question of women's rights, which was easily and unproblematically exploited in nationalist discourses. The situation in Egypt is different because the introduction of women's rights and gender equality at the beginning of the twentieth century as a contested sociohistorical question coincided with the feminized political articulation of the nation (as woman/mother). Moreover, in light of the specific sociolinguistic place of gender in Egyptian culture, this trope has its own complex history, different from its history in Europe.

Jābir ʻUṣfūr, a famous Egyptian literary critic, has examined this interaction between the concepts of woman and nation in an attempt to contextualize Egyptian narrative in the first twenty years of the twentieth century. ʻUṣfūr sees the exploration of the question of women in fiction as an expression of political and cultural inevitability. "Is it just a coincidence," exclaims ʻUṣfūr, in his book *Zaman al-Riwāya* (Time of the Novel), "that female names and attributes are the main titles of all the novels that emerged [at the beginning of the twentieth century], shaking the literary foundation of genres in Arabic literature?"[1] According to ʻUṣfūr, the connection between the emergence of the Egyptian novel and the rise of the women's rights movement with regard to such intellectuals as Qāsim Amīn is so clear that no serious critic should speak about one without addressing the other. The appearance of novels with titles like Haykal's *Zaynab* (1913–14), ʻĪsá ʻUbayd's *Thurayya* (1922), Niqūlā Ḥaddād's *Fātina-t- al-Imbrāṭūr* (The Emperor's Enchantress) (1922), Amīn al-Rīḥānī's *Khārij al-Ḥarīm* (Outside the Harem) (1922), Maḥmūd Ṭāhir Lāshīn's *Ḥawwāʾ bi-lā Ādam* (Eve Without Adam) (1934), and al-ʻAqqād's *Sāra* (1938) solidifies this socioliterary interconnectedness. Absent from Uṣfūr's study is the important fact that over the last two centuries Arab women authors played important roles not only in advocating for women's rights, but also enriching the so-called Arab *nahdah* (renaissance). These women include authors like Hanā Kūrānī (1870–1898) and Anīsa al-Shartūnī (1886–1906), in addition to journalists of the late eighteenth and early nineteenth centuries such as Hind Nūfal, Maryam Maẓhar, and Iskandarah Khūrī. A second generation of remarkable *nahdah* and women's rights advocates includes authors such as Ā'isha al-Taymūriyya (1840–1902), Zaynab Fawwāz (1846–1914), and Malak Ḥifnī Nāṣif, aka Bāḥitha-t- al-Wādī (1886–1918). More specifically in Egypt, at the beginning of the twentieth century, Nabawiyya Mūsà (1886–1951) stood out as the first Egyptian woman to receive a high school diploma and to be hired as a teacher at ʻAbbās Elementary School in Cairo. Male advocates for the women's rights movement, including Rifāʻa Rāfiʻ al-ṬahṬāwī, Aḥmad Fāris al-Shidyāq, and Qāsim Amīn, redefined in a historic move the relationship between men and women as well as between the public and the private. Haykal

[1] Jābir ʻUsfūr, *Zaman al-Riwāya* [*The Time of the Novel*] (Syria: Dār al-Madá lil-Thaqāfa wa al-Nashr, 1999), 96.

was a great admirer of Amīn and wrote about him extensively on various occasions.[2]

The emergence of the Women's Rights Movement and of the novel as an advocate of those rights can be seen as a sign of change in modern Egypt. If women have the right to choose their husbands and lead a life beyond the private realm of the household, then the demand for the liberation of women moves with the historical grain at the very moment that it conflicts with domestic ideologies. The increasing use of the woman as a trope of national identity would eventually lead, as was the case with European nationalisms, to the emergence of the Women's Rights Movement. In Egypt, the emergence of this movement became symbolic of the rise of Egypt as a nation, as in the famous example of *Nahḍa-t Miṣr* (Egypt's Awakening/Rise Statue). *Nahḍa-t Miṣr*, whose name connotes an Egyptian renaissance, shows a peasant woman unveiling as she stands next to the Sphinx. Created by the French-educated Egyptian sculptor Maḥmūd Mukhtār to bolster Egypt's nationalist momentum during the fight for independence, *Nahḍa-t Miṣr* was originally raised in Ramses Square in 1928, but now appropriately stands in front of Cairo University.

But if the movement for women's rights and its emergence on the Egyptian cultural scene are signs of a major change, then what space does the Egyptian woman of the 1910s *actually* occupy in Egyptian politics? Although this question has been ably investigated by many scholars of early Arab feminism, it still invites further research.[3] As evident in the case of *Zaynab*, if we consider the novel as a metaphor for Egypt, much like Mukhtār's statue, then there is a striking historical irony. Although the women of the novel, primarily Zaynab (the peasant) and 'Azīza (the protagonist's intended bride) are marginalized and suffer the kind of cultural and intellectual repression that

[2] One of Haykal's essays on Qāsim Amīn appeared in the newspaper *al-Sufūr* on February 25, 1916. There is also a reference to Amīn in *Zaynab*, p. 254. In addition, Haykal authored a book on Rousseau in Arabic; see Jān Jāk Rūsū (Cairo: NP, 1923).

[3] See Marilyn Booth, *May Her Likes be Multiplied: Biography and Gender Politics in Egypt* (Berkeley: University of California Press, 2001); Beth Baron, *Egypt as a Woman: Nationalism, Gender, and Politics* (Berkeley: University of California Press, 2005) and *The Women's Awakening in Egypt: Culture, Society, and the Press* (Yale University Press, 1994); Boutheina Khaldi, *Egypt Awakening in the Early Twentieth Century: Mayy Ziyadah's Intellectual Circles* (London: Palgrave Macmillan, 2012).

was the major focus of Egypt's project of modernity, it is they who must take on the role of symbols for the resurgence of a fresher nationalism in a new Egypt. In any case, in the hands of prominent male authors the trope of the land as woman in those early decades, irrespective of the actual condition of women, marked a watershed moment of literary modernity in Egypt.

As the British began to settle in Egypt, the rapid expansion of foreign-owned publishing and printing houses shifted the country's sociocultural dynamics. By 1910, a printing industry was established, with a concomitant rise in book sales. A middle class eager for all sorts of culture, its own as well as European, soon formed a small but enthusiastic society of readers, translators, and writers largely confined to metropolitan Cairo. It was during those times that the *adīb* (man of letters) began to assume the status of a "national voice," and the small reading public expanded to include other emerging cultural centers, such as Alexandria, Port Said, and Tanta. This period witnessed a noticeable rise in literary and, particularly, novelistic production, as well as an increase in the number and variety of literary periodicals. During that decade, Egyptian criticism was not yet regarded as an independent practice,[4] though with the poet/critic 'Abbās Maḥmūd al-'Aqqād, the modern Egyptian literary field was just beginning to distinguish between literary and non-literary texts on the one hand, and between the social, moralistic, and communal norms that determine the cultural value of those texts on the other. Out of this distinction, a separate vocation called *al-naqd al-adabī* (literary criticism) would eventually arise.

However, there were serious limitations to the role of *al-naqd al-adabī* in the public discourse of the time. This is evident in the esoteric intellectual complexity of al-'Aqqād's style, which attempts to compensate for a lack of depth within the Egyptian cultured

[4] A few important works of literary criticism were produced sporadically in Egypt in the early twentieth century, which are essentially historical and comparative in nature, foreshadowing Ṭāhā Ḥusayn's *Fī al-Shi 'r al-Jāhilī* [*On Pre-Islamic Poetry*] (1926). See for instance Rūḥī al-Khālidī, *Tārīkh 'Ilm al-Adab 'inda al-Ifrinj wa al-'Arab wa Victūr Hīgū* [*A History of the Field of Literature in France, the Arab World, and in the works of Victor Hugo*] (Cairo: Matba 'a-t- al-Hilāl, 1904). See also Aḥmad D[underdot]ayf, *Muqaddima li-Dirāsa-t- Balāgha-t- al-'Arab* [*An Introduction to the Study of Arabic Rhetoric*] (Cairo: Mat[underdot]ba'a-t- al-Sufūr, 1921). Both works emphasize the connection between literature and society.

community. There is in al-'Aqqad's writings a tendency toward difficulty for its own sake, with a thickening of language. A desire for abstraction positions him as a writer aspiring to a different status or *class* of rhetoric and literary composition, one that refuses to "descend" into any topic or theme that is non-philosophical, non-moralistic, non-metaphysical, or especially non-melancholic. No wonder a new and ill-defined genre like the novel was to prove discomforting for him.

Haykal, commonly known as the first Egyptian novelist, was born into a traditional well-off feudal family strongly connected to the ruling class, and, as such, he seemed to embody the cultural tensions typical of modern Egypt and of the genre of the novel that was to become its literary expression. Part of the first generation of Egyptians to be educated at Cairo University, Haykal graduated in 1909 with a law degree. Immediately after graduation, he traveled to Paris for three years and obtained a Doctorate of Philosophy in Law from the Sorbonne in 1912. The tension between Egypt and France in his ground-breaking novel, *Zaynab*, is evident from the fact that the idea of writing a novel about the Egyptian countryside first occurred to him while in France. He is even said to have started the novel in French before deciding to write it in Arabic. In 1921, he embarked on an ambitious three-volume project on the life and works of Rousseau, which he never completed. In 1922, the year which marked Egypt's nominal independence from British Rule, Haykal joined a group of the Egyptian elite and landowners in founding the not so popular *Ḥizb al-Aḥrār al-Dustūriyyīn* (Liberal Constitutionalist Party). Haykal also played a leading role in launching and becoming the editor-in-chief of *al-Siyāsa* (*Politics*), the Liberal Constitutionalist Party's daily paper.

Early twentieth century Egyptian *udabā'* (litterateurs) were thus not only mirrors of their society, but social reformers. In this context, it is not surprising to see how Haykal's role in *Zaynab* becomes that of an intellectual whose duty is to express, as subtly as possible, his denunciation of certain Egyptian traditions that he vehemently opposed. Just as in France with Flaubert in 1855, so it was in Egypt with Haykal in 1914: every Egyptian reader of *Zaynab* was required to form an opinion, explicitly or otherwise, about the novel's issues and about the novelist's success in giving them imaginative expression. *Zaynab* invites readers to become critics and thinkers, not passive consumers. With *Zaynab*, Egyptian literature takes on a new function. An Egyptian *adīb* becomes not simply a mediator between work and audience, but a critic as well. If the work fails to express the views of the public, it certainly does not fail to impress those views by laying bare the social customs repressed in the cultural unconscious of modern Egypt. In this sociological spirit, *Zaynab* is one of the first straightforward and unadorned Egyptian narratives to acknowledge the general state of repression and to dwell on its dire social consequences.

Unlike deliberately esoteric authors like al-ʿAqqād, Haykal shared a common taste with his people, and wrote *Zaynab* with an intuitive sense of what would be expected and appreciated by a general Egyptian audience. But he placed himself outside as well as inside the Egyptian community, responding attentively from its inside as he offered his opinions from the outside. This "outside" owes much to French culture, as many critics, including Allen and Hilāl, have pointed out. But *Zaynab* is neither a crude case of influence nor the result of naïve fascination with French literary models. Its form complements its intent of critiquing the conditions of Egyptian life.

When the first edition of *Zaynab* was published in 1914 (or 1913, according to Ḥamdī al-Sakkūt),[5] the author used the subtitle "Manāẓir wa-Akhlāq Rīfiyya" (Rural Sights and Ethics), and the *nom de plume* "bi-qalam miṣrī fallāḥ" (penned by an Egyptian *fallāḥ* [peasant]), thus avoiding any reference to his own name. Commenting on his novel after the fact, Haykal claims he was speaking not just *from the point of view* of a "*miṣrī fallāḥ*," but *as* one. The word *fallāḥ*, particularly after the events of Denshawai of 1906, had acquired a special resonance. *Fallāḥ* in nascent Egyptian nationalism connotes the native who sacrifices himself, the real and authentic true-blooded Egyptian who has the right to his country. Despite the nationalist implication of the subtitle, there is a blatant irony in Haykal's choice of words, considering the low degree of literacy among Egyptian *fallāḥīn* at the time. The pseudonym *miṣrī fallāḥ* (an Egyptian, a peasant/an Egyptian peasant) imbues its author with a voice of communal bonding, as if this novel could only be written by

[5] See Ḥamdī al-Sakkūt, *The Arabic Novel: Bibliography and Critical Introduction (1865–1995)* (Cairo: The American University in Cairo Press, 2000).

and for the Egyptian *fallāḥ*, and as if the author were a mere observer expressing a spirit of collectivity. The extent to which Haykal succeeds in achieving this end and in reflecting the spirit of the Egyptian peasant remains a matter of critical assessment.

The novel's title draws upon a famous Muslim female name, inviting the reader to dwell on the sacred connection of the title with the Islamic tradition. *Al-Sayyida Zaynab* is the name of one of the largest and most renowned mosques in Egypt, located in the city of Cairo, and which according to Sunni Muslims is considered the burial site of Zaynab, daughter of ʿAlī and Fātima and granddaughter of Prophet Muhammad. The title is supplemented with a subtitle that frames the text as rural and moralistic, highlighting valued habits and sceneries of the Egyptian countryside, as implied in the term "Manāẓir" (sights, shapes, images, scenes, aspects). The work departs from previous novelistic attempts in that it does not focus on a traumatic event (like Ḥaqqī's *ʿAdhrāʾ Denshawāi*) or critique the present using historical characters or events (like al-Ṭahtāwī, Ibrāhīm, and al-Mūwayliḥī). Rather, it takes the present Egyptian society as its main topic, with its problematic social conditions, complex class structures, and intricate gender and interpersonal relationships.

The plot bluntly addresses the social malaise of the countryside and juxtaposes its squalor with its beauty. *Zaynab* is a novel about a woman who embodies both these qualities. She is a poor, sick Egyptian *fallāha* (female peasant) who, in love with one man yet forced to marry another, ends up dying a miserable death. On her deathbed, Zaynab's heart still pines for Ibrāhīm, her first love, who left Egypt as a forced conscript in the Occupation Army to fight the Sudanese mutiny in the South. The narrative is told in the third person from the perspective of Ḥāmid, the son of the landowner who employs both Zaynab and Ibrāhīm, and who is the focus of the novel's subplot. Ḥāmid is a student at the new Egyptian University; he spends the summer at his father's house in the village. Haykal depicts Ḥāmid as torn between moral values and love, but more importantly, between his own "modern," self-acquired culture and the traditional culture of his own people.[6] Ḥāmid is divided between

[6] Cf. G.W.F. Hegel, *Phenomenology of Spirit*, trans. A.V. Miller (New York: Oxford University Press, 1977), 268–294 passim – i.e. Antigone's deed *vis-à-vis* the tensions of the self and its tearing itself away from its own people – an action involving loss. Also, note that Haykal wrote *Zaynab* before e.g. Kojeve's lectures on Hegel in France.

what appears to be an arranged marriage with his intellectually bankrupt and tedious traditionalist cousin, 'Azīza, and his burning physical desire for Zaynab. Though struck by Zaynab's captivating beauty, he is fully conscious of the social gap between them. Ḥāmid exemplifies all the contradictions of the modern Egyptian middle class male caught between modernity and traditions. His class consciousness is evident whenever he talks to Zaynab, for he never fails to remind the reader that Zaynab is a peasant woman working for his father. An alert reader will not miss the condescension in his tone whenever there is an episode that brings both of them together in the novel. Here is an example:

> She [Zaynab] remembered at that moment of pain and chagrin the days of joy and happiness she had earlier spent with him [Ḥāmid]. He is the best of all and the closest to her heart, and she would have unhesitatingly surrendered to him had she known that her modest heart was worthy of him.[7]

This is just one example in which the reader encounters the heavy emphasis on Ḥāmid's class consciousness: a sense of deep respect and reverence for him on the part of Zaynab, one which is exaggerated to the point of almost undermining her own commitment to Ibrāhīm. If we agree that Ḥāmid is the voice of Haykal, then the novelist's glorification of the Egyptian middle class is itself at stake. Despite its internal focus and seeming dismissal of the colonial situation, *Zaynab* is a product of its time and a symbol of Egypt's socioeconomic conditions under British rule at the outset of the First World War. The narrative seems to acknowledge that only the sons of landlords and rich merchants could afford to go to the Egyptian University, while the sons of peasants will always be peasants, often subjected to unfair labor, punitive governmental recruitment, and forced military conscription. Ḥāmid, like Haykal, belongs to the first Egyptian generation receiving an education after the university was opened in 1907.

Ḥāmid's modern outlook on love, human relations, and marriage is due to this education, which thus becomes the first obstacle to

[7] Muḥammad Ḥusayn Haykal, *Zaynab, al-Ṭabʿa al-Sādisa* (al-Qāhira: NP, 1967 [1921]), 213. Unless otherwise noted, all translations from Arabic into English are mine.

tradition with its rigid package of conventional practices, such as imposing the veil, the separation of the sexes, the unquestioned male right to education, and the automatic relegation of women to domestic labor, as well as forced marriages. The Egypt of the 1910s was a segregated society in regard to gender relations, and chances for men and women to meet and socialize prior to marriage were almost impossible. The only conceivable way for marriages to come about was through the almost defunct profession of salafi origins: that of *al-Khāṭ[i]ba* (the matchmaker), a socially intra-familial and well-connected woman, who has access to domestic spaces otherwise denied male Muslim non-family members, enabling her to mediate between families to match suitable mates. Zaynab, the poor, sickly, uneducated Egyptian peasant who, like Sitt al-Dār in Ḥaqqī's novel, is also a *ḥurma* (a belittling Egyptian reference to a woman), overwhelmed by the weight of tradition, is destined to listen and to obey without ever contradicting her male "superiors."

Ḥāmid strongly denounces the *khāṭ[i]ba* tradition by calling for the emancipation of men and women from dogmatic rules so that they can get to know one another and base marriages on love and mutual respect rather than class compatibility and family approval. Ḥāmid's position is explicitly anti-traditionalist; in fact, he views tradition as an enemy of the nation. Tradition denies Zaynab the chance to choose her husband, and ultimately causes her affliction and death. Tradition also ruins Ḥāmid's conjugal ambitions. At first, he thinks 'Azīza will make an ideal wife, but he is soon disillusioned by her exaggerated guilt and hyper-religiosity.

In a way, 'Azīza is not much different from Zaynab – despite the former's privileged bourgeois status. Both are victims of patriarchal mapping: fettered, channeled, and fashioned by their own restrictive social conditions to follow a specific prescribed path from which they could never deviate. Egyptian tradition, in the novel, has transformed itself into a kind of fossilized patriarchy refusing to see the benefits of social reform that may be the only option available for Egypt's advancement in the world. Whatever the outcome of its imperial struggle, the Egypt of *Zaynab* is a country doomed to impede gender equality, social equity, and human progress by pursuing its long-standing class hierarchies.

The novel ends with Ḥāmid reconciling himself to remaining unmarried. This choice is a symbolic blow against an outmoded tradition subscribing to an obsolete social logic. Evidence of this lies in the letter Ḥāmid writes to his parents upon his return to Cairo:

As I started to think about love and came to meet my cousin ['Azīza], I wanted to marry her. But when I saw her and saw how impossible it was for me to talk to her in private, I became more indignant with our society and its customs than those who have to simply accept and learn to live with the cruel restrictions it inflicts on them. I have come to have serious doubts about marriage. I believe that a marriage not based on or nourished by love is not worth being called marriage at all.[8]

One can easily tell that this letter is not simply addressed to Ḥāmid's parents. This epistolary insertion, typical of eighteenth-century European novels, testifies to the European influence on Haykal's novel. Habermas writes that the eighteenth-century bourgeois novel developed an epistolary device in letters exchanged as part of the "conjugal family's intimate domain."[9] Since the letters play a role in the plot of the novel, they naturally acquire a more public status. This is exactly what Ḥāmid's letters do in *Zaynab*.

Read in this context, the novel appears to be not simply a transformation of the private into the public, but a living document and a public witness to the Egyptian domestic sphere of the time. Above all, Ḥāmid's letter expresses his feelings about his own life and the social codes that encompass him. Although there is non-confrontational timidity inherent in the very act of choosing to write a letter that saves Ḥāmid the embarrassment of a parental showdown, the protagonist's message is clear. His letter is the perfect confessional subgenre that conveys truth to Egyptian readers and invites them to rethink interpersonal relationships in Egypt. It is also a call for reconstructing calcified traditions into more flexible forms compatible with the sociopolitical changes of the time. In setting an Egyptian protagonist against the backdrop of British colonialism, Haykal enacts an oppositional relationship between the public sphere of Egypt's colonial presence on the ground and the more abstract question of the country's sociopolitical future. The novel exposes inherent contradictions in Egyptians' social practices and, if it does not offer alternatives to them, it at least questions their logic.

[8] Haykal, *Zaynab*, 268–69.
[9] Jürgen Habermas, *The Structural Transformation of the Public Sphere*, trans. Thomas Burger (Cambridge, MA: MIT, 1991), 28.

Haykal's work confronts pre-First World War Egyptian society not simply with the pressing issues of class, gender, and power, but with the way in which class, gender, and power are understood. The ways in which Egyptians themselves internalize and normalize these issues are crucial. Just as the ideology of British colonialism serves to conceal the exploitation of the Egyptian society, the ideology of social relations as explored in *Zaynab* serves to conceal a different kind of dogmatic colonialism, one imposed by Muslim Egyptians on their own. The Egyptian community of *Zaynab* replaces the anti-colonial with the anti-modern and acknowledges no rational identity beyond its own boundaries. What caused First World War Egypt to be colonized, Haykal warns us, is precisely its unassuming adherence to traditionalism.

However, it is important to emphasize that Ḥāmid, despite his critique of traditionalism, does not wholeheartedly embrace Western ideology. We learn that he is a sharp critic of life in the West, its descent into materialism, its ill-conceived ideas of empiricism, the poor conditions of its working classes, and the suffering brought out by both its imperialism and its related subordination and denigration of non-Western cultures. When Haykal's protagonist exposes the limits of the Egyptian marriage system, he is speaking from a point of view of universal ethics, not necessarily a Europeanist or colonialist one. This censure is clear in the protagonist's scathing tone and especially in his vow of celibacy, with which Ḥāmid transcends the local milieu he criticizes. This perhaps could be the objective of Egyptian modernity: a well-informed, rational critique of the present and a concomitant move to change it with a view toward the "new," even though Ḥāmid's remains passive and non-confrontational at the end of the novel. In *Zaynab*, then, by virtue of the plot, the portrayal of social customs, and character development, the new genre of the novel acts as a practical mediator between family and society.

There is little or no doubt that *Zaynab* changed the practice of Egyptian literature from a heavy reliance on oratorical recitations and flamboyant verses – ones that are no less heroic in their call for social reform and their critique of power, be it represented in the Khedive or the British, but often marked by the subtlety and indirectness characteristic of the poetry genre – to a *narrative* of social criticism. Poised precariously between Egyptian colloquialism and revolutionary thought, Haykal's novel represents an early attempt to modernize Egypt, its literature, and the readership for that literature. Given Egypt's multiple religious and secular ideologies of the time, the readership of early twentieth-century Egypt was extremely varied in its reading practices and expectations. The unprecedented circulation of the press produced different kinds of readers: "news readers," "poetry readers," "politics readers," "Islamist readers," etc. Irrespective of their priorities, *Zaynab* demanded a highly literate modern readership whose engagement with the novel far exceeded that demanded by journalistic scoops. Merely knowing how to read Arabic or follow a narrative was not enough. A willingness to address issues of tradition and national pride critically and self-critically was required. *Zaynab* is a work in which the novelist finds himself addressing an audience that might or might not be ready to understand his message or technique. Not surprisingly, then, *Zaynab* was not fully appreciated upon its publication, not until the late 1920s.

If we treat *Zaynab* as a secular critique, then what appears to be wrong in colonial Egypt is a lack not of morality but of reason, and the only chance that Egypt has to de-colonize itself is by a radical dissociation from accepted social norms and values, which persist only in debased forms. What could be more destructive than a way of thinking devoid of reason in a nation whose social and interpersonal practices are inseparable from its colonization? In other words, Haykal issues a clarion call for nationalist Egyptians to step outside the circle of dogmatic stagnation and to reform many of their social practices, especially those regarding marriage, gender relations, and education. These concerns are no less important than gaining independence from British rule.

The passage from tradition to modernity, as the novel suggests, is also a passage from Islamism to moderate Islam, and one that does not involve the bourgeois society alone: it comprises Egyptian society at large.[10] Encircled and assailed by foreign interests, internally divided among nationalists, Ottomanists, and colonizers, Egypt is compelled to assess its own destiny in a new ideological light. The call for social reform, gender equality, and education for all cannot be attempted without acknowledging the will to class solidarity and

[10] See Aḥmad Zalaṭ, *Muḥammad Ḥusayn Haykal bayn al-Ḥaḍāratayn al-Islāmiyya wa al-Gharbiyya* [Muḥammad Ḥusayn Haykal Between Islamic and Western Civilizations] (Cairo: al-Hay'a al-Miṣriyya al-'Āmma lil-Kitāb, 1988).

to a multi-layered Egyptian identity in the face of a dangerous political threat. Reason is a necessity, not a luxury. Providing education for all is not an act of extravagance, nor is the application of secular reason to Egypt's traditionalism the whim of a Europe-educated elite, but a crucial catalyst in the *nahḍa* (awakening) of the modern Egyptian society as a whole.

Zaynab has received extensive critical acclaim by many Egyptian and non-Egyptian critics. Why, one may ask, has this novel gained a unique position among many other novels in Egypt that preceded and followed it? Answers to this question vary. Some regard it as *awwal riwāya fanniyya* (the first narrative to offer full-fledged representation of the novel as a genre) in Arabic literature, mainly because of its mature treatment of characters and events.[11] Roger Allen, for instance, contends that the novel's distinctive feature is its "realistic backdrop," a quality lacking in previous novelistic attempts. "Haykal places his reader right in the midst of the Egyptian village," Allen argues, "and proceeds to elaborate on natural phenomena – the fields and crops, the sunrise and sunset, and so on – at great, almost tedious length."[12] Al-Musawi, on the other hand, sees the novel as an indication of the Arab intellectual's critique of the "subordination of women." To al-Musawi, *Zaynab*'s significance lies in "its social consciousness and subversion of patriarchal structures."[13] This is a valid observation, but it should not escape our cultural memory that the novel's uncritical acceptance of gendered nationalism raises issues about the relationship between the culture of modernism in Muslim colonial Egypt and the continued subordination of women. Nonetheless, it is clear that Haykal's critique of Egypt's social conditions and his choice of a woman-centered title, irrespective of the implications of feminizing the nation, marks a shift in Egyptian intellectual and literary discourse.

[11] See for instance Qadriyya Zakī, *Muqaddima fī al-Adab al-Ḥadīth* [*An Introduction to Modern Literature*] (Cairo: Ghuzlān Press, 1990) 120–141; Ali Jad, *Form and Technique in the Egyptian Novel: 1912–1971* (London: Ithaca Press, 1983); see also Samah Selim, *The Novel and the Rural Imaginary in Egypt: 1880–1985* (New York: RoutledgeCurzon, 2004).

[12] Roger Allen, *The Arabic Novel: An Historical and Critical Introduction* (Syracuse: Syracuse University Press, 1982), 31–2.

[13] Muhsin Jassim al-Musawi, *The Postcolonial Arabic Novel: Debating Ambivalence* (Leiden: Brill, 2003), 59.

Haykal, consciously or not, repeats or accepts the pattern of European colonialism that Egypt, much like any colonized country, must question in its anti-colonial struggle against Britain. He does so by promoting categories of progress and reason. Partha Chatterjee, using the Indian example of nationalism, and drawing on the work of Edward Said and Anouar Abdel-Malek, argues that this problematic "is exactly the reverse of that of Orientalism." Whereas in Orientalism, Chatterjee explains, the Oriental is a passive subject, in nationalism the object becomes the active "subject," one that remains tied to such categories as "progress," "reason," and "modernity." What this means is that instead of being acted upon by these alien categories, the nationalist subject *internalizes* them and believes them to be autonomous and natural. Nationalist thought unquestionably accepts the binary distinctions between "East" versus "West" and "us" versus "them." This is precisely the inherent contradiction of so-called "Third World" nationalism: to accept the model of the very power it arose to resist.

However, one must still take into consideration the distinction that Chatterjee makes between "that part of social ideology which asserts the existence of certain historical possibilities" and that "which seeks to justify those claims by an appeal to both epistemic and moral principles."[14] For Egypt's specific cultural model, it is useful to underscore that *Zaynab* was meant to be more of a moral story than a novel, part of the vast discourse of humanism. *Zaynab* will be understood best if considered as a project of a bourgeois cultural politics seeking to interrogate and secularize the entire social structure of colonial Egypt, including its political and educational destiny, the status of women, family relations, the landowners' attitudes toward their servants, master–servant relationships, and the question of love-based conjugality.

If the task of literature is to assess social values from a humanist perspective, then the Egyptian novel must have emerged with a mission and as a mission: to alert every *miṣrī fallāḥ(a)* (Egyptian peasant), whose connection to Egypt stems from the native land, to the dangers of the ideological turmoil and political vulnerability that could very well erase one's identity. This is a harsh price that Egypt

[14] Partha Chatterjee, *Nationalist Thought and the Colonial World: A Derivative Discourse* (Minneapolis: University of Minnesota Press, 1993), 38–9.

may have to pay if the simple principles of reason are not to be applied to gender, class equality, and justice. If Egypt is to seek freedom and independence from foreign rule, it must first break free from itself.

Such a humanism, which also carries a germ of nationalism, with its emphasis on ethical and emotional responsibilities, individual freedom, and the triumph of free will, was not commonly addressed in Egyptian life. The unprecedented courage of Ṭāhā Ḥusayn's 1926 *Fī al-Shiʿr al-Jāhilī* (*On Pre-Islamic Poetry*) followed by his provocative 1927 autobiography *al-Ayyām* (*The Days*), represents a critical moment of enlightenment in a modernity where reason, in the face of the most sacred of traditions embodied in its dominant Islamic institutions, like al-Azhar, must dominate, and where the free exercise of secular reason, unshackled by defensive dogmatisms, should finally produce a richer, more diverse, and intellectually tolerant cultural milieu. It is a sign of the times that a revolutionary modernity would appear, revealing itself in critical works like *The Days*. It is also a sign of the times that those watershed texts would be labeled as sacrilegious.

3 *Blindness and Insight: Challenging the Sacred/Secular Divide in Ṭāhā Ḥusayn's* The Days

The director stood in the embrasure of the window, his back to the light

James Joyce, *A Portrait of the Artist as a Young Man*

France was kind to Ṭāhā Ḥusayn. During his four years of graduate studies there, which coincided with the First World War, he obtained a license in classics and a diploma in history. In addition, he received a doctorate from the Sorbonne, supervised by the renowned sociologist Emile Durkheim, on the topic of Ibn Khaldūn. Most notably, he was probably the first Azharite Muslim graduate of his time to meet and marry a Catholic French woman. A decade later, in his autobiography, he refers to his wife, Suzanne Brisseau, as *al-ṣawt al-'adhb* (the sweet voice), and says that once he heard this voice, anguish never again entered his heart. But this sweetness was received bitterly. Marriage to a foreign and Christian woman was not greeted with tolerance in a hardened, orthodox Muslim society, but with ridicule and disgust among the sheikhs and ministers. In her own autobiographical account, Madame Suzanne Taha Hussein [sic] recalls one of her husband's sordid exchanges with some sheikhs ridiculing their interreligious marriage:

"Doctor Taha, are you married?"

"Yes, of course, sir."

"Would you bring your wife to the meeting [a homage to another sheikh]?"

"Well, no, sir, because she is in France."

"In France? And you let her travel there all alone?"

"Well yes, sir; she's a French woman."

"And why then did you marry a French woman? If it were up to me I would pass a law exiling every Egyptian who married a foreign woman."

"Please, sir, pass that law right away; I'm tired of hearing such discourse and would just as soon be out of here."

The gentleman broke out laughing, and everyone joined in, at my expense. Sheikh Bekhit spoke again:

"All the same, Doctor Taha, I'd like to understand the serious reasons which led you to marry a foreigner. You are a good Egyptian, a good patriot, very intelligent; how in the world could you do such a thing?"

"I met a young woman, and I loved her; I married her. If I hadn't done it, I'd have remained a bachelor, or I would have hypocritically married an Egyptian woman whom I would have made miserable because I loved another woman."

"I can't fathom that!"

"That you will never be able to fathom, your Excellence; we will never understand things in the same manner."[1]

As if these vicious attacks were not enough, Madame Hussein tells of the humiliations Ḥusayn endured at the hands of the Islamic establishment owing to his book on pre-Islamic poetry, which was banned by al-Azhar immediately upon release. Deeply troubled, personally, by the hatred, the shunning, and the death threats he received from the fundamentalist community of 1926 Cairo, as well as professionally, by the adverse reaction of his colleagues to his Cartesian approach to pre-Islamic Arabic literature, Ḥusayn feared for his life and arranged for an armed guard outside of his house. Fearing the worst, Madame Ḥusayn took her husband to France so that he could regain his bearings and recuperate. It was in the southeastern village of Haute-Savoie, which borders Switzerland and Italy, where Ḥusayn composed the manuscript of the first part of his autobiography, *Al-Ayyām* (*The Days*), in nine full days.[2]

Ḥusayn's response to the critical impasse and public hostility encountered following the publication of *On Pre-Islamic Poetry* (1926), invites the question of how the confessional nature of his autobiography is to be regarded. Is it an *iʿtithār wa kaffāra*, an act of

[1] Suzanne Taha Hussein, *Les 'Souvenirs' de Madame Suzanne Taha Hussein* (*Memoirs of Madame Suzanne Taha Hussein*), ed. J. P. Lachèse, trans. T. K. Kraft (Paris: Mélanges Institut Dominicain d'Études Orientales [MIDEO], 15, 1982), 19. See also Suzanne Taha Hussein, *Avec Toi* [*With You*] (Paris: Editions du Cerf, 2011). Cf. www.dacb.org/stories/egypt/hussein_suzanne-taha .html (Submitted by Fr. Thomas Kevin Kraft O. P., Roman Catholic priest, member of the Order of Preachers [Dominican Friars], Lecturer at Tangaza College (Nairobi, Kenya, 2012).

[2] Hussein, *Les 'Souvenirs,'* 20.

expiation expressing a feeling of *dhanb* (guilt) for a transgression; or is it an *'udhr wa tabrīr*, an act of justification acknowledging no sense of guilt at all? Did Ḥusayn want to be forgiven for what was perceived as an act of heresy, or was he seeking *tabri'a* (exoneration, i.e. clearing his name of those accusations)? In other words, was it an apology or an apologia? And why does the difference between these two matter?

To begin, what must be historically recorded is that Ḥusayn's prosecutor found nothing particularly incriminating about the text itself,[3] yet insisted that Ḥusayn was nevertheless guilty of a transgression. The prosecutor was right: Ḥusayn was to blame for choosing systematic logic to debunk traditionalism, in what was clearly recognized as the challenge of familiar and sanctified dogma by critical scholarship. Ḥusayn, "one of the epoch's great defenders of rationalist tradition,"[4] as Fatima Mernessi calls him, knew that *On Pre-Islamic Poetry* would be widely acknowledged as one of the most controversial books in modern Arabic literary and cultural criticism; with that knowledge, he had to come to terms with the fact that he entered the scene of modern Arabic cultural and Islamic thought, once and forever, as the author of *On Pre-Islamic Poetry*. Little did he know that this heartrending experience would propel him to compose *The Days*, one of the most poignant cultural expressions in modern Egypt, a work of art whose magnetism would continue to attract extraordinary responses over time. Not only has it been translated into many languages, including English, French, Hebrew, Chinese, Russian, German, and Persian,[5] and serialized on Egyptian television, but some of its words, such as *al- fatà* (the young adult) and *al-ṣwat al-'adhb* (sweet voice), have become an iconic part of Egyptian and Arab-Islamic culture. Indeed, the aura surrounding the name of Ṭāhā Ḥusayn has continued to be powerful

[3] See the appendix of Ḥusayn, "Taqrīr al-Niyāba ḥawl Fī al-Shi 'r al-Jāhilī" [The Public Prosecutor's Report on *On the Pre-Islamic Poetry*] in *Fī al-Shi'r al-Jāhilī* (*On Pre-Islamic Poetry*).

[4] Fatima Mernissi, *Islam and Democracy: Fear of the Modern World*, trans. Mary Jo Lakeland (New York: Basic Books, 2002), 47.

[5] See Ṣalāḥ 'Aṭṭiyya, *Ṭāhā Ḥusayn wa Ma 'ārikuhu al-Adabiyya* [*Ṭāhā Ḥusayn and his Literary Quarrels*], vol. 1 (Cairo: Dār al-Jumhūriyya lil-Ṣaḥāfa, 1954), 18.

despite, or perhaps because of, Islamists' persistent attacks on his legacy.[6]

The aftermath of *On Pre-Islamic Poetry* – the trial coupled with a growing sensationalism – may have also prompted Ḥusayn to build a bridge away from, and to seek solace outside of, the specialized world of literature and culture, and to pursue a more direct dialogue with the reading public through journalistic writings. Owing to his court interrogation by the public prosecutor, Ḥusayn became a public event. The court – itself already a modern judicial phenomenon in colonial Egypt – brings to the mind of the cultural comparatist a watershed year of literature on trial in nineteenth-century France, namely, the 1857 trial of Gustav Flaubert's *Madam Bovary* for "indecency" and of Charles Baudelaire's *Les Fleurs du mal* (Flowers of Evil) for "erotic and irreligious imagery." The idea of subjecting a work of art – a work based on freedom of expression or on a specific understanding of history – to the scales of justice and the silent grandeur of the courtroom, is a hallmark of modernity. More specifically, in the case of Ḥusayn it stands at the crux of a fundamental moment in the battle between Islamism and secular modernity in the Arab-Muslim world.

In the aftermath of the trial, Ḥusayn slowly began to secure a considerable influence and reputation – both of which were much needed for an embattled intellectual like himself. Given both the intensity of the psychological and intellectual duress he endured as a result of his

[6] Numerous Islamists have considered Ḥusayn's book to be the mother of all battles against secular thought, and some even dedicated their scholarship to an attack on Ḥusayn's legacy. A case in point is the Islamist Anwar al-Jundī, who authored at least three books in defamation of Ḥusayn's legacy, including *Ṭāhā Ḥusayn: Ḥayātuhu wa Fikruhu fī mizān al-Islām* [*Ṭāhā Ḥusayn: His Life and Thought on the Balance of Islam*] (Cairo: Dār al-I 'tiṣām, 1976). See also Khayrī Shalabī, *Muḥākama-t- Ṭāhā Ḥusayn* [*The Trial of Ṭāhā Ḥusayn*] (Beirut: al-Mu'assasa al-'Arabiyya lil Dirāsāt wa al-Nashr, 1972); Jamāl al-Dīn al-Alūsī, *Ṭāhā Ḥusayn bayn Anṣārihi wa Khuṣūmihi* [*Ṭāhā Ḥusayn between Proponents and Opponents*] (Baghdad: Maṭba 'a-t- al-Irshād, 1973); Sāmih Kurayyim, *Ṭāhā Ḥusayn fī Ma'ārikihi al-Adabiyya* [*Ṭāhā Ḥusayn at His Literary Quarrels, 1*] (Cairo: al-Hay'a al-Miṣriyya al-'Āmma lil-Kitāb, 1974); Jābir Rizq, *Ṭāhā Ḥusayn: al-Jarīma wa al-Idāna* [*Ṭāhā Ḥusayn: Crime and Punishment*] (Cairo: Dār al-I 'tiṣām, 1985); Ibrāhīm 'Awaḍ, *Ma'araka-t- al-Shi'r al-Jāhilī* [*The Skirmish over Pre-Islamic Poetry*] (Cairo: Maṭb 'a-t al-Fajr al-Jadīd, 1987). For a more historical/archival approach to Ḥusayn's cultural legacy, see also Abū Bakr 'Abd al-Rāziq, *Wathā'iq Qaḍiyya-t- Ṭāhā Ḥusayn* [*The Documents in Ṭāhā Ḥusayn's Case*] (Beirut: al-Maktaba al-'Aṣriyya, 1991).

book and the concomitant rise of an oppositional Islamist current against him, Ḥusayn began to devote himself more to journalism, which was the customary beginning of a proper literary career in Egypt from the late 1920s to early 1930s. The initial motivations for writing publicly were not particularly artistic; it was, in fact, only through autobiography that Ḥusayn found the way back to the heart of Egyptian readers. From the time *The Days* was first serialized in *al-Hilāl* newspaper, between July 1926 and July 1927, it was met with tremendous – merited – appreciation and success.

The Days provides an exceptional outlook on Ḥusayn's formative years as a literary scholar as well as on the various currents of literary criticism that he learned to incorporate into his work, or from which he learned to break away. Even a cursory reading will reveal that Ḥusayn's motivations in *On Pre-Islamic Poetry* are far from irreligious or irrational or anti-Islamic. As it turns out, the exposure of the corrupt system of al-Azhar and the opportunism of certain *sheikhs* (religious leaders), as expressed forcibly and irreverently in this timely autobiography, served Ḥusayn's revolutionary academic purposes even more effectively than his perhaps overly positivistic *On Pre-Islamic Poetry*. The victory of *The Days* became a victory of nonconformity, delivered with an exquisite confessional style that shocked at the same time as it elevated its readers.

Ḥusayn's main goal in *On Pre-Islamic Poetry* was to incorporate what one generally refers to in literary theory as "context." According to the *Oxford English Dictionary*, *context* is a "weaving together," a "connection or coherence" defined as the "whole structure of a connected passage regarded in its bearing upon any of the parts which constitute it; the parts which immediately precede or follow any particular passage or 'text' and determine its meaning."[7] Context is thus primarily textual and constitutes the broader "reality" of text itself in a manner that informs understanding. This does not mean that Ḥusayn contradicts the Derridean formula "*il n'y a pas de hors-texte*" ("there is no outside-text").[8] On the contrary, to Ḥusayn, as well as to Derrida, who himself is just one generation shy of the graduate education Ḥusayn received in Paris, the only available

[7] "context, n." OED Online. June 2017. Oxford University Press.

[8] Jacques Derrida, *Of Grammatology*, trans. Gayatri Chakravorty Spivak (Baltimore: The Johns Hopkins University Press, 1976), 158.

context is (in) the text itself, and critics must endeavor to develop the linguistic skills and the meticulous methods that enable them to grasp the meaning of the text to the best of their abilities. Thus in the text lies the very history, the very *hors d'oeuvre*, that we vainly seek outside of it.

Seen in this light, *The Days* is the con-text, the sub-text, and indeed the belated pre-text of *On Pre-Islamic Poetry*, a necessary addendum to its broader intentions. In *The Days*, Ḥusayn's aesthetic brilliance returns, more persistently, though more covertly, than in his venture in *On Pre-Islamic Poetry*, as a boomerang effort to throw the theoretical text back against itself. The implication is that we could only understand *On Pre-Islamic Poetry* if we clearly comprehend the context of its composition. This context is available in *The Days*. For *context* is precisely the sociolinguistic key that opens up the text and saves it from falling prey to the very conventional judgment it seeks to deconstruct. *The Days* is thus more than the sum of its narrative. *The Days* is the necessary *matn* (marginalia) of *On Pre-Islamic Poetry*. It is an account of the suppression of freedom and the predominance of calcified thought. It is the forgotten context of the untold number of Egyptians who, on a daily basis, suffer abject poverty, government negligence, un-accommodated disabilities, and deteriorating health conditions – the Egyptians who, now, could read *in context*, but could not write themselves, every word Ḥusayn has penned so deeply.

This confessional account, presented in the third-person narrative mode, reveals that Ḥusayn is not the Trojan horse he was portrayed to be, or the betrayer of his tradition and religion as some have painted him, but a true scholar dedicated to illuminating the context of the society in which he lives. As transgressive and irreverent as his theoretical venture may appear, it is, in essence, the expression of a rational scholar adopting reason as an inalienable scholarly right. Like Haykal's *Zaynab*, Ḥusayn's text rejects traditionalism not so much because of its ahistoricity, but because of its irrationality. To conquer dogmatism, Ḥusayn has to cling to rationalism like "a shipwrecked man clinging to a spar," to borrow a line from Ibsen.[9] One only needs to ponder the psychotic religiosity of Ḥusayn's time – and

[9] Henrik Ibsen, *A Doll's House: A Play in Three Acts*, trans. William Archer (London: Methuen Drama, 2009): Act 3, p. 82.

of our own – to comprehend the enormity of the task of the intellectual in steering society away from its own self-destructiveness.

A shocking work of intellectual density like *On Pre-Islamic Poetry* was perhaps not the best way to begin a dialogue with the Egyptian readership in the 1920s, especially not in the aftermath of the demise of the Islamic Caliphate. While Ḥusayn's connections with academic circles were close, and he spoke a language they understood, Egypt's broader masses needed to be prepared and approached differently, all the more so since he was dealing with a grave matter of larger sociological and theological implications. *On Pre-Islamic Poetry* started Ḥusayn on the wrong foot, as it were, creating a negative ferment and leading to popular discontent and accusations of sacrilege. Ḥusayn needed a textual supplement consistent with Egyptian cultural sensibilities, a local narrative to illuminate the context and restore public confidence in him, or at least public empathy.

There is already a precedent for *The Days* in the authenticity and local color of Haykal's *Zaynab*, which, despite its heterodoxy, gained remarkable success and popularity, mainly owing to its plot and subplot lines, as well as to its captivating, conversational narrative style. It is precisely through conversations that the protagonist becomes disillusioned with his society's dogmatic doctrines, and eventually comes to renounce them. In addition, the novel not only raises, in the minds of the modern Egyptian public, ironies of fate but also strengthens the association of the curse of conventionalism with corruption and injustice. Zaynab, an Egyptian peasant woman of low social status, is able to inspire Ḥāmid and plant the seeds of love in his heart. Suffering unrequited love, being given in marriage to someone else because of wealth, forced to bear inhumane social conditions that rob her of her freedom: this is the fate of Zaynab, which is not much different from the fate of her lover, Ibrahim, who is separated from his beloved, conscripted in a war he does not understand, and ultimately dies for a cause not his own.

A nascent genre, the novel had nonetheless already established itself in Egypt as the successful literary project of social critique par excellence; a decade after the publication of Haykal's tragic romance, the time was ripe for a fresh type of novelistic writing. Perhaps a shocking realism, detailing the difficult realities of the quotidian and the struggle to overcome physical hardships, would be a strong dose to swallow, but what could be more sympathetic than a narrative of a poor, blind child from an unknown village in the Egyptian south elbowing his way through massive physical and institutional challenges determined to achieve his dreams? And to a society accustomed to propriety and conservativeness, what argument for social progress could be more credible than a personal account of the gestation of an enlightened human being beginning with the tribulations of an underprivileged family, the days of hunger, the nights of uncertainty, and the years of institutional oppression and cruelty?

There could have not been a more opportune year for the publication of the first volume of *The Days* than 1927, the year following the appearance of *Pre-Islamic Poetry*. For nothing could have been more relevant to the torment Ḥusayn had been forced to endure than the contrast between his wretched beginnings as a blind and impoverished young boy in the south of Egypt and his current embattled status as the leading intellectual figure of the entire cultural scene of modern Egypt. His attackers – who were primarily from conservative upper middle class and Islamist backgrounds, so different from his own – had no sense of who he was or of what boyhood challenges and institutional discrimination he had encountered. The publication of the volume in 1927, then, was a brilliant and timely move to link his autobiography with his scholarly study so that the Egyptian reader of the late 1920s could view him and his work with greater understanding and sympathy.

The first volume of *The Days* portrays a world full of calamities and narrow escapes, and teeming with ignorance and unthinking traditionalism; the story it tells provides an explanation of the rigid antirationalism of a dogmatic society that he had set out to challenge in *On Pre-Islamic Poetry*[10] – and a defiant response to it. Like *Zaynab*, *The Days* departs from the model established by such early-century classics as Aḥmad Shawqī's romance novels or al-Manfalūṭī's moral and sentimental tales. Ḥusayn is even more realistic than Haykal. Although *Zaynab* strives to depict an authentic image of the Egyptian countryside, it is not free of a French-inspired literariness, most notably in the Dumasian flourish, in the fashion of *La Dame aux Camélias*, of Zaynab's hyperbolic handkerchief death scene at the

[10] See 'Abd al-Hamīd Yūnus, *Ṭāhā Ḥusayn Bayn Dhamīr al-Ghā'b wa Dhamīr al-Mutakallim* [*Taha Dhamīr al-Mutakalliml-Ghān: Methuen Drama, 2009): Act 3*,] (Cairo: Dār al-Hilāl, nd.).

end of the novel. No such literary flourishes mitigate the impact of Haykal's exposure of religious exploitation, and of the crushing of the dignity and aspirations of the most forgotten in the Egyptian society whose lives and dreams get trampled and squandered either by ruthless materialism or hardened traditionalism.

The first lines of *The Days* are pragmatically Egyptian; they immediately take the reader into the innermost feelings of a blind boy, born to a disadvantaged family in one of the deepest pockets of illiteracy in the Egyptian South. Because of his blindness, the narrator is frequently unable to specify exactly when events occur. This inability is an important *leitmotif* in the autobiography

> He cannot remember the name of the day nor is he able to place it in the month and year wherein God placed it. In fact he cannot even remember what time of the day it was exactly and can only give it approximately.
>
> To the best of his belief, the time of the day was either dawn or dusk. That is due to the fact that he remembers feeling a slightly cold breeze on his face, which the heat of the sun had not destroyed.
>
> And that is likely because notwithstanding his ignorance as to whether it was light or dark, he just remembers, on leaving the house, meeting with soft, gentle, delicate light as though darkness covered some of its edges.[11]

Nonetheless, the autobiography depicts vivid scenes of *al-Qarya* (the village), of its society, and its ways of life. Ḥusayn's recollection of the village is a complex one, at times rancorous, at times cynical, and at times humorous, but never romantic or idyllic. Superstition roams unchecked as the reader relives moments of trauma and night horror with the young boy who fears that *ʿafārīt* (demons) and "terrifying apparitions" will seep through his sheets "unless he wrapped himself up inside the coverlet from head to toe."[12] He is convinced that "if he uncovered his face in the course of the night or exposed any of the extremities of his body, they would be at the mercy of one of the numerous evil sprites which inhabited every part of the house, filling every nook and cranny."[13] The young boy's personal trauma is amplified by the external conditions of an impoverished countryside whose only redeeming feature is the griot, the roaming poet and

[11] Ṭāhā Ḥusayn, *The Days, Taha Hussein: His Autobiography in Three Parts*, trans. E. H. Paxton, Hilary Wayment, and Kenneth Cragg (Cairo: The American University in Cairo Press, 1997), 9.

[12] Ibid., 11.

[13] Ibid., 10.

storyteller who would recite "in a wonderfully sweet tone" the exploits of folkloric Egyptian heroes such as "Abu Zaid, Khalifa, and Diab."[14]

The young boy lives a life full of events – sometimes suddenly poignant, more often prolonged and banal. But is it not precisely the banal that carries with it the pain of the tragic? The medical charlatanism of the local barber causes him to lose his eyesight at a very early age; his four-year-old sister contracts an agonizing disease and dies of medical neglect; the cholera breakout of 1902 sweeps entire villages and takes many innocent lives in its course; the young boy's eighteen-year-old brother, a would-be physician, also dies, while trying to save cholera-infected patients in Cairo. Religion, magic, and superstition blend indistinguishably and are an integral part of the villagers' lives, only intensifying the tragedy of their existence. "Religious" men benefit commercially from the horror of the cholera outbreak by selling *Ta'wīdhāt* (charms and amulets), incantations, and lists of the Prophet's relics as protections. And the young boy's father is no better; he too seeks to benefit from his son's physical disability by asking him to recite repeatedly the Yāsīn Chapter, expecting God to be more charitable because "it would not be acceptable for Allah to turn down the appeals of a blind child reciting the Quran."[15] His disillusionment with the tedium of religious rituals increases after he has committed the entire Qur'ān to memory by the age of nine and realizes that the eagerly awaited title of "shaykh" comes with neither a cap nor a gown.

Ḥusayn, then, seems predestined to a limited career: either as a local imam (religious leader) or neighborhood shaykh (sheikh), or if he has the voice, as a Qāri' (Qur'ān reciter) at funerals and other social functions of his community. This would have been a good occupation for an early twentieth-century Upper-Egyptian peasant. Joining al-Azhar and receiving the best traditional education available in the Arab world for a specialist in Islam and Arabic literature would, in itself, have indeed been a remarkable success given his disability and humble beginnings. But to obtain his doctorate from Egypt's first-ever secular university, to travel to France and receive a PhD from the Sorbonne, and then to become the doyen of Arabic

[14] Ibid.
[15] Ibid., 12.

literature and the intellectual frontrunner of an entire century of modern Egyptian thought – this is a truly remarkable achievement and a living refutation of the fatalism of the rigid traditionalism that he came to challenge in his scholarly work.

von Grunebaum has correctly described Ḥusayn as "the intellectual leader of the next generation,"[16] and his influence remains so extraordinary that even today the profundity of his thought is difficult to appreciate. In fact, the complexity of his intellectual growth and scholarly contributions is so extensive that even Pierre Cachia's groundbreaking *Taha Husayn: His Place in the Egyptian Literary Renaissance* (1956), based on his 1951 dissertation, the first in English on a modern Arab literary scholar and public intellectual, failed to fully capture the extent of his contributions. Years later, Cachia himself acknowledged that "a corrective to my early assessment of Taha Hussein lies in the historical perspective which the lengthening years have brought."[17] Those lengthening years have allowed Cachia finally to come to see Ḥusayn as the intellectual he really was, the man who "provided Arab Modernism with its most appealing formulation: not innovation but renovation, the revitalization of a great cultural heritage by bringing the best modes of Western thinking to bear upon on it, and this in emulation of forefathers who, in the heyday of Islam, had drawn freely on the resources of Greek civilization."[18]

Although still not adequately acknowledging the innovative nature of Ḥusayn's intellectual venture, Cachia's "corrective" more adequately acknowledges Ḥusayn's far-reaching impact. Ḥusayn remains the legitimate heir of a new spirit of modern secular thought in Egypt extending far beyond Islamic boundaries, and the first autobiographer in modern Egypt whose literary work delineates a reality reflective of his own intellectual endeavor. Here is a scholar condemned by traditionalism yet triumphantly rising above it, showing no hesitation in attacking its methods of criticism, and defiantly

[16] G. E. Von Grunebaum, *Modern Islam: The Search for Cultural Identity* (New York: Vintage Books, 1962), 312.

[17] Pierre Cachia, "Introduction" in *The Days, Taha Hussein: His Autobiography in Three Parts*, trans. E.H. Paxton, Hilary Wayment, Kenneth Cragg (Cairo: The American University in Cairo Press, 1997), 5.

[18] Ibid., 5.

calling for a re-examination of its dogmatic articulations of Islamic history and its political institutionalization of Islam.

Ḥusayn was in favor of a creative synthesis of Arabic and Western literatures.[19] He shared with contemporary intellectuals such as Salāma Mūsà, Tawfīq al-Ḥakīm, Yahyà Ḥaqqī, Ismā'īl Maẓhar, Muḥammad Ḥusayn Haykal, Aḥmad Amīn, and Maḥmūd Taymūr a nationalistic but cosmopolitan understanding of Islam and of Egypt's past. In particular, they considered Alexandria part of the Mediterranean Basin and of the Hellenistic world; Egypt, therefore, is in historical and geographical harmony with the secular culture of Western Europe.[20] But it is a mistake to claim, as does H. A. R. Gibb, that Ḥusayn "has frequently stressed the result of this contrast [between Western and Arabic literature] by creating a dislike of Arabic literature in the mind of the students and strengthening their preference for Western literature."[21] When Gibb dismisses Ḥusayn's autobiography as a work of little cultural significance, claiming that "there is little to be gained from devoting a special study to it,"[22] he is no doubt influenced by his misunderstanding of Ḥusayn's true attitude toward Arabic and Egyptian literature. Gibb's superficial judgment invites a careful re-contextualization of Ḥusayn's work.

Ḥusayn's modern Egypt was tainted with apparently irreconcilable differences: Does Islamism have to be part and parcel of the nationalist project of modern Egypt, or is it one among many components? If it is a dominant component, does nationalist Islamism imply both a demonization of Egypt's non-Muslim minorities, especially Egyptian Jews

[19] For a detailed study of Ḥusayn's rapprochements between Eastern and Western cultures, see 'Abd Allāh Ibrāhīm, "Ṭāhā Ḥusayn: Tafkīk Mabda' al-Muqāyasa" [Ṭāhā Ḥusayn: Deconstructing the Principle of Analogy]. *Fuṣūl: Majalla-t- al-Naqd al-Adabī*, Vol. 15, No. 4 (Cairo: al-Hay'a al-Miṣriyya al-'Āmma lil-Kitāb, Winter, 1997):160–83.

[20] See Ṭāhā Ḥusayn, *al-Mu'allafāt al-Kāmila* (The Complete Works), vol. 9 (Beirut, Dār al-Kitāb al-Lubnānī, 1973), 58. See also 'Abd al-Muḥsin Ṭāhā Badr, *Taṭawwur al-Riwāya al-'Arabiyya al-Hadītha fī Misr* [*The Development of the Modern Arabic Novel in Egypt*], 4th ed. (Cairo, n.p. 1976), 376–97; and J. Brugman, *An Introduction to the History of Modern Arabic Literature in Egypt* (Leiden: Brill, 1984), 232–4.

[21] H. A. R. Gibb, "Studies in Contemporary Arabic Literature: II. Manfalūṭī and the 'New Style.'" *Bulletin of the School of Oriental Studies, University of London*, Vol. 5, No. 2 (311–22, 1929), 313.

[22] H. A. R. Gibb, "Studies in Contemporary Arabic Literature" *Bulletin of the School of Oriental Studies, University of London*, Vol. 7, No. 1 (1–22, 1933), 21.

and Copts, and a rejection of secularization? Does Islamism have to be synonymous with Arabism?[23] Is Islamism the new Hebraism of colonial Egypt, *à la* Matthew Arnold, implying a strong de-Pharaonicization of Egypt and a pronounced dissociation with its Hellenistic past? The capacity of modern Egypt to assimilate such seeming contradictions defined the battleground for the war over Egypt's social, cultural, and political future between the intelligentsia and the Islamists, putting Ḥusayn's secular project at the center of these cultural skirmishes and leading to major polarizations in the 1930s and beyond.[24]

Ḥusayn's autobiography provided a much needed basis for rethinking the premises and reconsidering the starting point of this culture war, inviting the conscious Egyptian reader to re-examine the outdated ideologies and practices of Egypt's dogmatic institutions:

> Between 1920 and 1940 it was much more a question of clearing the ground and preparing minds to receive than of building a new literature; it was especially a matter of "revising values," as they said, and of adjusting modern Western values to the traditional Eastern way of thinking ... In short, this generation took on the task of freeing the modern Arab mind from the chains of tradition as well as from the encroaching siege of Western materialism, by giving back to it, or more exactly, permitting it to find again its true personality.[25]

This act of "revising values" and "freeing the modern Arab mind from the chains of tradition" finds clarion expression in *The Days*, as well as in other important literary and historical interventions by

[23] On the issue of perceiving Islamism as synonymous to Arabism, see P.J. Vatikiotis, "Between Arabism and Islam," *Middle Eastern Studies*, Vol. 22, No. 4 (Oct., 1986), 576–86.

[24] For more on this particular epoch in modern Egypt's nationalist history, see Jamal Mohammed Ahmed, *The Intellectual Origins of Egyptian Nationalism* (London and New York: Oxford University Press, 1960); Albert Hourani, *Arabic Thought in the Liberal Age, 1798–1939* (New York: Oxford University Press, 1970); Israel Gershoni, "The Emergence of Pan-Nationalism in Egypt: Pan-Islamism and Pan-Arabism in the 1930s," *Asian and African Studies* 16(1): 59–94; "The Evolution of National Culture in Modern Egypt: Intellectual Formation and Social Diffusion, 1892–1945," *Poetics Today*, Vol. 13, No. 2 (Summer, 1992): 325–50. See also Gershoni, Israel, and James P. Jankowski, *Egypt, Islam, and the Arabs. Vol. 1, The Search for Egyptian Nationhood*, 1900–1930 (New York: Oxford University Press, 1986).

[25] Taha Hussein, "The Modern Renaissance of Arabic Literature" *Books Abroad*, Vol. 29, No. 1 (Winter, pp. 4–18, 1955), 13–14.

Ḥusayn and his generation. For instance, 'Abbās Maḥmūd al-'Aqqād authored *al-'Abqariyyāt*, pl. of *'Abqariyya* (Account(s) of Genius), a number of historical narratives on the genius of Prophet Muhammed and on some of his companions; Haykal wrote a history of the Prophet and the two first Caliphs, Abū Bakr al-Siddīq and 'Umar ibn al-Kaṭṭāb; and Ḥusayn wrote four volumes of narrative titled *'Alà Hāmish al-Sīra* (*On the Margins of the Prophet's Biography*). All those works revisit Islamic past, commending not only the justice, but the humanity of the Prophet, his mortality, and his unwavering commitment to equality and social justice.[26]

As Egypt's nationalist modernity created the need for both the introduction and consumption of new cultural expressions, the idea was to establish an appealing and provocative reservoir of cultural production capable of breaking through the familiar veneer of traditionalism in order to allow Egyptians to understand their Islamic history outside the dogmatic control of the *ulemas* and to see this history as a confirmation of the validity of hard-won constitutional rights, including the right to freedom of expression under the banner of a civic and secular society.[27] *The Days* is therefore an integral part of "a debunking campaign," as Mohamed al-Nowaihi once described the scholarly project Ḥusayn undertook in the 1920s, and a plea for a serious interrogation of the violation of these rights.[28] *The Days* was hailed by many critics not only as a work of great erudition but also as "the most satisfying artistic achievement in modern Arabic letters," as A. S. Eban has called it.[29] Yet in the eyes of some critics it was vulnerable to the charge of subjectivity, and, by implication, of historical inaccuracy, a charge that has dogged the genre of autobiography from its very beginnings.

In the Arab-Islamic tradition, autobiography has a long history, both classical and modern. Many critics, including Chokri

[26] Ibid., 15.
[27] Ibid.
[28] Mohamed Al-Nowaihi, "Towards the Reappraisal of Classical Arabic Literature and History: Some Aspects of Ṭāhā Ḥusayn's Use of Modern Western Criteria." *International Journal of Middle East Studies*, Vol. 11, No. 2 (Apr., pp. 189–207, 1980), 196.
[29] A. S. Eban, "The Modern Literary Movement in Egypt." *International Affairs* (Royal Institute of International Affairs 1944), Vol. 20, No. 2 (Apr., pp. 166–78, 1944): 175.

al-Mabkhout,[30] have addressed this history in varied degrees of detail.[31] However, writing the self has always been a precarious undertaking. From the time of Ibn Khaldūn's *al-Ta'rīf* (*Identifying the Self*), autobiography carries the germ of the confessional, yet in autobiography, the historical accuracy of the author's confession – whatever its sincerity – is always in doubt. Because it blurs the boundary between historical events and personal impressions of those events, some readers find the genre of autobiography disturbingly broad and loose, as it wavers between history, memory, fact, and fiction.

If the autobiographical has played a persistent and defiant role in modern Arabic and Islamic thought, it is at least in part because of its fluidity, which allows it to present itself in an urgent, dialectical fashion: freedom and orthodoxy, self-determination and dogmatic predestination. It is precisely because of the "wavering" between the historical and the novelistic that autobiography as a cultural category of self-expression – be it as "witness," "educational," or "adventurous" writing, to use al-Mabkhout's terms[32] – becomes a figure of

[30] See Chokri al-Mabkhout, *Sīra-t- al-Ghā'ib Sīra-t- al-Ātī: al-Sīra al-Dhātiyya fī Kitāb al-Ayyām li-Taha Ḥusayn (A Biography of the Absent, A Biography of the Advent: Autobiography in Tāhā Ḥusayn's The Days)* (Tunis: Dār al-Janūb, 1992).

[31] For the history and categorization of autobiography in classical, medieval, and modern Arabic literature, see the following: Hātim al-Ṣakr, *Al-Bawḥ wa al-Tarmīz al-Qahrī fī al-Kitāba-t- al-Sīrdhātiyya: Tanwī'āt wa muḥaddadāt* [*Confession and Repressed Symbolism in Autobiographical Writings: Variations and Limitations*] (Cairo: Al-Hay'a al-Miṣriyya al-'Āmma lil-Kitāb, 2014); Yahyà Ibrahīm 'Abd al-Dāyim, *Al-Tarjama al-Dhātiyya fī al-Adab al-'Arabī al-Ḥadīth* [*Autobiography in Modern Arabic Literature*] (Beirut: Dār Iḥyā' al-Turāth al-'Arabī lil-Ṭibā'a wa al-Nashr, 1994); Muḥammad al-Bāridī, *'Indamā Tatakallam al-Sīra al-Dhātiyya fī al-Adab al-'Arabī al-Ḥadīth* [*When Autobiography Speaks in Modern Arabic Literature*] (Damascus: Manshūrāt Ittiḥād al-Kuttāb al-'Arab, 2005); Iḥsān 'Abbās, *Fann al-Sīra* [*The Art of Biography*] (Amman: Dār al-Shurūq lil-Nashr wa al-Tawzī', 1988); and 'Abd al-Qādir al-Shāwī, *Al-Kitāba wa al-Wujūd* [*Writing and Existence*] (Morocco: Dār Afrīqiyā al-Sharq, 2000). See also Chokri al-Mabkhout, 24–6 and Ihsān 'Abbās, 123–4, 136–8.

[32] Al-Mabkhout distinguishes three types of autobiography: *shahāda* (witness), *tarbawiyya* (educational), and *mughāmarāt* (adventurous). Notable examples in the "witness" category include Ibn Khaldūn's *al-Ta 'rīf* [*Autobiography*]; the "educational" category autobiographies include al-Ghazālī's *al-Munqidh min al-Ḍ[underdot]alāl* [*Deliverance from Loss*]; and finally the "adventurous" type includes works like 'Usāma Ibn Munqidh's *Kitāb al-I 'tibār* [*The Book of Contemplation*]. See Chokri al-Mabkhout, 24–6.

necessity, because in speaking of the self it speaks of all other matters that are at the heart of Egypt's struggle with fundamentalism and Islamist hegemony.

This "wavering" is particularly characteristic of *The Days*. The Egyptian literary critic, 'Abd al-Muḥsin Ṭāhā Badr, argues that Ḥusayn's text includes "internal" as well as "external" links that are at the same time subjective and objective, novelistic and historical.[33] Badr's account is primarily socio-historical, but it bears a strong resemblance to Paul de Man's deconstructionist account of autobiography in general as an act of "de-facement."[34] To de-face is to take away the features, the face of the autobiographer, with the result that what might at first sight appear as an act of narcissism and an indulgence in self-memorialization turns out to be the opposite. Since autobiography is, paradoxically, a negation of the self, any treatment of it should not indulge in assumptions about its accuracy – about the primacy, in Badr's terms, of the external over the internal, the historical over the novelistic.

De Man goes on to argue that autobiography is neither a "genre" nor a "mode," "but a figure of reading or of understanding that occurs, to some degree, in all texts."[35] It is a trope like any other, and, as de Man emphasizes, its interest is tropological, not historical: "the interest in autobiography is not that it reveals reliable self-knowledge – it does not – but that it demonstrates in a striking way the impossibility of closure and of totalization of all textual systems made of tropological substitutions."[36] It is therefore crucial that we focus on the tropological function of Ḥusayn's autobiography, not on its "reliability."

Al-Mabkhout deciphers Ḥusayn's text as a relationship of "persuasion" between the author and the reader.[37] In De Man's articulation

[33] Badr structures the development of the Egyptian novel in relation to five major themes: Didactic; Pleasure; Artistic (a.k.a. Novelistic); Analytical; and Autobiographical. See 'Abd al-Muḥsin Ṭāhā Badr *Taṭawwur al-Riwāya al-'Arabiyya al-Ḥadītha fī Miṣr: 1870–1938* [*The Development of the Modern Arabic Novel in Egypt: 1870–1938*] (Cairo: Dār al-Ma'ārif, 1968), 112, 297, 306.

[34] Paul de Man, "Autobiography as De-facement." *MLN*, Vol. 94, No. 5. *Comparative Literature* (Dec., 1979, pp. 919–30).

[35] Ibid., 921.

[36] Ibid., 922.

[37] Al-Mabkhout, *Sīra-t- al-Ghā'ib Sīra-t- al-Ātī: al-Sīra al-Dhātiyya fī Kitāb al-Ayyām li-Ṭāhā Ḥusayn*, 105.

of this kind of intricate negotiation, "the reader becomes the judge, the policing power in charge of verifying the *authenticity* of the signature and the consistency of the signer's behavior."[38] As the ultimate authority on the author's authenticity, the reader's "interest in [the] autobiography" is not in the accuracy of Ḥusayn's memory retrieval – which is inherently unverifiable – but in the cultural expression for which his representational narrative is a trope. Ḥusayn writes (about) himself, but the self is defaced in a much larger and open-ended discourse of Islamism and a metanarrative of a secular epistemological break with tradition. Ḥusayn's autobiography, in this sense, is as much novelistic as historical, and there is no essential difference in this regard between the "real" protagonist in *The Days* and the "fictional" ones in *Zaynab*.

Readers' responses to "the impossibility of closure" in *The Days* will inevitably affect the reception and assessment of the text. In a study on the role of reading in *The Days*, al-Mabkhout categorizes the reader as either accepting/unassuming or real, and divides the act of reading into *'ādiyya* (regular) and *yaqitha* (alert/conscious), which echoes Barthes's distinction between *lisible* (readerly) and *scriptable* (writerly) texts and between *plaisir* and *jouissance* in *S/Z*.[39] To al-Mabkhout, reading Ḥusayn is not simply a pleasurable act performed by a passive reader, but an act of historical education. Al-Mabkhout sees Ḥusayn as "a revolutionary author,"[40] one whose primary aim, in a text apparently about himself, is not to speak about himself but to address and challenge the "conscious reader,"[41] with the ultimate motive of effecting a revolutionary change in the mindset of his traditionalist society. The return of autobiography as a de Manian figure of "de-facement" in modern Egypt thus plays a crucial role in the rise of a new mode of cultural uprising, in the creation of a radical, alternative form of a disfigured human subjectivity in the face of the dominant traditionalism of al-Azhar.

Like a *Bildungsroman*, *The Days* builds a structure of negotiations between irreconcilable elements in the developmental life of its

[38] Paul de Man, "Autobiography as De-facement," 922.

[39] Al-Mabkhout, *Sīra-t- al-Ghā'ib Sīra-t- al-Ātī: al-Sīra al-Dhātiyya fī Kitāb al-Ayyām li-Ṭāhā Ḥusayn*, 140–2; Roland Barthes, *S/Z: An Essay*, trans. Richard Miller (New York: Hill and Wang, 1974), 4–5.

[40] Ibid., 142.

[41] Ibid., 143.

protagonist. But in its insistence on the triumphant virtue of its protagonist against all the forces of adversity arrayed against him – including squalor, blindness, the loss of siblings – it can seem closer to a somewhat clichéd melodrama than to a true *Bildungsroman*. However, one of the challenges that *al- fatà* faces comes as an unexpected shock: his maltreatment by his Azharite superiors. It would be expected that the clergymen of a reputable religious institution like al-Azhar would be sympathetic to a blind man seeking knowledge and enlightenment, would honor civil discourse and constructive debate, and would support him even if his outlook on tradition were not necessarily in harmony with their own. This shock constitutes the climax of Ḥusayn's narrative precisely because it disrupts both the status quo, generally, and, more specifically, the accepted view of al-Azhar as a benevolent and magnanimous Islamic institution. *The Days* speaks out against canonization and launches an ethical war on the institutionalized Islam of al-Azhar, shattering an image and a state of affairs that for long seemed to be secure from challenge.

The question of the historical accuracy of *al- fatà*'s autobiography still remains. This question is directly related to the relationship between the reception of *Pre-Islamic Poetry* and the motivation for writing *The Days* – and to it there is no easy answer. But here is what is clear: Ḥusayn's autobiography is grounded in an unswerving method of reflections and recollections that converts the hackneyed cliché of "me against them" into a challenging narrative marked by subtle transitions and motions, and by the interplay of calamity and triumph. His mediations between village and city, tradition and modernity, reason and dogmatism, faith and heresy, are all brought together under the inalienable principle of academic freedom. Thus the overarching tropological function of *The Days* is as a metaphor for liberation, a trope coinciding perfectly with an important moment in Egypt's political history: its first constitution. "In 1923," writes Ḥusayn, "the first Egyptian constitution was promulgated. It guaranteed, among other things, liberty of thought, expression, and assembly. Thus it is that the history of Arabic literature from this moment, particularly in Egypt, exactly coincides with the history of Arab liberty."[42] The stigmatization, character assassination, and accusations of heresy that Ḥusayn suffered were the displaced modes for an

[42] Hussein, "The Modern Renaissance of Arabic Literature," 8.

intellectual impasse. Ḥusayn's autobiography puts to shame institutionalized religion and calcified thought to the exact extent that it seeks to mend his own public image. Whether or not Ḥusayn's inevitably subjective autobiography "reveals reliable self-knowledge," it remains a triumphant account of its protagonist who turned his disability into an enablement and conquered the blindness of thoughtless dogmatism with unrelenting resolve and unyielding insight.

4 *An Egyptian Sophocles: Qurʾānic Inspiration in Tawfīq al-Ḥakīm's* The People of the Cave

I am. I am, I exist, I think, therefore I am; I am because I think, why do I think? I don't want to think any more, I am because I think that I don't want to be, I think that I ... because ... ugh!

Jean-Paul Sartre, *Nausea*

Judith Butler has remarked that humans are "marked for life," and that this marking "becomes the condition by which life is risked, by which the questions of whether one can move, and with whom, and in what way are framed and incited by the irreversibility of loss itself."[1] This chapter examines the contours of such irreversible loss, whether the actual loss of humans or their inevitable loss to and from themselves. Drawing on modern Egyptian drama, a lost genre in its own right, it investigates the ontological, social, and political implications of loss, or what Jeffrey Sacks would call – "the archaic debris of a time said to be no longer,"[2] in Tawfīq al-Ḥakīm's *Ahl al-Kahf* (*The People of the Cave*). If no representation can capture history through catastrophic plots that make it sensible to us, then perhaps a theater of loss is capable of at least approximating the harsh realities of history by invoking the absence of such plots. The play discussed here explores multifaceted themes of loss – the dissolution of a sense of self, estrangement from place and from time, and, ultimately, death. My goal is to articulate and analyze the struggle between humankind and time in an original variation on the theater of loss: the performance of anachronism, the representation of mourning, and the staging of pain.

1 Judith Butler, "Afterward: After Loss, What Then?" in *Loss: The Politics of Mourning*, eds. David Eng and David Kazanjian (Berkeley: University of California Press, 2003), 472.

2 The complete quotation is as follows: "Loss, and with the dividing expansion of capital and the asymmetrical force of colonial, juridical violence, is to be left behind, the archaic debris of a time said to be no longer" (Jeffrey Sacks, *Iterations of Loss:* Mutilation and Aesthetic Form, al-Shidyaq to Darwish (New York: Fordham University Press, 2015), 1.

Although hailed by Ṭāhā Ḥusayn as the first work in Arabic literature that may be properly called "drama" and "an important event, not only in modern Arabic, but in the whole of Arabic literature,"[3] al-Ḥakīm's play failed to gain the appreciation of broad audiences, causing financial loss to the Opera House Theater where it was performed in 1935. While al-Ḥakīm attributes the failure of audience appreciation to the play's unsuitability for "action," there is more to this "failure" than mere belonging to *al-Masraḥ al-Dhihnī* (Theater of the Mind), as al-Ḥakīm himself proclaimed. It is also fair to say that after returning from Paris, al-Ḥakīm felt alienated from a society that could not understand him, which was eventually to lead to a major crisis in confidence.

Due to its abstruse philosophical foundations and intellectually challenging script, as well as the resultant difficulty in finding suitable and trained reviewers and critics, the play was demanding for an ordinary audience. Although it had been published two years before being staged, because of the difficulty of its language and its lack of action it had not developed a large readership. Some of the small audience who watched the performance at the Opera were reported to have fallen asleep, prompting the Egyptian dramatist Alfrid Farag to characterize the failure to appreciate al-Ḥakīm's play a "colossal loss for the theater."[4] Moreover, in a move detrimental to Egyptian culture, the theater industry restricted al-Ḥakīm's contribution to only four plays in the following two decades. But it was not only the public and the industry that failed to appreciate *The People of the Cave*; fellow dramatists failed to do so as well. *Masraḥ Al-Rīhānī* (Al-Rīhānī Theater) lobbied against it on the pretext that it was "a dangerous and blasphemous insult to the established norms of the stage."[5] This action led to a halt in the operation of *al-Firqa al-Qawmiyya lil-Funūn al-Masraḥiyya* (The National Company for Performative Arts), even after it went back to performing plays by Shakespeare and Sophocles; a major decline in theatrical performances was prevented only by the Revolution.[6] Critics of the time were split: ʿAlī al-Rā ʻī criticized *The People of the*

[3] Ṭāhā Ḥusayn, *Fusūl fī al-Adab wa al-Naqd* [*Essays on Literature and Criticism*] (Cairo, Dār al-Maʻārif, 1945), 102–6.
[4] Alfrid Farag, *Dalīl al-Mutafarrij al-Dhakī ilà al-Masraḥ* [*A Smart Viewer's Guide to the Theater*] (Cairo: Dār al-Hilāl, 1966), 80.
[5] Farag, *Dalīl al-Mutafarrij*, 87.
[6] See Jalāl al-ʻAshrī, *Majalla-t- al-Majalla* (May 1971), 45.

Cave as a poor work of literature, while Ghālī Shukrī praised it as "the first genuine," if not "the first original Egyptian tragedy."[7] It was, however, to be well received when it was eventually produced in Italian at the Palmero Congress on Mediterranean Affairs in the 1950s. Moreover, a 1952 survey showed that, once it had been translated into French, Italian, Japanese, and Spanish, *The People of the Cave* was al-Ḥakīm's most popular play.[8]

What, then, is the nature of the complexity of *The People of the Cave* that posed such a challenge to its first audience and readers? To begin, it draws from a wide range of sources both eclectic and esoteric: For example, Plato's allegory of the cave; Greek Christian sources, such as Symeon Metaphrastes of the Byzantine Church in his *Lives of Saints of the Saints*; The Qur'ān's *Cave* Chapter (notably 18: 7–18: 22); *The Book of the Dead*; and the legend of the Seven Sleepers of Ephesus. However, perhaps the most important source of complexity and initial bafflement in the play is al-Ḥakīm's ironic and subversive use of motifs and techniques of Greek tragedy, especially as analyzed by Aristotle and represented by Sophocles. The play swerves dramatically from its Qur'ānic source as narrated evidence of God's ability to protect his believers and resurrect the dead, and offers us instead a staging of human isolation, of death interrupting itself, and of a lost ontological battle against time through scattered moments of inconclusive Aristotelian *anagnorisis* and which repeatedly fail to result in a conclusive *peripeteia*. Al-Ḥakīm offers us no answers, Qur'ānic or Sophoclean. In the end it is a question that we are left with: Of what reality is the theater of the mind represented in *The People of the Cave* precisely the image? Whatever the ultimate answer to this question, it is my view that in the play's representation of loss, political as well as ethical issues are at stake. Politically, the sleepers' final return to the cave can be seen as a symbolic rejection of Egypt's apathy towards its colonial destiny, its giving up to despair, while culturally the play addresses the antithesis between the sacred,

[7] See Muḥammad Mandūr, *Masraḥ Tawfīq al-Ḥakīm* [*The Theater of Tawfīq al-Ḥakīm*] (Cairo: Dār al-Ma'ārif, 1960), 41–7; and Ghālī Shukrī, *Thawra-t-al-Mu'tazil: Dirāsa fī Adab Tawfīq al-Ḥakīm* [*The Revolt of the Recluse: A Study of Tawfīq al-Ḥakīm's Literature*] (Cairo: Maktaba-t- al-Anglū al-Miṣriyya, 1966), 179–218.

[8] See Kermit Schoonover, "A Survey of the Best Modern Arabic Books," *The Muslim World*, vol. 42, No. 1 (Connecticut: Hartford, 1952), 44–55.

which Al-Ḥakīm has a rare capacity to connect to the issue of individual impermanence, and the larger drama of existence.

More than fifteen years after its publication, al-Ḥakīm makes the following disclaimer about *The People of the Cave*:

> In writing *The People of the Cave*, my goal was to insert tragedy in an Arab-Islamic narrative. My reference here is to tragedy in its classical Greek sense, which it has preserved throughout history: the conflict (struggle?) between humankind and a hidden superhuman (metaphysical?) power. I was careful not to choose a Greek myth to exemplify this conflict but the Qur'ān itself. My intention was not just to take a story from the Qur'ān and turn it into a dramatic performance. The goal was rather to view our own Islamic narratives from the perspective of Greek tragedy, that is, to arrange a "marriage" between these two literary traditions.[9]

The Ḥakīmian finished product is thus an Islamic drama of fate, *à la Oedipus*, where the protagonist cannot escape predestination, but can still pose some of the most perplexing questions about the meaning and end of life. In the Qur'ān, the Chapter of *The Cave* tells the story of some pious men and their dog seeking shelter in a cave and asking God to help them escape the grip of a heathen king and his people; al-Ḥakīm's play "from the perspective of Greek Tragedy," in contrast, is decidedly not a reiteration of God's power or a showcasing of His ability to protect the believers and then resurrect the dead. But if al-Ḥakīm is indeed re-telling his story from the perspective of Greek tragedy, as he claims, the perspective is strangely warped. Rather than invoking the fatal working out of a predestined pattern, he leaves us with the sense of a world, like that of Calderon's *Life is a Dream*, perched uneasily on the boundary between dream and reality, or like that of *King Lear*, perched equally uneasily on the boundary between Edgar's moralistic "The gods are just, and of our pleasant vices/Make instruments to plague us"[10] and Gloucester's nihilistic "As flies to wanton boys are we to th' gods./They kill us for their sport."[11] Or if this is a variation on the Faustus theme, which

9 Al-Ḥakīm, "Muqaddima" [Preface] in *al-Malik Ūdīb* [*Oedipus King*] (Cairo: Maktaba-t- Miṣr, 1949), 38.

10 William Shakespeare, *The Tragedy of King Lear* (Act 5, Scene 3: 160–1), ed. Jay L. Halio (Cambridge: The New Cambridge Shakespeare, Cambridge UP, 2005), 255.

11 Ibid. (Act 4, Scene 1: 36–7), 207.

Faustus are we then watching: Marlowe's, whose isolated and terrified protagonist is torn limb from limb at the end of the play, or Goethe's, whose Faust, representing humanity as a whole, ultimately achieves salvation? But even if there is no salvation, at least there is space to cry, to revolt, and to doubt, and this, itself, is perhaps a kind of redemption and a remarkable achievement by an Egyptian playwright.

In al-Ḥakīm's play, the three protagonists are Christians who seek shelter in a cave and awake after a long 300 years of slumber to find themselves in a completely different world in which they have become saints. The sleepers, once awakened, seek to reestablish their connections with the material world, but ultimately fail and return to the cave, only this time resigned to die. The play opens in a dark cave in the Raqīm Mountain (in the area of ancient Tarsus) where the shadows of two men can hardly be distinguished. We learn from their dialogue that they are two courtiers and ministers, Marnūsh and Mishlīniyā, who have run away from an evil hedonistic Emperor Decius (249–51) (in Arabic, Diqyānūs) during a dark era of the persecution of Christians in late Roman/early Christian times. As they are fleeing, they encounter a shepherd named Yamlīkhā, himself a Christian in hiding, who guides them to the cave, where all three of them, accompanied by Yamlīkhā's dog, seek refuge. They awake in the cave in the reign of the Christian Emperor Theodorus II (408–50).

When they awake and leave the cave they discover that they have slept for 300 years and that their once-persecuted religion is now the formal religion of the land. While Emperor Theodorus and the whole city hail them as holy men and venerate their resurrection as a divine miracle, the escapees-turned-saints cannot adapt to their new life; they lose interest in living among the living, and gradually seek refuge, and ultimately death, in the cave.

Paul Starkey situates *The People of the Cave* in relation to what he characterizes as a *leitmotif* of fantasy versus reality, which appears at intervals in al-Ḥakīm's work from the 1930s to the experimental writings of the 1960s and the 1970s.[12] While Starkey's claim is not inaccurate with respect to al-Ḥakīm's philosophical musings on the concept of time, it does not support his argument that al-Hakīm's

[12] Paul Starkey, *From Ivory Tower: A Critical Study of Tawfiq al-Hakim* (Oxford: Ithaca Press, 1987), 28.

oeuvre lacks development. This argument ignores the remarkable development of al-Ḥakīm's theatrical thought and his response to the changing social conditions of Egypt in the span of forty years. However, while M. M. Badawi rightly critiques Starkey for his reductionist approach to al-Ḥakīm, one must agree with Starkey that there are recurrent motifs in al-Ḥakīm's writings, on the stylistic as well as the thematic levels.[13] One of these is the paradoxical relationship between loss and humor. The protagonists wake up one day, thirsty and hungry, exhibiting clear mortal needs. Yet everyone they meet believes them to be saints – that is, to be holy and thus otherworldly. Hunger meets God in a drama where sainthood is not a choice, but an imposition of a society hungry for a miracle. In fact, Badawi dwells on this *leitmotif* without realizing that he seems to be echoing Starkey's claim, arguing that "the discrepancy between the characters viewed mainly as earthly creatures with human frailties and practical needs, and the saintly roles imposed upon them by those amongst whom they are resurrected give al-Hakim ample scope for the kind of humor in which he generally excels and which consists of long stretches of dialogue with characters talking at cross-purposes."[14] But, in fact, the repetition of the same blackly humorous pattern of imposing meaning of ("characters talking at cross-purposes") is not a bug but a feature of al-Ḥakīm's art; it is his central theme, the theme of the repeated but futile *anagnorisis*. The desperate people of the cave are like Pozzo and Lucky in *Waiting for Godot*, defenselessly tied to a historical context and a causality without which humanity is lost.

One after the other, the characters experience *anagnorisis* (the shock of recognition) without achieving *peripeteia*, redemptive or otherwise. In Act II, Yamlīkhā, still unaware of the passage of time, departs to locate his sheep, but soon realizes the frightening gap between his own time and the present. Even his dog, Qaṭmīr, is chased away by the dogs of Tarsus. Here, the dramatic irony stems both from the clever juxtaposition of humans and animals and from the blackly humorous realization that because there is no sainthood in the canine world, the sheer economy of survival and the basic instincts of friend versus foe determine the social dynamics of the society of dogs. Qaṭmīr's

13 M.M. Badawi, *Modern Arabic Drama in Egypt* (Cambridge: Cambridge University Press, 1987), 34–5.

14 M.M. Badawi, *Modern Arabic Drama*, 32.

anagnorisis has no more or less meaning, in terms of genuine recognition, than Yamlīkhā's or anyone else's in the play.

Marnūsh discovers that his home has disappeared and is replaced by a weapons market. One cannot help but see a remarkable similarity between Marnūsh's miserable situation and our own time, particularly when it comes to the global imposition of US military forces that, among other things, turn the homes of innocent civilians in countries like Iraq and Afghanistan into weapons markets and war zones; thus, the shattering and temporal loss of home continues to occur while the prospects of a safe and secure future with loved ones diminish in favor of a ruthless and shattering economy of violence. Dejected and alienated, he finds out that his own son "died a martyr at the age of sixty after he brought victory to the Roman armies."[15] At this point Marnūsh realizes the enormity and meaninglessness of his own tragedy:

> Mere life in itself is meaningless, because abstract life with no past, no connection to anything, no causation is less than nothingness. In fact, there is no such thing as nothingness. Nothingness is nothing but absolute life.[16]

Marnūsh's vision of nothingness is echoed by Yamlīkhā, the last of three Christian resurrectees to accept death by returning to the cave, as he testifies to God that he does not know if his life is a dream or a reality. Marnūsh follows, and dies a death "devoid of everything, naked as I came to this life, sans thoughts, sans feelings, sans belief."[17]

As if to emphasize the ironical distance between the classic Sophoclean form of his play and its distinctly un-Sophoclean vision, al-Ḥakīm respects the three traditional classical unities of place, action, and time. In regard to place, Acts I and IV are in the cave. Acts II and III take place in the palace and its surrounding pavilions. As far as action is concerned, all of the action of the play leads relentlessly to the same theme, to the realization that humanity wanes before the overarching force of time. The unity of time can be seen from two perspectives: in terms of plot and of theme. In Act I, the protagonists wake up one morning, thinking it is night time because of the darkness of the cave. Act II takes place at the end of the day, Act III at night, and Act IV the morning after. Thus the play occurs within the single

[15] Tawfiq al-Ḥakim, *Ahl al-Kahf* [*The People of the Cave*] (1933) (Cairo: Dār al-Hilāl, 1954), 61. All translations from the Arabic edition are my own.
[16] Ibid., 65.
[17] Ibid., 103.

revolution of the Sun, as Aristotle would say. But time also becomes the springboard for the play's most profound and complex question. *The People of the Cave* begins with a dialogue that takes place upon waking (the present), thus establishing a moment of time in time, a moment related to a memory of a yesterday or a few hours of sleep, a moment reminiscent of the escape from the emperor (past) that is also connected to their intention to leave the cave in search of food (the future). At the very moment this future becomes present, namely when Yamlīkhā seeks to purchase food, the experience of loss at the heart of the play begins to unfold as the present (Yamlīkhā) moves towards the future (the city of Tarsus), only to realize that his very movement in the space of the city is itself supernatural, a breach of the law of causality that governs earthly existence – a sacred ghost, a past on a collision course with its own past-ness.

There is one element in the play, however, that is a pure insertion of Ḥakīm's and which at first glance seems to have little in common with Sophoclean tragedy: the romantic love story of Prīskā and Mishlīnyā. As the plot develops (or rather dilutes itself) toward ineluctable defeat and death, an episode of love complicates the existential equation, as an old romance is rekindled, anachronistically, between Mishlīnyā and the great-great-granddaughter of his long-deceased true love and fiancée, Prīskā. When the "saints" are taken to the King, Mishlīniyā, who bemoans the loss of his true love Prīskā, sees the King's daughter, who is identical in appearance to Emperor Decius' similarly named and long-deceased daughter, and falls in love with her. When Mishlīniyā scolds Prīskā for spending an evening with a stranger – in actuality her father – she tells him not only that he is confusing her with her great-great-grandmother but also that he is in love with a mere semblance, for she belongs to a different era altogether. But when she expresses sadness that those powerful love feelings are not for her but rather directed towards someone else, Mishlīniyā's response reveals an amalgamation of resolve, poignancy, despair, confusion, and a total state of loss:

> Prīskā, dear, please come back, you are her. Oh. Lord. If you are not her, who would you be then? Am I asleep? Am I alive? Am I dreaming? Lord, Lord, oh Christ, Lord: Give me my mind back so I could see you, give me light, or give me death.[18]

[18] Al-Ḥakīm, *Ahl al-Kahf*, 80.

Then he tries to convince Prīskā that love is stronger than time:

It is only 300 years. What proof do you have that you are not her? What misery awaits me if I discover that you are other than her, and that there is a gap between us? None of this matters to me now.[19]

Princess Prīskā eventually reciprocates Mishlīniyā's love for her and even decides to die with him in the cave.

There is no mention of this love story in any of the sources al-Ḥakīm consulted, or any of the well-known Qur'ānic *tafsīr* (explication/exegesis) books of al-Ṭabarī, al-Zamakhsharī, and al-Qurṭubī; nor is there reference to this development in Edward Gibbon's study of the fable of the seven sleepers in *The Decline and Fall of the Roman Empire*, where he argues that this particular story "would furnish the pleasing subject of a philosophical romance."[20] And the sweet melancholy of this episode could hardly be more distant in tone from the Sophocles of *Oedipus*.

There is perhaps a suggestion that Prīskā's love for Mishlīniyā represents a spiritual bond that survives the ravages of time and that underlines by contrast the tragic fate of Mishlīniyā's companions in the cave who share no such faith. Yamlīkhā's experience of the present is so painful that he comes to doubt whether he is alive or not, whether there is former life before life on earth or not, thus shaking his Christian faith despite the strong display of faith he exhibits in Act I Marnūsh, unlike Yamlīkhā who exits with doubt, loses his faith completely and dies a disbeliever. In contrast, Mishlīnīyā, who lives for love, is grateful that his faith remains unshaken and his resurrection is somewhat successful (though his summing up of the defeat of love by time is hardly optimistic: "Our time is past, now we are the property of history. We wanted to return to time, but history is taking its vengeance."[21]) This is the moment Prīskā resolves to die with him listening to the call of her dreams and yielding to her belief that her soul is content in the company of her one and only beloved.

However, there are those who see Prīskā as more than a foil to the tragic male protagonists of *The People of the Cave*, who assign her a

19 Ibid., 88.

20 Edward Gibbon, *The Decline and Fall of the Roman Empire*, vol. 2 (New York: The Modern Library, 1932), chapter XXXIII (423–55 A.D.), 243.

21 Ibid., 98.

much more central role in terms of the cultural context of modern Egypt. Many critics, including Ghālī Shukrī, Paul Starkey, and ʿAbd al-Munʿim Ismāʿīl find the play to be uniquely modern and uniquely Egyptian in its symbolic representation of Egypt's colonial destiny, her fall from epochs of degeneration to the ambush of twentieth-century industrial modernity and its handmaiden of a militarily advanced Western civilization. In this figurative light, the Egyptian critic 'Abd al-Munʿim Ismāʿīl, drawing on the motif of "woman as nation" (see Chapter 2) interprets Prīskā as Egypt herself, condemned to infertility and a youthful death at the hands of those who claim to love her.[22]

When asked about his message from the play, al-Ḥakīm denied any such specific historical significance:

> One thing prompted me to choose this subject: the desire to write an Egyptian tragedy on an Egyptian basis. You know that the basis of Greek tragedy is "fate" – that terrible struggle between "humankind" and "fate." The basis of Egyptian tragedy as I conceive it is "time" – its source is the horrifying struggle between humankind and "time." Read *The Book of the Dead* and you will be aware of this immediately. With the Greeks it is "fate" and "destiny"; with the Egyptians it is "time" and "space."[23]

Although al-Ḥakīm's explicitly political novel *ʿAwda-t- al-Rūḥ* (The Return of the Spirit) and *The People of the Cave* were published a few months apart in 1933, he maintained that there was nothing political about *The People of the Cave*, thus dismissing the presumption that, like *The Return of the Spirit*, *The People of the Cave* embodies "nostalgia" for the past.[24] "The past is the past and must not shackle the present," and accordingly, says al-Ḥakīm, "this is how we must see the protagonists of *The People of the Cave*: they are the past incapable of competing with the present or playing a leading role in it."[25] However, although al-Ḥakīm's statement may be true of the play's male protagonists, it completely ignores the role of Prīskā in the play, especially her willful entrance into the cave for the first and

[22] 'Abd al-Mun'im Ismā'īl, *Drama and Society in Contemporary Egypt* (Cairo: Dār al-Kātib al-ʿArabī lil- Ṭibāʿa wa al-Nashr, 1967), 55.

[23] Al-Ḥakīm, *Muqaddima-t- al-Malik Ūdīb* [*Preface to Oedipus King*], 40.

[24] Muḥammad Ḥasan ʿAbd Allāh, *Al-Ḥakīm wa ḥiwār -al-Marāyā* [*Al-Ḥakīm and the Dialogue of Mirrors*] (Cairo: Dār al-Qibāʾ, 2000), 148.

[25] Ibid., 148–9.

final time while she does not belong to that past. If the past is in the past, as al-Ḥakim claims, what do we make of the future, i.e. young Prīskā, thrust into the midst of that dark cave?

In response to this question one might point out that for the past two centuries women have always been sacrificed to plots; one aspect of our analysis of *The People of the Cave*, then, proceeds in light of this fact with regard to gender.[26] From this perspective, it seems that al-Ḥakīm wanted to portray an exciting love scene at the expense of a young woman's future. Did al-Ḥakīm think that, by casting a youthful woman in the mix, surrendering her to death after a powerful melodramatic love scene, he would produce a more effective catharsis than the return of the men alone to the cave would have achieved?

Although there may be some truth to this claim, perhaps a reconsideration of al-Ḥakīm's emulation of Sophoclean tragedy might suggest a more central role for Prīskā and the cave. There is an uncanny resemblance between al-Ḥakim's Prīskā and Sophocles' Antigone, another loving young woman whose love leads to death in a cave, a resemblance that brings us back to Butler's intimations on loss at the beginning of this chapter. Instead of recasting Antigone as a character in defiance of the state personified in her uncle, Creon the King, who has deemed it illegal for her to give her brother Polyneices a proper burial, Butler, influenced by Georg Wilhelm Hegel, Jacques Lacan, and to some extent Luce Iragary, reads Antigone not necessarily as "a political figure, one whose defiant speech has political implications, but rather as one who articulates a pre-political opposition to politics, representing kinship as the sphere that conditions the possibility of politics without ever entering into it." Butler's Antigone is a "liminal figure" who falls in the middle ground between family and the state, life and death. Al-Ḥakim's Prīskā occupies this middle ground as well. She is, to be sure, a defiant figure, one whose liminality is neither wholly anti-familial nor anti-state. But if Butler views Antigone as a woman who claims her life in choosing to die in

[26] For a subtle critique of the demonization of Prīskā as a woman in *The People of the Cave*, especially in connection to her "jealousy" of her great-great-grandmother, see Rajā' ʿĪd's chapter, "al-Tafakkuk wa al-Taṣanuʿ fī *Ahl al-Kahf*" [Fragmentation and Affectation in *The People of the Cave*] in her book *Dirāsa fī Adab Tawfīq al-Ḥakīm* [*A Study of Tawfīq al-Ḥakīm's Literature*] (Alexandria: Mansha'at al-Maʿārif, 1977).

defiance of both the traditional family and the patriarchic state, what then is the claim of al-Ḥakim's Prīskā? In her death, Antigone hangs herself within the "cave" of her entombment, following the tradition of Jocasta, her own mother. When Prīskā enters the cave, she too chooses to end her own life in the love tradition of her own great-great-grandmother. In this alone, al-Ḥakim's Prīskā is Butler's Antigone. Both al-Ḥakim's Prīskā and Bulter's Antigone represent the shockingly unfamiliar in traditional families, those who stand for a non-normative claims and challenge not only the standard model of interpersonal relationships but also time and the state. Their passage into death, in both cases associated with the cave, their claim-of-death, becomes the victory and the fulfillment, the victory over traditionalism, legalism, and patriarchism, and the fulfillment of love, self-love, maternal love, grand-maternal love, of a wish long overdue for the great-great-grandmother and an homage to all maternal ancestors crushed by familial and patriarchal "norms" and deprived of love and the freedom to choose. Prīskā's last words are poignant "If they ask you about me – tell them I am no priest, I am a woman who fell in love."

Love then, or death in love, is Prīskā's claim, one in which she, like Antigone, intimately follows the footsteps of her own kin, the mother, the grandmother. Prīskā/Antigone is symbolic of the specter of death, of those who spend their lives outside the norms of Creon-veneered societies, the non-normative, the *pharmakon* of traditional family and kinship.

Philosophically, as well as anthropologically, emerging from the cave traditionally has signaled humanity's rise from savagery, barbarism, and ignorance to the light of progress and enlightenment. Emerging from the cave is the step humanity had to take to proceed towards civilization. But this is not the case here. It seems here that al-Ḥakīm is thinking outside of the paradigm of the cave. For al-Ḥakīm the protagonists are caught up in a complex paradox, at once the miracle and what Camus would call *la chute* (the fall), bringing divine light to the city while simultaneously suffering a severe existentialist crisis. Those whose very wakening proves God's powers of resurrection are the *pharmakon*, the sacrifice of God at the same time as they are the gift of God. And herein lies the aporia of loss and the aporia that is loss.

Loss has a fundamental presence in this text, which is directly related to three Christian protagonists. Loss functions like a dormant gene in the nucleus of existence itself, provoked into manifesting itself by humans' inevitable advancement towards death; that is, by the disbanding of our attachment to time as we age and grow disenchanted with all that is imposed upon us by the outside world. This is also the moment of modernism in al-Ḥakīm's play, the tension between the sacred and the secular. Because there is much to unpack here, I will simply attempt to make one last point, which is crucial for an epistemological contextualization of *The People of the Cave*.

If the history of philosophy, beginning with Book X of Plato's *Republic*, articulates a relationship between the real and the mimetic, or between the evanescent and the eternal, then it is not far-fetched that al-Ḥakīm's Christian protagonists would want to reflect on the meaning of life, on death, and on resurrection. However, one implication of this argument is that it places al-Ḥakīm squarely within the Western tradition; that is, the thematic reflections of his characters would make intuitive sense to someone steeped into the Western tradition. What remains peculiar is that the people of the cave choose death over life and decide to return to the cave instead of just thanking God for the miracle of resurrection and the gift of life, and just moving on. Is not resurrection at once the hope and the fear of humans? It is bewildering to see al-Ḥakīm engaged in a serious exercise of anxiety – related to time – when the causes do not necessarily lead to the results. So are we to believe that Yamlīkhā's loss of his cattle while his dog is chased to the end of the city by other dogs is enough reason for him to warrant a dramatic death wish? Is Marnūsh's loss of his wife, son, and home a sufficient rationale for abandoning the world and surrendering to the darkness of the cave? Do al-Ḥakīm's protagonists prefer death to the pain of loss? Is not learning to overcome loss a significant part of being human alive? And why is it that none of the sleepers seems to care about or celebrate their religion, Christianity, which is the primary cause of their persecution and consequent hiding in the cave? Or must Christianity, the religion of Coptic minority in Egypt and the quintessential pharmakon in this historical drama, be forever repressed and entombed in a predominantly Muslim society? Is this, then, the political unconscious and the trope of tropes in al-Ḥakīm's play? Otherwise, why not rejoice that God has delivered on his promise and protected them against a tyrant king, that a city of God is now in place, and that

Christianity has endured and become the dominant religion of the land, bestowing sainthood upon them for their persecuted lives and making them living proof of omnipresence, of the power of God to protect his faithful believers?

These questions lead me to believe that al-Ḥakīm's play is, as Ghālī Shukrī and Mandūr argue, a play of the time; however, I disagree with their exclusivist Marxist reading of the text as symbolic of a dark phase in Egypt's political history in the 1930s – i.e. the infamous Ministry of Ismā'īl Sidqī – and of Prīskā as Egypt condemned to the cave and hampered by a regressive politics of her own nation, etc. Absent from both Shukrī and Mandūr is the cultural discursiveness of a moment of reference, of philosophical turmoil, of a modernity of preference, so to speak – in which divinity, symbolized here in the Qur'ānic text, *becomes* no longer prescriptive and dictatorial, but a descriptor of human loss and an incubator for philosophical views on human existence that range from Plato to Sartre.

Al-Ḥakīm's play represents a remarkable address of the human condition and a bold confrontation between existentialism and the dictates of theology in a Muslim society new to the idea of drama and essentialist in its views of Nietzsche as a murderer of divinity. Appropriately enough, the existentialism debate flourished during al-Ḥakim's stay in France in the 1930s and continued with Sartre, Camus, and Simone de Beauvoir; al-Ḥakīm's play could have not been written any earlier or later. Soon enough, existentialism was to be replaced by structuralism and language theory, and the French cultural scene was to replace "nothingness" with culture and anthropology as a new wave of thought. In other words, French cultural and intellectual thought of the 1940s witnessed the beginning of the extinction of traditional philosophical concerns with boredom, alienation, the absurd, freedom, commitment, nothingness, or existential anxiety, as embodied in the late 1930s and the early 1940s. French intellectual and cultural theorists like Greimas, Barthes, Straus, Benveniste, Macherey, and Fanon would soon come to dominate the scene of cultural production, while major cultural and political events, including the French New Wave and the Algerian War of Independence, would usher the advent of the Other and the rise of postcolonial thought.

As if in anticipation of the loss of the intellectual in the tradition that had nurtured al-Ḥakīm in France, *The People of the Cave* can be read as a significant expression of the last wave of a dying existentialism, a repressed heroization of faithful Christianity on Muslim lands, and a Sartrean on a Qur'ānic theme. This is the modernity of al-Ḥakīm's contribution to the theater of loss, of its creative borrowing from the sacred, and its staging of the clash of the divine with secular modernity.

5 Writing the Mad Text: Freedom, Modernity, and God in Naguib Mahfouz's "The Whisper of Madness"

From the depth of the Middle Ages, a man was mad if his speech could not be said to form part of the common discourse of men. His words were considered null and void, without truth or significance, worthless as evidence, inadmissible in the authentication of acts or contracts. And yet, in contrast to all others, his words were credited with strange powers, of revealing some hidden truth, of predicting the future, of revealing, in all their naiveté, what the wise was unable to perceive.

Michel Foucault, *The Archaeology of Knowledge and the Discourse on Language*

In the previous chapter, I argued that a theater of loss is better able to evoke the harsh realities of history than catastrophic plots that attempt to mimic that history directly. In this chapter, I would like to make a similar point about another kind of loss, the loss of reason: it is the through the loss of reason – through madness – that a narrative of the irrational becomes a compelling representation of the socioeconomic conditions of Egypt in the 1930s.

Perhaps no other modern Egyptian writer has captured Egypt's oscillation between tradition and modernity or Islam and secularism as well as Naguib Mahfouz – also known as Najīb Mahfūz 'Abd al-'Azīz al-Sabīljī- (1911–2006). The only Arab to have been awarded the Nobel Prize in Literature (in 1988), Mahfouz has a uniquely deep understanding of human nature as it projects itself on the Egyptian psyche. Born in early twentieth-century Cairo, Mahfouz lived through the years of British colonialism in Egypt that left indelible scars on the city, which became the background for many of his works. With a solid education in the humanities and a degree in philosophy from Cairo University in 1934, he set out to produce works of fiction that focused on Islamic Cairo, not merely as a setting for an unfolding narrative but also as the subject of that very narrative. Islamic Cairo, for Mahfouz, is often the protagonist *par excellence* – sometimes the hero, sometimes the victim, but more often the silent witness and ubiquitous *mise en scène* of a rapidly changing culture and a dialectic between tradition and modernity. His narratives capture the pulse of the city's modern streets, as well as the dissolving relics of Old Cairo. In this novelistic Cairo, Mahfouz delineates the modern Egyptian self in its wavering between old and new – its equivocation between economic profit and religious contentment; spiritual sanctuary and financial security; work and thought; brothel and mosque; man and God; and, most relevant for the current discussion, madness and reason. There is room for everyone: the ascetic Sūfī and the hopeless sinner; the lover and the killer, the seeker and the loser; the good, the evil, and the indifferent; the sage and the mad – all inhabit the fictive world of Naguib Mahfouz.

Readers of Mahfouz's fiction, then, can hardly fail to see its richness as a record of a culture, as a literary reservoir of manners and things Egyptian. But it is more than that: it is also, in itself, an embodiment of a moment in the epistemological history of modern Egypt, of the practice and ideas that dominated the Islamic cultural scene before and during Nasserism. This is nowhere more evident than in his short story, "The Whisper of Madness."[1]

It may seem idiosyncratic to base a consideration of Mahfouz's relationship to Islam and the culture of modern Egypt on one of his very early short stories, which he began writing in the late 1930s. Why should one choose to consider what appears to be a minor work peripheral to Mahfouz's grand narratives as a way of access to the complex interrogations of the sacred and secular in his work as a whole? A good number of other less opaque and more fully elaborated texts that foreground Islam, God, and modernity may appear to offer a more promising approach. For example, a study of his so-called historical novels of the late 1930s and early 1940s, such as the *'Abath al-Aqdār* (*The Absurdity of Fate*), *Rādūbīs (Rhodopis)*, or *Kifāḥ Ṭība* (*The Struggle of Thebes*), could yield interpretive insights. Or one could consider later and better known texts in the 1940s and 1950s, such as *al-Qāhira al-Jadīda* (*Modern Cairo*), *Zuqāq al-Madaq* (*Midaq Alley*), and *al-Thulāthiyya* (*The Trilogy*). Another work, *Awlād Ḥāritnā* (*Children of the Alley*), which Mahfouz wrote in the aftermath of the July Revolution of 1952, would appear to offer a

[1] Naguib Mahfouz, *Hams al-Junūn* [*The Whisper of Madness*] (Cairo: Maktaba-t-Miṣr, 1938).

more direct and informative introduction to his lifelong exploration of the clash between the sacred and the secular. However, the often neglected short story corner of Mahfouz's canon offers us a kind of shortcut, a more direct approach to an understanding of Mahfouz's dialectical interrogations of the divine and the human than the usual critical approach, which reaches for a grand synthesis, either by starting from general categorical classifications and moving through periods of development, or by dwelling exclusively on the complexities of particularly long narratives.

One of the distinguishing characteristics of Mahfouz's narrative is the way it problematizes the idea of representation in the very moment of representation. This problematization leads to a reformulation of questions of culture, religion, freedom, and politics that permeate his work. It is through this aspect of textuality that one may begin to reevaluate the imbrication of literary and historical figuration in Mahfouz with regard to socio-historical and ethico-political concerns, especially in light of the fact that this very imbrication results in a kind of writing that aims to challenge not only canonical versions of history but also the mode of their representation.

Critics have not always risen to this challenge, mistaking Mahfouz's deliberate problematization of traditional narrative as a problem with the narrative itself. An example of this unreflective approach is the harshly contemptuous dismissal of "The Whisper of Madness" by Trevor Le Gassick:

> The lack of sophistication of Mahfouz's first collection is evident from the stories' dearth of ideas and weakness of artistic structure. "Whisper of Madness," the story from which the collection takes its title, is a simple moralistic tale that tells directly of the activities of a madman who steals food, is violent to others, assaults girls and tears his clothing. Its long introduction about madness exceeds the needs of the short story, which demands concentration and economy. The story then proceeds to external description of characters, these characterizations being superficial and lacking in artistry.[2]

The lack of sophistication of this very critique reflects an unquestioning acceptance of the traditional function of literary criticism as an exercise of power through categorization. Le Gassick's categories

[2] Trevor Le Gassick, *Critical Perspectives on Naguib Mahfouz* (Washington, DC: Three Continents Press, 1991), 11.

("weakness of artistic structure," "moralistic," "lacking in artistry," etc.) reflect his misplaced confidence in his role as an Olympian arbiter of the work of an immature artist as yet unsure of his craft; it obscures the fact that critical as well as literary productions are conditioned socially and ideologically by their historical situation. That is why, from one year to the next, Mahfouz's prolific writings over the span of sixty years, which he began with the collection containing "The Whisper of Madness," are of crucial importance for a continual reinterrogation of Egypt's modern history. A serious reader, rather than categorizing and dismissing "The Whisper of Madness" once and for all, according to spuriously "timeless" categories, might prefer to ask challenging questions: How can one character be symbolic of a certain generation or a dominant trend in that very generation? How can one read a work of art as a comment on, as well as a product of, history? What did the work say about our society then? What does it say about it now? And – more specifically with respect to "The Whisper of Madness" – what are the "rational" forces that the actions of its unnamed madman are set against? When and how does a critique of madness turn into madness as a critique? Any comments on "the needs of the short story" which do not address such questions will inevitably be superficial.

"The Whisper of Madness" is not alone among texts in which the experience of madness in modernity has become a major concern. Most notably, Michel Foucault's archaeological history of madness in *Madness and Civilization* shares many characteristics with "The Whisper of Madness." Both Mahfouz and Foucault tell us that madness and the experience of modernity in the city are strongly interrelated.[3] They are so not because the practice of everyday life in the modern city is conducive to madness, as some may argue; rather, they are mutually informing, because the modern city hides the potential for insanity under the garb of reason and order. But to assume that the treatments of madness in Mahfouz and Foucault are comparable in every respect is to overlook significant complexities and to ignore the different conditions of modernity that produced both texts; it is to miss an opportunity to figure, from a broader perspective, how, in two dissimilar cultures belonging to two disparate world

[3] See Michel Foucault, *Madness and Civilization: A History of Insanity in the Age of Reason*. trans. R. Howard (New York, NY: Random House, 1965).

orders and modes of representation, madness is constituted, understood, and represented.

Taking into consideration the period of its production in the 1930s, a period that Mahfouz revisits in the sharp existential satire of *Modern Cairo* to reveal the corruption and absurdity of social opportunism as well as the fallacy of administrative modernity, we can see that "The Whisper of Madness" reveals the remarkable ability of the young Mahfouz to speak both about and for the mad, which is itself a modernist phenomenon. This mode of representation invites myriad questions: How can Mahfouz attempt to write about madness? Does not his task amount to the paradoxical if not impossible project of trying to use language to penetrate beyond language? Is Mahfouz taking the side of the dominant form of modern rationality, or is he rather writing a text to show the artist's sensitivity to madness and sympathy for the mad – those ignored, silenced, devoiced, and crushed under the ruthlessness of (capitalist and colonial) modernity? Does Mahfouz's text carry similar condemnations to the ones that Foucault levies against the dictates of power in modernity that have been largely successful both in conflating *folie* and *déraison* and in reducing them to pathological madness, if not at times to mere muteness? If madness, as some might argue, cannot speak for itself, and if the mad person is deprived of the logos of shared understanding, how can their language even be thought to exist? As the language of the mad points to a realm of meaning or non-meaning beyond reason, how can reason comprehend, and thus capture, madness? And even if a representation of madness is interpreted as a metaphor for social criticism or a critique of representational logic, madness still challenges the limitations of representation itself. Can there ever be a representation of madness? Who could write it? Could there ever be a cultural text that expresses madness with accuracy, nuance, and comprehensibility? Or would such writing, by definition, render madness un-mad? In order to attempt to answer some of these questions, it is useful to position Mahfouz's narrative in relation to the overarching triangulation of madness, religion, and modernity.

A strong vein of Platonism is detectable in "The Whisper of Madness." It could be rightly argued that in his early writings (in the 1930s), Mahfouz was more concerned with elaborating a systematic philosophical doctrine than with putting language to the test of portraying social malaise, as opposed to asserting it. In the Greek tradition, Plato is the first recorded philosopher to address madness. Contending that madness is not always evil, especially when given by the gods, Plato describes madness in *The Phaedrus* as "a nobler thing than sober sense" because "madness comes from God, whereas sober sense is merely human."[4] Madness in Plato is deeply connected to divine love, a gift from the gods that could yield "great benefits":

> And the conclusion to which our whole discourse points is that in itself and in its origin this is the best of all forms of divine possession, both for the subject himself and for his associate, and it is when he is touched with this madness that the man whose love is aroused by beauty in others is called a lover.[5]

Plato's madman, described by Socrates, lives in a state of "mingled pleasure and pain" and is "perplexed by the strangeness of his experience."[6] Like Mahfouz's protagonist, Plato's madman "remains still by day, but his longing drives him wherever he thinks he may see the possessor of beauty … the convention of civilised behavior, on whose observance he used to pride himself, he now scorns."[7]

The central character of Mahfouz's short story is a man affected to his marrow by the incomprehensible insanity of modern Cairo. The number of social shocks he goes through exposes the fragmentary nature of his own personality: a mad city and an alienated self are mirror images of each another. By virtue of its narrative economy, Mahfouz's text offers a vague yet artistically compelling description of the indefinable state of mind of an anonymous protagonist who, in contradicting the laws of probability and in breaking the "sacred" chain of cause and effect, acts without any purpose or direction.

On one level, Mahfouz's treatment of madness appears to be generic, conforming to a broad definition of insanity as that which does not comply with the dictates of reason known to shape our communal coexistence. But if we delve deeper into the life of Mahfouz, we learn that he lived his early life in the neighborhood of al-'Abbāsiyya, where Egypt's most famous al-Khānka (lunatic asylum, also commonly known among Egyptians as '*al-Sarāyā al-Ṣafrā*' – "the Yellow Mansion") still lies. Mahfouz's account may echo his own biography.

[4] Plato, *Phaedrus and the Seventh and Eighth Letters*, trans. Walter Hamilton (New York, NY: Penguin Books, 1973), 47.
[5] Ibid., 56.
[6] Ibid., 56, 58.
[7] Ibid., 58.

Geographically, residents of al-'Abbāsiyya are the closest Cairo-dwellers to madness as both a physical condition and a medical reality. What lies behind the walls of the *Yellow Mansion* has always been a mystery to most Egyptians. Such geographical adjacency might have fascinated young Mahfouz and driven him to approximate the experience of madness in fiction. But fiction, like history, can only represent madness relationally, that is, in connection to something else that speaks about it, critiques it, laughs at it, or learns from it. But this something is its opposite. Writing is the discourse of rationality, a discourse that takes many forms, all aiming to expel madness. Is it possible, one may ask, as does Foucault, that madness itself has been subject to the caprices of reason throughout history? While there can be no positive answer to this question, it remains a fact that the representation of madness confuses both culture and history, primarily because madness is the most extreme limit of our culture; it becomes an emptiness toward which language – the only medium that enables fiction and history – is drawn to find its justification. How does language work in Mahfouz's text?

Young Mahfouz's representative language of madness has two parallel characteristics: it establishes an order of representation (the madman's mind), and at the same time, controls this very order and stands outside of it (the logic of narrative). The text begins at the end, that is, after madness, when Mahfouz's protagonist is back to sanity – or at least thinks he is – and is now trying to grasp in flashes some echoes of his elapsed mad experience. In something akin to a cinematic flashback, Mahfouz, working backward, traces the events that led to his protagonist's mental break, refusing to give closure or a neat rounding-up of the events by letting the madman go on his way.

Stylistically, the language of Mahfouz's short story is conscious of the unconscious that it claims to represent. This mode of narration, which, in a stream-of-consciousness, echoes the flow of thoughts in the mind of his protagonist, makes it difficult to tell when Mahfouz is speaking in his own voice or merging with the voice of his madman, In Mahfouz's depiction of the process of thought within his madman's mind, the mental filter that determines socially appropriate behaviors does not work any more; thought is always action. Mahfouz's madman is everything that Shakespeare's Hamlet, for example, is not. In fact, if he were in Hamlet's shoes, one would think he would have killed Claudius immediately and saved seven other lives! Yet the difference between sanity and madness lies in the immediate, uncontrollable externalization of spontaneous human thoughts. After putting the short story down, the reader might agree that most of the madman's reactions are not entirely insane. For example, it is not madness to think of the absurdity of scattering and removing sand after an Egyptian president's or minister's procession passes by, or to wish to feed chicken to a group of young impoverished paupers, or even to be provoked by a bully's behavior. On the contrary, each of these incidents is a normal human response that must have crossed our thoughts at one time or another.

A closer look at how these incidents build up to the climax of mental breakdown reveals a depth of thought: the traditional festive rituals of sand-scattering to honor dignitaries passing through city streets reflect the pointless extravagance of regimes and the ludicrous lavishness of those in power; the chicken and the paupers incident is a brilliant symbol of the situation of the impoverished majority of Egyptian citizens in the 1930s, economically depressed, stricken by squalor and unemployment, and under a corrupt monarchy that must be blamed for widening social inequalities and the deepening gap between the classes. The incident of the bully is another example of an irrational and unjustifiable exercise of power, a regression to the rule of the jungle.

The protagonist's reaction to each of those four incidents in "The Whisper of Madness" qualifies him as mad not because he thinks the unthinkable, but because he crosses the critical line between repression and expression. In dealing with these provocative situations, Mahfouz's gifted madman, *à la* Plato, conveys an un-wisdom that questions traditional understandings of wisdom. But anyone who writes about madness must eventually encounter the dilemma of representation. Mahfouz attempts to challenge this representational impasse and to use language to speak about and for madness, stepping onto that dangerous terrain between writing as a linguistic manifestation of rationality and madness as a metalinguistic, irrational phenomenon. This relationship has always been precarious. Whereas language deals with regularity, consistency, and grammaticality in its logic of formation, of cause and effect, and of hierarchy, madness lies outside the norms of sound reasoning that language offers. The problem lies not only in how a work of art represents madness, or in the project of treating madness as an object of study (for this treatment would always be subordinated to the logic of language itself); more importantly, it lies in how one gives voice to a long-silenced, non-reasonable Other, in the paradox of making madness speak its mind. This logic tells us that once a text undertakes to transgress the borderlines between sanity and madness, the text itself becomes a psychological document. Or, to put it differently, a text cannot be produced from within madness that is, by definition, the negation of reason and order.

Yet the language of fiction does not claim to accurately represent a reality that lies outside of it; at least it has no obligation to do so. The function that only literature can perform is to produce an *impression* of madness, of representing madness without actually representing it, and more importantly, without the transcendental imperative of any historical reference. However, although literature does not need the justification of historical referentiality to make its point, this does not mean that literature lacks historicity, especially in its response to or critique of social phenomena. So when Mahfouz chooses to represent a mad character, readers and critics are free to treat this representation as an artistic expression and a social statement, irrespective of its accuracy as a historical document. Through narrative (which is roughly defined as a certain logical sequence in which parts relate to each other through a series of causally related events taking place in space and time) Mahfouz tests the limits of representation as he accepts the challenge of navigating the mind of a madman who is experiencing the unthinkable moments of a mental breakdown. Mahfouz's text does more than making representable something that can neither be conceived nor represented.

Storytelling is, above all, a narrative perspective and a way of organizing thought and giving it form, even if the sequence is radically disjunctive. In other words, narrative cannot function without some kind of order. Even if what is represented in language is an instance of radical disorder, like mental illness or death, the moment this instance is approached it can only be articulated in a sequenced narrative, inviting us into a process of rationalizing the irrational – of giving clear form to muddled content. We are thus led to read Mahfouz's text for what lies beyond it. Here the essential tension in Mahfouz's text between reason and unreason, functioning metaphorically, offers the possibility of revealing more than what it talks about. How do we understand this metaphor?

The story invites us to regard the omniscient narrative voice as the voice of understanding, which, by virtue of its omniscience, captures the inconsistent thought process within the protagonist's mind. This effort to think the opposite of thinking, i.e. madness, through the sentential logic of narrative – i.e. syntax and semantics – begins to approximate the experience that Mahfouz's protagonist is going through. The narrative voice, then, expresses the void between reason and the truth it claims to convey. Yet, it could well be claimed that every act of writing is necessarily an inscription of hope for something better. If this claim holds, then Mahfouz's text could be seen as arguing that narrative reconstitutes itself as a hope for an alternative.

Reason itself is always established through a relation with the other. Therefore, reason moves by changing what it makes of its other reason, here instantiated by Mahfouz's protagonist. This may lead us to conclude that, as a work of art, "The Whisper of Madness" does not seek to represent madness directly as much as it attempts to gesture towards it through the dynamic relationship of reason to its other. The imaginative dimension of art does not explicitly claim any direct historical referentiality outside itself (Aristotle's formula of constructive imagination as mimesis). It might be safe to argue, then, that art – by virtue of its mimetic function or by its separation from the yoke of representing what Aristotle describes as the particular truth of things[8] – excludes the external referent, and that in representing madness through the medium of narrative it finds a way, as Mahfouz does in his text, to judge the world and to lay bare its nonsense rather than to provide the world with a way of knowing madness.

In "The Whisper of Madness," Mahfouz manages to penetrate his madman's mind in an attempt to provide him with justification for his "abnormal" thinking and actions, whether they result from boredom, from the discovery of the absurdities of life, or simply from medical imbalance. This is what makes the text so provocative: at a time when the field of medicine claimed that it had managed to neutralize madness by defining it, Mahfouz gives madness an important social, or perhaps a socio-psychological, dimension, precisely by refusing to define it. The implication is that if we are not sure what madness really is, then we can no longer be sure what norms of freedom are. Mahfouz opens his story with a defiant question – the first

[8] Aristotle, *Poetics*, trans. Richard Janko (Indianapolis, IN: Hackett, 1987), p. 12.

question that philosophy asks, that is, the question of essence – which paradoxically threatens Mahfouz's entire project of representation: what is madness? He then proceeds to offer a definition:

> It appears to be a mysterious case just like life and death, you can know a great deal about it if you look at it from the outside, but the inside, the essence, remains secret. Our man knows he was a resident of the sanatorium for some time. He now remembers his own past in the same manner all sane people do; he is also well aware of the present. But this short interval of his life – thank God it was short – perplexes his mind; he really cannot make any sense of it at all. The whole thing was for him like a journey to a marvelous ethereal world, so foggy and full of many featureless faces that haunt his memory. No sooner does he try to shed some light of remembrance on these memories than they vanish and sink into complete darkness. Sometimes his ears would catch sounds like murmurs, but as soon as he tries to listen to them, they disappear and retreat, leaving behind them only silence and confusion. That magical time with its pleasure and pain is now lost forever, even those who witnessed it have kept silent about it for a very obvious reason. That time has been completely dropped from memory as if it had never happened. No one single truthful historian could tell us about its wonders. How did it all take place, we wonder. When? How did people come to realise that this reason of his had become something other than reason and that he had become an abnormal individual that had to be confined and isolated from the community as if he were a carnivorous monster?[9]

Madness thus appears to be born out of nothingness and functions as the opposite of reason's narrative sobriety. As is usually the case with Mahfouz's fiction, there is in this tale an equation between its apparent theme and a universal quest for meaning and justice. Mahfouz's text touches from afar on the idea that madness is a condition of human existence *a priori*, namely, that madness is inextricably linked to social malaise. Even at its very end, Mahfouz's story insists on the idea that his madman is a victim of social injustice and the enslavement to tradition, and that modern social ethics and political codes are likely to provoke madness in the first place. To this effect, Mahfouz seems to write not so much *about* or even *for* the mad, but *with* them, not only delineating the threatening realm that his protagonist and those like him inhabit, but also entering into it, becoming the internal voice of the madmen while keeping his own external narrative voice intact.

[9] Mahfouz, *Hams al-Junūn*, 4.

By means of the schizoid monologism of his narrative voice, Mahfouz manages both to trace a break between reason and unreason and to establish an ironic connection between them that is far from traditional. The madness that appears in Mahfouz's text is not the conventional kind of madness we see in Western literary representations. Traditional representations of madness – from Sophocles' *Ajax* and Euripides' *Bacchae* through *Leyla and Majnun*, *Don Quixote*, *Jane Eyre*, and Gogol's *Diary of a Madman* to Sylvia Plath's *The Bell Jar* and Emile Habibi's *The Secret Life of Saeed the Pessoptimist* – take a bewildering multiplicity of forms; but they all have in common the fact that they mark an irreversible exclusion from "real" society. Shakespeare creates a varied cast of mad characters of whom this is true – Ophelia, Lady Macbeth, King Lear, Poor Tom – but even in the case of his most famous "mad" character, Hamlet, whose madness is profoundly ambiguous, the ambiguity does not arise from the relationship between madness and reality but from the question of whether, or to what extent, Hamlet's madness is itself real or merely assumed. Real madness is, as the Doctor summoned to treat Lady Macbeth's says, a "disease … beyond my practice" which "more needs … the divine than the physician."[10] In Mahfouz's story, madness is of interest, not as the disordered opposite of reason, but as a climax to acts of social injustice and cultural, if not religious, despair. In other words, Mahfouz does not focus on the relationship between the mad and the sane. What seems important to him, at least in this text, is the relationship between the legitimate limits of reason and the violation of those limits. It is possible to see in "The Whisper of Madness" a desire to understand the meaning of life (as in al-Ḥakīm's *The People of the Cave*), a seeming nostalgia for a lost Cairo (as in Mahfouz's next work, his novel *al-Qāhira al-Jadīda* [*Modern Cairo*]),[11] a fear of social psychosis, or even a wish for a utopian state of life. However, at the heart of this symbolic narrative is a total condemnation of the social structure and the complacent religiosity of modern Cairo.

There is a significant turning point in the narrative testifying to this condemnation, namely, when Mahfouz's silent man decides – in a

[10] Shakespeare, *Macbeth*, Act V, Scene 1: 59; Act V, Scene 1: 62.

[11] See Mohammad Salama, "Mahfouz's Cinematic Cairo: Depictions of Urban Transformations in Twentieth-Century Egypt" in *Cinematic Cityscapes: Global Approaches*, ed. Reena Dube (Nebraska: The University of Nebraska Press, 2018, forthcoming).

revolutionary act against his own habits – to break free from his self-incurred silence:

He was a quiet man, so quiet that his quietness could be described as absolute. Perhaps this is why he tended to like quiescence and indolence and to avoid socialization and activity ... His quietness was on all levels, internal and external, physical and mental, sensory and imaginative. He was a statue of flesh and blood that appears to be observing people, whereas he is isolated from life altogether ...

At last, he reached the café, sat conveniently on his chair as usual, but this time he could not lock his hands against his knee or surrender to his habitual silence; somehow his psyche could not be motionless anymore and lost the ability to be immobile, so he rebuffed his chair, and started to rise.[12]

The decision to "rise" from the chair of silence stirs in Mahfouz's madman's mind a spontaneous love of the idea of freedom. Here, the connection between passion and freedom is far from vague:

He is free to do whatever he likes, however he likes it, and whenever he likes without submission to any power, any external force, or any internal drive. In a second, he was able to solve the question of human will and save it with excellent vigour from the toils of reasoning.[13]

We are now confronted not so much with the question of madness as with a broader issue of freedom. Mahfouz's protagonist is no longer responsible for making his own decisions or deciding to think responsibly. Thinking is deciding, and reflection cannot be separated from action – there is no space between. The act of deciding, for Mahfouz's madman, entails thinking, and thinking curtails freedom, because it "suppresses," as Jean-Luc Nancy once put it, "the undecidable that renders decision possible and necessary."[14] It is a decision against commitment and decidability, a decision to leave nothing more to be decided or worshipped or followed. Madness here, appears to be a rejection of the constraints of religion, a *tabula rasa*, a discovery of behavior and thought as non-committal, and a cancellation, though not a denial, of the existentiality of existence. This state of freedom from God, from law and order, appears to be the only way out: an unforced choice and resistance to logic that tests the

12 Mahfouz, *Hams al-Junūn*, 4.
13 Ibid., 6.
14 Jean-Luc Nancy, *The Experience of Freedom* (Stanford, CA: Stanford University Press, 1993), 162.

limits of logic, so that the madman's freedom lies outside theology and cultural appropriateness. In short, his freedom takes him outside religion, outside the theological dictates of good and evil, to a decision free from judgment – precisely because it originates as an "authentic"[15] decision, but one that does not know, nor cares to know, that it is authentic or that it is even a decision.

Mahfouz's political affiliation is no secret. In his early youth, he was an ardent member of the Wafd Party, which brought Egypt's nominal independence from England in 1922. He knows that what his party's leader, Sa'ad Zaghlūl did – not only in 1919 but throughout his life, indeed until his death in 1927 – was a revolution. Freedom also informs revolutionary thought, and revolution is a kind of madness and a kind of freedom from an existing system, a dominant way of thinking. Mahfouz's text was written in the early 1930s and published in 1938, that is, eleven years after Zaghlūl's death and two years after the formation of a new Egyptian Democratic Party. Written in an atmosphere of political havoc and economic depression, "The Whisper of Madness" could also be speaking for the sociopolitical malaise of the time. Arthur Goldschmidt reminds us of the socioeconomic conditions of Egypt in the 1930s:

> The income gap between rich and poor Egyptians grew wider. Along with poverty went ignorance and disease. The 1923 constitution had made primary education compulsory, but poor peasants could not pay tuition to send their children to school, because they could not do without the meagre income they gained from their children's work in the fields. Mortality rates, especially for babies and small children in rural areas, were among the world's highest ... Many vagabonds slept in doorways, under bridges, and on railroad rights-of-way. Most Egyptians endured hardships patiently, but these conditions could not be borne forever. Eventually, some would question the system by which the benefits and burdens of citizenship were parceled out by 1936 Egyptian democracy was in question.[16]

If this argument holds, then it is possible that Mahfouz's anonymous character is itself a trope, a metonymy that stands for a larger whole: social codes that are devoid of sense and meaning in a decaying monarchy; the institutional monopoly of religion; and the suppression of

[15] Ibid.

[16] Arthur Goldschmidt Jr., *A Brief History of Egypt* (State College, PA: Pennsylvania State University Press, 2008), 125.

individual values and of social consensus – all negations of the feelings of freedom and autonomy of which only a madman is capable. Mahfouz's "The Whisper of Madness," then, has nothing to do with the catastrophe of an isolated case of lunacy. The madman's story uniquely corresponds to a moment of religious, social, and political madness. The kind of madness that Mahfouz's protagonist experiences is neither deluded nor based on false convictions. He is not incapable of logic. In fact, he does show a purposeful logic when faced with social inequality:

> On the sidewalk of the restaurant, he saw a table loaded with delicious food, where a man and a woman were sitting on each side eating and drinking in mirth. Not very far from them sat a group of young paupers, almost naked except for some shabby rags, their faces and skins covered with thick layers of dust and dirt. The incompatibility between the two sights made him uncomfortable and his newly gained sense of freedom aggravated his sense of annoyance, so he decided not to let it pass. But what can he do? His heart replied in determination and faith, "the kids should eat with the others."[17]

However, one will never understand, for certain, the protagonist's lapse into madness and with it the freedom from the fetters of conventional reason, for, as Nancy argues, "incomprehensible freedom makes itself understood at the limit, in a very precise sense of this expression, as a self-comprehension independent of the comprehension of understanding."[18] For Mahfouz, thinking madness requires thinking not the idea of madness but a particular happening, an event, the process that his protagonist has to undergo, just as it requires carrying thought to its limits, a process that has enabled the final revolt of the madman against reason and all inherited traditions of his culture, be it Islamic, fundamentalist, or secular. One is free to be mad, then, to be in a state of madness which preserves freedom, but also in a state of madness that cannot be an object of thought. The freedom of madness, or the madness that is the ultimate expression of mental freedom, the freedom from the dictates of custom and indoctrination, is dialectically inseparable from reason, and becomes a freedom that exposes itself to itself, a reason after reason, or even a split reason. Nancy tells us that "all liberations (national, social, moral, sexual, aesthetic) are ambiguous, and

[17] Mahfouz, *Hams al-Junūn*, 7.
[18] Nancy, *The Experience of Freedom*, 49.

also arise from manipulations."[19] But because the seeds of revolution are always planted in the individual, the recognition – or, more precisely, the epiphany – of the possibility of choice that has dawned upon Mahfouz's madman, marks the beginning of alterity and promises the dissemination of free thinking from the individual to the collective. After all, revolutions are also considered a sort of madness; they seek to break a seemingly consistent order or regime.

The genius of Mahfouz's narrative manifests itself not only in facing the challenge of transforming knowing into telling, or in finding words for that which is difficult to articulate, but also in writing a story that becomes a model of alternative thinking and in offering different ways of looking at the world not as what it is, but as what it is not. The experience of madness evokes "the experience of freedom," and thinking freedom "should mean," as Nancy insists, "freeing freedom from manipulations, including, first of all, those of thinking."[20]

Mahfouz's protagonist does not fit the Marxist profile of a victim of class oppression, nor does he strike us as a man fully aware of his displacement and separation from the means of production. Only in the paupers incident could it be argued that he enacts a Robin Hood-like socialism and achieves the anti-capitalist move from "the things of logic to the logic of things," as Pierre Bourdieu would call it.[21] But in more than one incident, the text invites a reading of madness as a metaphor for social resurgence, one that might not have a heroic revolutionary model, but that reopens the question of the model itself. Narrativizing madness in this sense becomes a kind of storytelling that requires what the sociologist Richard Harvey Brown refers to as "a political economy and collective psychology in which a sense of lived connection between personal character and public conduct prevails."[22] After all, people continue to suffer under brutal regimes, and in many cases people die of hunger, repression, and despair, which all whisper madness in the ear of Mahfouz's protagonist, as they must have in the ear of Mahfouz himself.

[19] Ibid., 164.
[20] Ibid., 164.
[21] Pierre Bourdieu, 'The Essence of Neoliberalism', *Le monde diplomatique* (Dec, 8, 1998), 2. http://mondediplo.com/1998/12/08bourdieu
[22] Richard Harvey Brown, *Society as Text* (Chicago, IL: Chicago University Press, 1987), 144.

6 *Islamism Writes Back: 'Alī Aḥmad Bākāthīr's* The Red Revolutionary *and the Dismantling of the Secular*

We have an incapacity for proving anything which no amount of dogmatism can overcome. We have an idea of truth which no amount of scepticism can overcome.

Blaise Pascal, *Pensées*

By the late 1930s, Ḥusayn had already sketched the blueprints for the future of culture in Egypt, both in his seminal 1938 work *Mustaqbal al-Thaqāfa fī Miṣr* (The Future of Culture in Egypt) and in *The Days* trilogy, which he completed in 1939. Those were the years when the novel genre came to assert itself as the secular *bête noire* of Islamic fundamentalism, winning the hearts of readers and of the audiences of cinematic adaptations. Novels would soon be interrogating the sacred and taking bold steps away from the divine to the human. The generation of the 1930s thus succeeded in hitting the mark of secular modernity, and, for a time at least, seemed to have quelled the surge of Islamism, despite the strong support for the increasingly popular Muslim Brotherhood in its tender years. Major authors like Ḥusayn, al-'Aqqād, al-Ḥakīm, Haykal, Mūsà, and now Mahfouz formed a unique cohort of pioneering Egyptian intellectuals who joined forces in delivering a sharp blow to fundamentalism and giving birth to a nascent humanism – in an epoch of cultural richness that comes at the tail end of what Pierre Cachia once called a "literary Egyptian renaissance."[1]

Thus by the time the Indonesian-born Egyptian author of Yemeni origins, 'Alī Aḥmad Bākāthīr, came to publish *Al-Thā'r al-Aḥmar* (*The Red Revolutionary*) in 1949, the Egyptian cultural scene was already set on a massive collision course with the divine, one that was narrowly avoided in the ending of Yaḥyà Ḥaqqī's 1940 masterpiece, *Qandīl Umm Hāshim* (*Umm Hāshim's Lamp*), which represents a

[1] Pierre Cachia, *Ṭāhā Ḥusayn, His Place in the Literary Egyptian Renaissance* (London: Luzac and Company Ltd., 1956), 1–42.

reconciliation between religion and science. Yet a collision would inevitably materialize in the late 1950s, most importantly in Mahfouz's *Awlād Ḥāritnā* (*Children of the Alley*), a thematic expansion of "The Whisper of Madness," conceived as an allegory of the history of God (Jabalāwī in the novel), which al-Azhar immediately banned upon its release and which became the most controversial novel in the history of modern Arabic literature.[2]

The time had come for introducing a new, Islamist variation on the theme of the Egyptian peasant: a devout believer, a faithful lover, and a grateful son of the Egyptian *qarya* (village). The idea behind the invention of the Islamist peasant is to fight against the secular and reclaim the future of Egypt; in response to the disillusioned humanist we see in Ḥusayn's *The Days* or the non-conformist anti-traditionalist peasant of Haykal's *Zaynab*. Indeed, Sayyid Quṭb, the godfather of the Muslim Brotherhood, had attempted to debunk both Haykal's critique of traditionalism in the Egyptian village and Ḥusayn's exposure of the village's charlatanism, ignorance, and squalor. In a lesser-known novel, an alternative autobiography to be sure, Quṭb announces that his recollections of his own village are different from those of Ḥusayn's. In fact, in a twist of cultural irony, Quṭb dedicates his memoirs of his own village to Ḥusayn himself:

> To the author of *The Days*, Dr. Ṭāhā Ḥusayn. These, sir, are days just like yours, lived by a child in a village. Some of those days resemble yours, but most of them are different from yours, just like the difference from one generation to another, from one village to another, from one life to the other, or from one perspective to another. But in the end, they are days.[3]

For the embattled Islamists of the Muslim Brotherhood, the time had come to be on the side of God instead of acquiescing to secularism, and to forge a counter propaganda campaign for Islamism. The Islamist novelistic project of the 1930s and 1940s thus resembled the morality plays of fifteenth-century Western Europe, where allegorical

[2] See Muṣṭafà 'Abd al-Ghanī, *Naguib Mahfouz al-Thawra wa al-Taṣawwuf* [*Naguib Mahfouz, Revolution and Sufism*] (Cairo: al-Hay'a al-'Āmma lil-Kitāb, 2002); George Ṭarābīshī, *Allāh fī Rihla-t- Naguib Mahfouz al-Ramziyya* [*God in the Symbolic Journey of Naguib Mahfouz*] (Beirut: Dār al-Ṭalī'a, 1988); Ṣalāḥ Faḍl, *Shafrāt al-Naṣṣ* [*The Codes of the Text*] (Cairo: Dar al-Fikr lil-Dirāsāt wa al-Nashr wa al-Tawzī', 1993).

[3] Sayyid Quṭb, *Ṭifl min al-Qarya* [*A Child from the Village*] (Beirut: Dār al-Shurūq, 1946), 1.

representations of good and evil allowed the plebeians to heed the path of God and renounce the secular world and the ungodly temptations offered by the Renaissance. From the perspective of an overpowered Islamism, the need was urgent for an Islamist counterculture, one which the exhortations of the Muslim Brotherhood's leading Imam and founder Ḥasan al-Bannā or the critical rebuttals of Quṭb could not confront alone.[4]

When Bākāthīr wrote his novel, the socialist current in Egypt had begun to soar. The Egyptian Socialist Party, which was established in 1920 but had lasted only four years, reinstated itself again in 1949 under the name of *al-Ḥizb al-Shiyū'ī al-Miṣrī* (The Egyptian Communist Party).[5] In addition, the publication of *al-Thā'r al-Ahmar* in 1949 coincides with the assassination of al-Bannā. Although hardly emphasized in Western scholarship on the Muslim Brotherhood or in current discourses on Islam in Egypt, what sparked the rise of the Muslim Brotherhood in 1928 was the perceived injustice visited upon al-Bannā's fellow factory workers in the city of al-Suwīs. The Muslim Brotherhood, then, was formed as a labor union (with a religious flavor) against oppression visited upon workers. As this chapter demonstrates, there is a remarkable parallel between Bākāthīr's novel and the formative moments of the Muslim Brotherhood – a parallel that manifests itself not only in the fight for social justice but also, and more prominently, in the rejection of Western solutions to workers' rights. If this argument holds, then it would not be far-fetched to consider Bākāthīr's novel the first apologetic work of historical fiction in modern Arabic literature – an apologia for one of the world's largest and most effective Islamist organizations in the twentieth century.[6]

[4] See Sayyid Quṭb, 'Naqd Kitāb Mustaqbal al-Thaqāfa fī Miṣr li-Ṭāhā Ḥusayn' [*Critique of [Ṭāhā Ḥusayn's] Book The Future of Culture in Egypt*], *Ṣaḥīfa-t-Dār al-'Ulūm*. Issue. 4, April, 1939.

[5] Ṭāhir 'Abd al-Karīm, *Al-Shakhṣiyya al-Waṭaniyya al- Miṣriyya* [*Nationalist Egyptian Character*] (Cairo: Dār al-Fikr lil-Dirāsāt wa al-Tawzī', n.d.), 194.

[6] There is evidence that Bākāthīr supported the Muslim Brotherhood movement. His collection of plays *Masraḥ al-Siyāsa (The Theatre of Politics)* were first published individually in the *al-Ikhwān al-Muslimūn* (Muslim Brotherhood) and al-Da'wa (The [Muslim] Call) magazines in the 1940s and 1950s. See 'Abdullah Bāṣabrīn, "Rā'id al-Adab al-Islāmī 'Alī Bākāthīr: Wājib al-Adīb al-'Arabī Tabṣīr al-'Umma bi- al-Akhṭār allatī Tatahaddaduhā" ("Alī Bākāthīr: The Pioneer of Islamist Literature: The Duty of the Arab Author Is to Alert the Nation to the Threatening Danger"). *Al-Ayyām*, (28 June 2003), 8.

Bākāthīr's historical novel takes us centuries back to one of the most contentious political periods in the history of Islam in the 10th century AD, namely, an escalation in political rivalries consisting, among other events, of the rise of the Ismaili *Ḥaraka-t- al-Qarāmiṭa* (The Qarāmita Movement, also known as Carmathians, Qarmathians, or Karmathians) and a perceived rise of Jewry as an organized force against the Islamic caliphate.[7] This heightened rivalry, moreover, coincided with the increasing vulnerability of the Abbasid caliphate near the end of the third Hijrī century, during the rule of al-Mūwaffaq bi-Allāh in Iraq (June 870 AD–June 891 AD). As with every work by Bākāthīr,[8] a prolific poet, dramatist, and novelist with deep sympathy for the Muslim Brotherhood, this novel is didactic in intention. As a result, it is highly anachronistic, since long-dead movements and individuals are made to stand in for what Bākāthīr sees as their contemporary equivalents, which, in fact, bear little resemblance to their supposed historical prototypes. The historical, highly melodramatic *mise en scène* is meant to foreshadow the struggle of the forces of Marxism and communism against Islam in the modern world, a struggle in which the forces of the human intellect, with all its trendy theories, will inevitably fall short of eternal divine justice.

The didactic elements of *The Red Revolutionary* appear very clearly in the quotes from the Qur'ān at the beginning of each of the novel's three sections, which are intended to usher the reader into the labyrinthine tale of the protagonist Ḥamdān and his divided world. Using theological terminology, those three sections are referred to as

7 See Ibn al-Nadīm, *al-Fihrist* [*Chronicles*] (Beirut: Maṭba'at al-'Arabī lil-Tawzī' wa al-Nashr, 1991), 385–6. See also Ibn al-Athīr, *al-Kāmil fi al-Tārīkh* [*The Complete [work] on History*] (Beirut: Dār Sādir, 1966). Vol. 8, 469; and Maḥmūd Shākir, *al-Qarāmiṭa* [*The Caramites*] (Beirut: al-Maktab al-Islāmī, 1979), 1.

8 For more on the Islamist tendencies in Bākāthīr's work, see the following: Marvin Carlson, *The Arab Oedipus* (New York: Segal, 2005) and 'The religious Drama of Egypt's Ali Ahmed Bakathir', in *Religion, Theatre, and Performance: Acts of Faith*, ed. Lance Gharavi (New York: Routledge, 2012); M. M. Badawi, *Modern Drama in Egypt* (Cambridge: Cambridge University Press, 2005); Bākāthīr, *Muḥāḍarāt fī al-Fann al-Masraḥī min Khilāl Tajāribī al-Shakhṣiyya* [*Lectures on Theatrical Art through my Personal Experience*] (Cairo: Dār al-Ma'ārif, 1958); Urlike Freitag, 'Dying of Enforced Spinsterhood: Hadramawt through the Eyes of Ali Ahmad Ba Kathir', *Die Welt des Islams*, Vol. 37, No. 1 (Mar. 1997): 2–27; Eeqbal Hassim, 'The Significance of Quranic Verses in the Literature of Ali Ahmad Bakathir: Case Studies of al-Silsila wa al-Ghufran and al-Duktur Hazim.' *NCEIS Research Papers* 1.3 (2002): 1–27.

asfār (volumes), a word used in the Qur'ān for the books of the Old Testament.[9] Every *sifr* (volume) is prefaced with a Qur'ānic verse epitomizing the main theme of that volume and connecting it with the larger message of the novel as a whole, thus imposing a liturgical structure on the entire work akin to the structure of the Christian morality plays of medieval Europe.

Volume One is prefaced by a verse from *sūra-t- al-Isrā'* (The Chapter of the Nocturnal Journey):

> And when We want to perish a township, We will allow the moral depravity of its well-to-do to increase so that the saying befits it and We destroy it utterly.[10]

Not only does this verse sum up the main conflict in the novel between rich and poor, it also advocates equitable distribution of income at the same time as it warns against inequity and the monopoly of financial resources held by a corrupt faction of society.

Similarly, Volume Two is prefaced with the following Qur'ānic verses:

> And Recite unto them the story of the one to whom We gave Our revelations, but he divorced himself from them, and the Devil overtook him and he became among the astray. And had We willed We could have raised him by their means, but he sought eternity on earth and followed his own airs. His likeness is as the likeness of a dog: if you weigh in on him he pants with his tongue out, and if you let him be he pants with his tongue out. Such is the likeness of the people who belied Our revelations. Relate unto them such history so that they may reflect.[11]

The two verses summarize the theme of that particular chapter, namely, the going astray of Ḥamdān and his deviation from the path of God.

[9] *Qur'ān*, 62:5.

[10] *Qur'ān*, 17:16. My approximation of the meanings of this verse differs from common translations. I follow Abū 'Ubayda's interpretation/pronunciation/reading of the verb *amarna* as *amirna*, where he changes the reading of the verb *amarna* (we will decree/command/order) to read *amirna* (increase), thus differing from the reading that makes the verb an imperative (for the rich) to act in such a corrupt manner toward one another that *increases* their immoral behavior. Abū 'Ubayda's theological leanings advocate that he interprets the Qur'ān from the point of view of divine justice, lest God be attributed with provocation and therefore unfairness. See Abū 'Ubayda, *Majāz al-Qur'ān*, ed. Muḥammad Fu'ād Sarkīn, Vol. 1 (Cairo: Maktaba-t- al-Khānjī, 1970), 372.

[11] *Qur'ān*, 7:175–6.

Volume Three includes three different verses:

And Allah has favored some of you over others in providence. Those who were favored would not hand over their providence to those in their care so they would be equal to them. Is it the grace of Allah they deny?

Allah has given a likeness of an owned slave who has no control over anything, and (the likeness of) whom We have given good providence of which he spends in secret and in public. Are they the same? Praise be to Allah! Verily most of them do not know.[12]

And Allah has given a similitude of two men, one of whom dumb with no control over anything and is a burden on his care giver wherever he ask him to go, he brings no good. Could he be equal to the one who advocates justice and follows a straight path.[13]

These verses, which present inequality among humans as divine and not as a human creation, point to the central theme of the novel even more clearly: that both communism, which challenges inequality, and capitalism, which promotes it, are the result of human endeavor, and are therefore, by their very nature, ungodly – inherently corrupt systems of governance that ultimately harm rather than benefit wretched workers, and society as a whole. Both movements, the argument continues, are alien to the sensibilities of God-fearing Muslims in Egypt. No human-made system of social justice will ever be fair to all humans. The fact that both capitalism and communism originated in an Islamophobic West is reason enough to doubt their value as means of achieving social justice and equitable governance, whether politically, economically, or socially. Islam, together with its divinely inscribed social laws, remains the one and only religious system fit to rule the Egyptian society and to administer a God-inspired lasting and comprehensive justice for all. From this perspective the question of inequality and how or whether to eradicate it becomes irrelevant.

The Red Revolutionary is a loosely historical novel that focuses on Ḥamdān Ibn al-Ash'ath, also known as Ḥamdān Qarmaṭ, the founder of the third-century *Ḥaraka-t- al- Qarāmiṭa* in the Iraqi city of al-Kūfa (Kufa). Its adherents, the Qarāmiṭans, were a syncretic Islamic group that drew on elements of Ismā'īlī Shī'ism and revolted against the Abbasid Caliphate. They are mostly remembered for their invasion of Mecca, the robbery of the Ka'aba's famous Black Stone, and the

12 *Qur'ān*: 16:75.
13 *Qur'ān*: 16:76.

sacrilege of the sacred Well of Zamzam during the pilgrimage days of the Hijrī year of 930 (1524 AD), events which postdate Ḥamdān's life and play no direct role in the novel, but hover in its background. *Qaramaṭ* translates in the Nabataean language (a Western Aramaic variety) as "the red-eyed one"[14] and it is probably as an allusion to this meaning that Bākāthīr called his novel, *Al-Thā'r al-Aḥmar (The Red Revolutionary)*, anachronistically blending the socio-linguistic associations of the movement's historical origins with the modern associations of the color red with Marxism and communism.

The novel begins with Ḥamdān, a peasant working in serf-like conditions for Ibn al-Ḥaṭīm, a wealthy landowner. Gradually, Ḥamdān grows indignant at the social and economic conditions in Kufa. He understands that what he and his family earn from this hard, backbreaking toil in a desert climate, laboring under the burning heat of the sun and the bitter cold of the night, is barely adequate for the cheapest food and the roughest clothes.[15] Bākāthīr disingenuously aims to win over the reader by arousing sympathy for the degrading conditions of the peasants, which eventually becomes the rationale for Ḥamdān's rebellion against the injustice visited upon him, his family, and his class by the brutality of an exploitative system. This tactic on Bākāthīr's part is disingenuous precisely because, in the course of the novel, it becomes clear that the struggle for social justice is not his primary concern; rather it is the superiority of Islam, as he conceives it, over any attempt on the part of human beings to transform the divinely ordained order of the universe through their own powers. The parallel with the Muslim Brotherhood, which similarly began by arousing sympathy for the socially oppressed and focusing on the rights of workers, can hardly be ignored.

Ḥamdān is the sole supporter of his family, which consists of his mother and his two sisters, Rājya and 'Āliya. The latter is engaged to

14 A useful reference here is Ibn al-Athīr's text, *al-Kāmil fī al-Tārīkh* (*The Comprehensive Book of History*). Ibn al-Athīr dates the Qarāmiṭa movement back to the hijrī year of 278; but the fourteenth-century Muslim intellectual historian Ibn Khaldūn contends that the Qarāmita movement appeared in the heart of Kūfa city in the year 258. Qarmaṭ is also lexicalized in Ibn Manẓūr's *Lisān al-'Arab* (*The Language of the Arabs*) under the referent Qarmūṭ. This term is explained as *zahr al-gha i* (the flower of the ghaḍā bush), which also happens to be red in color.

15 Alī Aḥmad Bākāthīr, *Al-Thā'r al-Aḥmar* [*The Red Revolutionary*] (Cairo: Maktaba-t- Miṣr, 1949), 5.

his cousin 'Abdān, and to deepen the sense of injustice even further, the henchmen of his employer, Ibn al-Ḥaṭīm, kidnap her and add her to Ibn al-Ḥaṭīm's ever-increasing harem. This abduction becomes the turning point for Ḥamdān, for it triggers a journey of revenge, regret, and self-discovery that leads, eventually, to his return to Islam and his disillusionment with non-Islamist systems of governance.

Before following Ḥamdān on this journey, however, it is worth pausing for a moment to examine the role of 'Āliya and the other women in Bākāthīr's novel. 'Āliya's abduction is clearly intended to illustrate the evils of a society based on inequalities of wealth and social class, and from that perspective it might well support a communist critique of social injustice. But any sympathy with this critique that we might have is later blunted by a comment by a member of a proto-Communist, anti-Islamic group that 'Abdān and Ḥamdān will later join. Having lost 'Āliya, 'Abdān plans to marry the daughter of a member of this group, but is told that he can have her without bothering with marriage if he wants:

> "[W]hy worry about marriage, she is all yours; you can have her today, do whatever you wish to do with her."
>
> "But this is against..."
>
> "Against what? Religion? Do you still believe in religion? Do you want to go back to your old backward ways?"[16]

'Abdān, like Bākāthīr, finds this proposal utterly despicable and irreligious.[17] We, as readers, are meant to believe that the highest moral principle of communism is that everything belongs to everyone, in an absolute interchangeability that extinguishes humans as individual beings, condemning humanity to an endless cycle of promiscuity. This double-barreled attack on both capitalism and communism is not only reductionist; it indicates how blind Bākāthīr is to the results of the version of "Islam" that he promotes and whose effects are evident all around him in his own time and place. In this he is not entirely unlike some of the otherwise progressive authors we have already considered in our discussion of the symbol of the woman as the land. Bākāthīr sees women primarily as objects of male pleasure to be "protected" against destruction and corruption. Without male protection they die, they are abducted, they are raped, they become

[16] Ibid.
[17] Bākāthīr, *Al-Thā'ir al-Aḥmar*, 66.

members of harems, etc. The rationale is clear: it is the conservatism of a society that sacralizes marriage and the subservient role of women as a humane and civilized institution against debauchery and prostitution. But in his inability to conceive of women as anything but passive objects of men's actions, even as he is accusing both communism and capitalism of being their oppressors, Bākāthīr allows the existing *episteme* to write his critique for him.

On the first step of his journey, reminiscent of the crude attempt at redistributive justice that we noted in the chicken episode of Mahfouz's "The Whisper of Madness," Ḥamdān meets with some *'Ayyārīn* (literally, equalizers or scale-eveners, men whose job is to steal money from the rich and give it back to the poor, *à la* Robin Hood). It is not surprising, after all he has seen in his life, that he would want to join this group: "All I know is that God has sent them to punish the rich for denying *zakāt* [alms] and charity and for squandering the rights of laborers like myself who work their lands."[18] On hearing this statement, one of the organizers, 'Abd al-Ra'ūf, commends him as a true equalizer: "Wonderful! You seem to be a naturally born equalizer."[19] But Shaykh Bahlūl, the leader of the equalizers, is skeptical:

> No, 'Abd al-Ra'ūf, he is not an equalizer yet. An equalizer is someone who feels his injustice and responds by taking matters in his own hands by retaliating against his oppressor. Ḥamdān is done injustice to, but he hasn't done anything about it, so he is more like half an equalizer now.[20]

Ḥamdān eventually does take the final step, pledges to become an equalizer, and is joined by his cousin 'Abdān. Yet Ḥamdān does not last as an outlaw for long; soon 'Abdān kills all the police officers who raided the house to arrest them due to their ties with the equalizers. Pursued by other members of the police, they both flee to Baghdad. Shortly after, Ḥamdān's wife dies. Believing that her death is God's punishment for his ill-doings, Ḥamdān leaves the gang, rents a few bulls, and, for the time being, takes to work as a peasant in Kufa.

The argument of the novel becomes more explicit when 'Abdān begins frequenting *ḥalaqāt al-'ilm* (learning circles) in Baghdad and develops a keen interest in the relationship between theory and

18 Ibid., 41.
19 Ibid.
20 Ibid.

practice. On the matter of *zakāt*, for instance, the following debate takes place between him and his fellow students in the learning circle:

"Don't you see if the rich gave *zakāt* then no one will be left without food or wanting clothes," emphasized 'Abdān.

"Yes," replied the students.

"Why then are the poor left without food and clothes? Why is this aspect of religion neglected?", responded 'Abdān.

"There is nothing we can do to fix things. We live in corrupt times. Our job is to explain the rules, not to guarantee their fair execution, replied the students."[21]

This passivity does not satisfy 'Abdān, and his dissatisfaction leads him to a crucial moment when Marxian thought (inflected with anti-Semitism) begins to seep into this anachronistic tale.[22] Ja'far al-Karamānī, deputy of Maymūn al-Qaddāḥ, the founder of the Qarmatian-Isma'ili doctrine – who is known in the novel as *al-Yahūdī (the Jew)*, in reference to the Islamist claim that he was a Jew who feigned conversion to Islam in order to attack it from within – immediately seeks to inculcate into 'Abdān the idea of *al-'Adl al-Shāmil* (comprehensive justice), Bākāthīr's thinly-veiled version of communism. 'Abdān feels that he has finally found a solution for the malaise of humanity, and at long last resolves to make an argument for comprehensive justice:

The earth will be shared by all of us equally. No one can be richer or poorer than the other. Wealth will be distributed evenly among us all. But in order to achieve this utopian vision, we must first revolt against and tumble down the existing state and replace it with one founded solely on the principles of comprehensive justice.[23]

With this economic version of communism comes the negation of religion. Bākāthīr delivers a strong message by offering a scathing criticism of current secular thought represented in the rise of Marxism in Egypt in the 1940s. Bākāthīr's novel coincides with the Egyptian critic 'Abbās al-'Aqqād's condemnation of Marxism in his book, which carries the same title as Marx's famous statement "*Die Religion... ist das Opium des Volkes*" (*Religion is the Opium of the Masses*), where al-'Aqqād

[21] Ibid., 56.
[22] Ibid., 70.
[23] Ibid., 63.

characterizes Marxism as the very opium of modern human thought.[24] So it is easy to see how the epistemic discursiveness of the time is reflected in Bākāthīr's work. For instance, in the novel's fifth chapter, Ja'far, the mouthpiece of communism, rebukes 'Abdān as an old-fashioned religious man: "Are you still using religion as your reference? Why don't you say that if religion was indeed right, then it would come up with a theory just like the one you believe is right?"[25]

At 'Abdān's urging, Ḥamdān becomes a follower of Shaykh Ḥusayn al-Ahwāzī, whom Bākāthīr describes, in a possible allusion to Lenin's vanguardism, as dividing his followers into two categories: elite and public. The elite group has access to all the secrets and tools of power, with absolutely no need for rituals or daily prayers, while the public group is ordered to pray fifty times per day (not just five), for according to *Sīra* (the biography of the Prophet), God originally prescribed fifty prayers per day to the Prophet Muḥammad during his *mi'rāj*, his ascension to heaven on his nocturnal journey. The cynical rationale behind this prescription is threefold. First it ensures that the public members of the group will be too preoccupied with their own ritualistic duties to consider the true aims of the elite and perhaps to ever revolt against them. Second, based on the premise that most of the public followers are peasants and workers, they will not have time to do their work efficiently and will end up arousing the indignation and brutality of their masters. As a result, the public will be furious that the performance of one of God's most sacred rituals is not being honored by the rich landlords. Third, by citing the original prescription, at the time of the *mi'rāj*, of fifty daily prayers, the elite will throw into question one of the foundations of the Islamic faith, thus leading to a slow but sure reduction of *ṣalāt* (prayers) until prayer is abandoned altogether.

When the Caliph Mu'taḍid finds out about Ja'far al-Karamānī's seditious movement, he sends Abū al-Baqā' al-Baghdādī – a charismatic leader whom he had earlier imprisoned because he feared his wide popular support – to help him suppress the movement and arrest its leaders. Known among his followers as *Muḥibb al-Dīn* (lover of (the Islamic) religion), Abū al-Baqā' is an adherent of the strict Ḥanbalī school of

[24] 'Abbās Maḥmud al-'Aqqād, *Afyūn al-Shu'ūb: al-Madhāhib al-Haddāma* [*The Opium of the Masses: On Destructive Doctrines*] (Cairo: Maktaba-t- al-Anglū al-Miṣriyya, n.d.), 8.

[25] Bākāthīr, *Al-Thā'ir al-Aḥmar*, 66.

jurisprudence, which would later become an inspiration for Salafis and Islamists, of whom he is an all too obvious prototype. However, in another twist of the plot, Ḥamdān manages to escape and succeeds in establishing his own kingdom in Mahībād, attracting hundreds of followers, mostly peasants. In this new kingdom, nobody has private ownership of the land, and nobody is too rich or too poor. At first, all is well in the kingdom, but after a while, it begins to be revealed, *à la Animal Farm*, that not everyone is equal after all, and not everyone gets the same kind or amount of food. To emphasize the non-Islamic nature of this ungodly kingdom, prayers are no longer allowed.

However, by the end of the novel, somewhat surprisingly and with no historical basis, Ḥamdān, after being defeated by al-Baghdādī, becomes a born-again Muslim, not necessarily in the theological sense of the term, but rather in a Joycean fashion: through an epiphany by which he recognizes that al-Baghdādī, and, by implication, the Salafi Islamism that he represents, has always had his best interests at heart. "I love him and I hold him in high esteem, especially when by deposing me he serves to establish the banners of justice for all."[26]

Ironically, more than Ḥusayn's *The Days*, *The Red Revolutionary* deliberately imitates European models, especially the *Bildungsroman*, where we follow the psychological and intellectual development and growth of a character on his life journey, whose denouement provides us with a clear moral. The moral of Bākāthīr's convoluted narrative is certainly clear enough: neither capitalism nor communism works for the Muslim Egyptian peasant. However, *The Red Revolutionary* is not a true *Bildungsroman*; it is a morality play disguised as one. A true *Bildungsroman* is dynamic and dialectical, tracing the ever-developing history of an individual as he or she confronts obstacles, overcomes them, and, most importantly is transformed by them. A morality play, with its allegorical representation of the unquestioned truths of the faith is, in contrast, static and ahistorical. The protagonist encounters a series of antagonists who are classified as evil because of their opposition to the Truth, and there is no suggestion that the protagonist's – or our own – sense of the truth can be in anyway transformed by these encounters, since the Truth is true. In the logic of Islamism (though not of Islam), everything that is not *customary* to Islam is considered *contradictory* to Islam, and therefore dismissed as

[26] Bākāthīr, *Al-Thā'r al-Aḥmar*, 177.

heretical without further consideration. The profound limitations of this approach can be seen if, to compare small with great, we turn for a moment to Dostoyevsky. Dostoyevsky was every bit as rigid an adherent of religious orthodoxy as was Bākāthīr of Islamism, and, if anything, more reactionary in his politics. But Dostoyevsky, as an artist, acknowledged the power, and, indeed, the value, of the views against which he reacted, and was not afraid to recognize their historical importance and to give them their due. In *The Brothers Karamazov*, there can be no doubt where Dostoyevsky stands in the ongoing debate between the worldly, skeptical Ilya and the unworldly, devout Alyosha. But Ilya's rejection of Alyosha's view of a benevolent deity is represented with such power and eloquence ("It is not God that I don't accept, Alyosha, only I most respectfully return Him the ticket.")[27] that Dostoyevsky runs the risk of being defeated by the enemy. This is not a risk Bākāthīr takes. As a result, in place of Dostoyevsky's dynamic dialogism, we are left with a static muddle.

For Bākāthīr, each category perceived to be contradictory to Islam as he understands it is presented as a complete abandonment of the word of God, played out childishly, ridiculed, and defeated; social classes disappear and the life of the society as a whole suddenly becomes harmonious in "Islam." Bākāthīr describes a peasant "paradise" in which human consciousness surrenders completely to God's law on earth. The narrative may seem at first to be concerned with the unjust power of money and the abuse of workers, but in fact Bākāthīr's real concern is to reject both communism and capitalism as ways of dealing with such issues, as do his Islamist contemporaries, who saw them both as threatening the principles of Islam by the very fact that they are human, not divine, creations. If Sayyid Quṭb's warning against capitalism and communism, as well as his passionate call for an Islamist state, were to be adapted into fiction, the result would be *The Red Revolutionary*. Zafar Ishaq Ansar sums up this doctrinal tendency in Islamist Egypt quite saliently:

> Orthodox Islamic thought rests on the assumption that Islam can ensure not only success and felicity in the hereafter, but can also ensure a judicious ordering of worldly affairs. This is natural in view of the belief of Muslims that Islam is the embodiment of the Divine Wisdom and the final and

[27] Fyodor Dostoyevsky, *The Brothers Karamazov*, trans. Constance Garnett (New York: The Modern Library, 1929), 301.

superbly perfect version of *Hudà* [Divine Guidance] revealed to mankind through the last of His prophets ... The contemporary sociopolitical ideologies are therefore, a priori, regarded by the Islamically-oriented thinkers as defective and erroneous, being the product of the frail and fallible human intellect and devoid of Divine Guidance.[28]

Both al-Bannā and Quṭb have repeatedly emphasized total Islamicization of Egypt as the only route to its economic and spiritual salvation in the world.[29] In his book, *al-ʿAdāla al-Ijitimāʿiyya fī al-Islām* (*Social Justice in Islam*), one of the most significant contributions to Islamism in modern Egypt, Quṭb emphasizes the sociopolitical edicts of Islam as indispensable to social justice, which he characterizes as an all-embracing principle of Islam:

The faith of Islam, which deals with the whole field of human life, does not treat the different aspects of that life in the mass, nor yet does it split up the field into a number of unrelated parts. That is to say Islam has one universal theory which covers the universe and the life and humanity, a theory in which are integrated all the different questions; in this Islam sums up all its beliefs, its laws and statutes, and its modes of worship and work.[30]

In the end, committed as he is to the Islamist cause, Bākāthīr is unable to give convincing form to this vision: the novel's abrupt ending does not solve Ḥamdān's problems. Instead, it comes at a point of exhaustion and surrender. Even Chokri al-Mabkhout's "conscious reader," discussed in Chapter 3, may find it difficult to understand the purpose and role of the novel's hero-turned-victim-turned-Robin Hood-turned-victim again turned-villain, and eventually, turned-repentant Muslim. There could be no more baffling and jumbled depiction of a hero.

Whatever its artistic success or failure, *The Red Revolutionary* clearly represents Bākāthīr's attempt, as a good Islamist, to dramatize the motto of the Muslim Brotherhood, *Al-Islām huwa al-ḥall* (Islam is the Solution). However, perhaps an even better motto for his novelistic variation on the morality play, comes from the New Testament: "godliness with contentment is great gain" (1 Timothy 6:6). But does the historical record since the death of Prophet Muhammad really

28 Zafar Ishaq Ansar, "Contemporary Islam and Nationalism: A Case Study of Egypt" *Die Welt des Islams*, New Ser., vol. 7, Issue 1/4. (1961), pp. 4–5.

29 Ḥasan al-Bannā, *Mushkilātunā fī Ḍaw' al-Niẓām al-Islamī* [*Our Problems in Light of the Islamic System*] (Cairo: n.d.), 38–68.

30 Sayyid Quṭb, *Social Justice in Islam*. Translated by John B. Hardie (Washington, DC: 1955), 16.

illustrate that "true" Islam is a religion of contentment in its own godliness, which sees no gain in engagement with the Other? Is it true that Islam has always won the battle against "false" versions of Islam and has, as a result, been able to achieve comprehensive justice consistent with *fiṭra insāniyya* (human nature) *à la* Quṭb? One does not need to read al-Ṭabarī or Ibn Khaldūn to know that this has never been the case. Bākāthīr, however, chooses to construe capitalism and communism as fixed and unchanging principles, opposites not just of one another, but of Islam itself. It seems that Bākāthīr, with his vision of a reified Islam, cannot understand the positive potential of secular systems of governmental rule because he cannot accept that even when flawed, such systems may give rise to a dialectical process that may lead to a better, though never perfect, life as history unfolds. A critical view of capitalism or communism from an Islamic perspective can be constructive as long as, in its critique of these alternatives, it can see a possibility of self-examination, transformation, and growth. If a Bākāthīrian version of Islam, immune to the vicissitudes of mortal change, did, in fact, once exist on the face of the earth, how did its corruption set in, in the first place? And what do Muslims make from the prophetic hadith "*antum a'alamu bi-umūri dunyākum*" (You know the matters of your own world/you know how to manage your world affairs best)? Bākāthīr is calling for a future that can only be achieved through a return to a supposedly perfect past, but the past he invokes, like all pasts, was already at odds with itself. In fact, what Bākāthīr is invoking is an *impression* of a past, which has nothing to do with the past itself. Bākāthīr offers "Islam" as a cure for the ills of the present (poverty, harsh work conditions, broken family ties, interpersonal relationships, abduction, war), without realizing that the past whose blessings he invokes is no different from the present he seeks to cure. Thus he became the spokesman of the Islamist nostalgia that both al-Bannā and Quṭb promoted and whose attraction to the Egyptian people grew more compelling with the rise of political tyranny, the spread of poverty, and economic deterioration as Egypt moved steadily towards Westernization in the aftermath of the Second World War.

In the end, the novel's attack on so-called godless and permissive theories is, in fact, an attack on positions that had no serious proponents in contemporary Egyptian literary and cultural criticism, which had begun to incorporate secular (social and positivistic) theories in its generally respectful investigation of tradition. Blatantly God-denying epistemologies are not to be found, even in the writings of controversial secular authors like al-Ḥakīm, Mahfouz, or Ḥusayn. By creating a melodramatically one-sided version of communism as the embodiment of evil, Bākāthīr acknowledges no value in its critique of a society that is, in fact, seriously corrupt and oppressive. Such a critique is rejected as the work of heretic villainy that taints the least deviation from the principles of Islamic faith, supposedly embodied in an ideal Islamic society under attack. In other words, according to Bākāthīr, any concern with achieving a society that provides adequate food, shelter, and a decent standard of living moves inexorably towards disbelief and immorality. But to be sure, it is not Islam that Bākāthīr is defending – only his own parochial version of it. In fact, his single-minded urge to resist the secular and the foreign at any cost turns his morality play against itself, exposing the very banality of the fundamentalism it advocates. This does not mean that secular systems of governance are immune to critique. Capitalism, as Timothy Mitchell argues in his study of economy and the constructed power of techno-science in Sadat and Mubarak's Egypt, is indeed a false utopia: "[I]t survives parasitically, like the *Plasmodium falciparum*, taking up residence in human bodies and minds, or in sugarcane or private property, drawing its energy from the chemistry of others, its force from other fields, its momentum from others' desires."[31] But the invocation of an distant past, portrayed in Bākāthīr's equally utopian account as an Islamist Egyptian version of Muslim piety, is just as parasitical when it seeks to transform anachronism into an empty hope of things to come. Any such hope, Yūsuf Idrīs will remind us, remains empty if it does not recognize that it – like the reality behind the impressionistic, selective past it harkens back to – is always already internally contested and narratively fragmented. The question becomes not one of perspective or even politics, but of possibilities: might a utopia that takes critique not as an end but as a dialectical point of departure present precisely the conditions for the possibility of social transformation, rather than mere historical pastiche?

[31] Timothy Mitchell, *Rule of Experts: Egypt, Techno-Politics, Modernity* (Berkeley, University of California Press, 2002), 303.

7 *Secular Realism and Utopian Irony in Yūsuf Idrīs's* Faraḥāt's Republic

The greatest works of art do not exclude the lowest depth, but kindle the flame of utopia on the smoking ruins of the past.

Theodore Adorno

Nothing has roused Egypt's Islamist movement to action in the last century more than the external threats and political challenges posed by European imperialism. By the beginning of the twentieth century, Egypt, together with Africa and a predominantly Muslim Arab world, found itself in the grip of an alien occupation that challenged its fundamental principles and values. The pressure of this foreign modernity, with its military superiority and ostensibly secular values, contributed to the rapid development of a sense of Arab nationalism that spread throughout Africa and Asia.[1] The struggle was harsh and long and the impact of European colonialism has been profound and long-lasting. The geopolitical map of the Arab-Muslim world changed dramatically as Arab countries began to assume their independence. All independent Arab nations successively became members of the Arab League, which at its inception in the 1950s, was controlled by Gamal Abdel Nasser, the Egyptian leader who disseminated the ideology of pan-Arabism: the movements of pan-Arabism, Arab nationalism, and, most significantly for our purposes, Islamism. From this historical perspective it is arguable that the rise of political Islam is not merely a *post*colonial phenomenon, but an *anti*colonial one *ex post facto*.[2]

[1] Arab nationalism has not been completely Islamic in character. One of the points of focusing on Arab identity was that it avoided making Islam the automatic factor uniting the Arab world.

[2] For various treatments of the relationship between colonialism, nationalism, and the rise of Islamic fundamentalism see: S. Al-Ḥuṣarī, *Al-Bilād al-'Arabiyya wa al-Dawla al-'Uthmāniyya* [*Arab Countries under Ottoman Rule*] (Beirut: n.p., 1966); C. Ernest Dawn, *From Ottomanism to Arabism: Essays on the Origin of Arab Nationalism* (Urbana: University of Illinois Press, 1973); Arthur Goldsmith, Jr., *A Concise History of the Middle East* (Boulder, CO: Westview Press, 1979); John Waterbury, *The Egypt of Nasser and Sadat: The Political*

While it is true that Islam is neither the first nor the only religion of Egypt, the culture of modern Egypt is predominantly Muslim. Egypt is also a cultural space whose demographics, ideologies, and political identities have in many ways been deeply tied to the Islamic faith, albeit in varied and oftentimes conflicting degrees. Most notably, the Muslim Brotherhood's influential leading figures, such as al-Bannā (d.1949) and Quṭb (d.1966), as well as Islamist sympathizers such as Bākāthīr, managed to carve a fundamentalist identity and push their version of Islam into the great game of cultural politics in mid-twentieth-century Egypt.

The competition over Egypt's political and economic future was both urgent and fierce, and influential authors like Haykal, Ḥusayn, al-Ḥakīm, Mahfouz, Bākāthīr, and Yūsuf Idrīs were all participants in this great game. As such, they were shaped by, and contributed to the production of some of the most vigorous cultural movements in modern Egypt. The most notable of these movements were secularism, nationalism, communism, republicanism, and, of course, Islamism. Islamism, especially in the Muslim Brotherhood's version, promoted a return to supposed origins and a "revival" of fundamentalist Muslim unity with the aim of instituting divine law on earth as the one and only solution to the political corruption and economic depression of postcolonial Egypt. Thus the war over which version of the "Egyptian peasant" (Haykal's, Ḥusayn's, Bākāthīr's, Quṭb's) is worthy of leading Egypt and steering it away from the chaos of decolonization persisted during the period of Nasserism. Nasser himself regarded Quṭb's Islamism as a step backward, a serious threat to postcolonial Egypt and a hindrance to its economic progress and competitiveness in the world. Instead, *à la* Ataturk, he opted to recast Egyptian history as an

Economy of Two Regimes (Princeton, NJ: Princeton University Press, 1983); Tareq Y. Ismael, *International Relations of the Contemporary Middle East* (Syracuse, NY: Syracuse University Press, 1986); Georges Corm, *Fragmentation of the Middle East: The Last Thirty Years* (London: Hutchinson Education, 1988); Adeed Dawisha and I. William Zartman, eds. *Beyond Coercion: The Durability of the Arab State* (London: Croom Helm, 1988); M. E. Yapp, *The Near East Since the First World War* (London: Longman, 1991); Albert Hourani, *A History of the Arab People* (New York: Warner Books, 1991); Roger Owen, *State, Power and Politics in the Making of the Modern Middle East* (London: Routledge, 1992); Mohammad Salama, 'Arabs, Islam, and the Arab World' in *Encyclopedia of the Modern World*, ed. Peter N. Stearns (Oxford: Oxford University Press, 2008).

essentially secular history of the Egyptian nation, dismissing the broader historical context of the Islamic caliphate in its final manifestation as the Ottoman empire.[3]

But in the aftermath of the Second World War, Egypt faced numerous challenges. There was, of course, the difficult struggle for decolonization and the challenging transfer of power that the country thereafter underwent. But in addition, there were such factors as the call for pan-Arabism (for solidarity with all Arab and African nations fighting for independence), the Algerian War, the Arab–Israeli conflict (beginning in 1948, and persisting to the present day), the persistence of autocracy, and the radical downturn in economic conditions in the aftermath of decolonization. Amid these challenges, the fear of losing the postcolonial bid for an economically stable country grew stronger among the Egyptian intelligentsia. The cultural elite of Egypt in the mid- and late 1950s grew increasingly suspicious of Nasser's ability to deliver a strong economy, especially after his abrupt nationalization of the Suez Canal and the subsequent tripartite invasion of France, Britain, and Israel in 1956.

Yūsuf Idrīs's *Jumhūriyya-t- Faraḥāt* (*Faraḥāt's Republic*), published in 1956, is a sharp allegorical critique of utopian Nasserism in the aftermath of decolonization. The circumstances that witnessed the composition of this novella were rife with suspense and doubt, and Idrīs delineated this uncertainty through his poor, mediocre, over-worked protagonist. As part of this project, Idrīs felt compelled to make use of colloquial Egyptian Arabic as a reflection of the pulse of the street. When Ḥusayn wrote the Introduction to Idrīs's collection of short stories, which included *Faraḥāt's Republic*, he was the first to point to this as a pivotal stylistic shift in the history of modern Egyptian fiction, but it was a shift of which he did not entirely approve.

Ḥusayn's reservations are not surprising. Seen as the figurehead of Egypt's cultural renaissance and as a scholar whose work and professional career were devoted to the cause of linguistic propriety and the revival of pure Arabic, Ḥusayn is an interesting literary phenomenon. Owing to his education in classical Arabic, he achieved an unrivalled mastery of pre-Islamic poetry, the Qur'ān, and medieval and post-medieval Arabic literature; and his graduate work at the Sorbonne

[3] Timothy Mitchell, *Rule of Experts: Egypt, Techno-Politics, Modernity* (Berkeley, CA: University of California Press, 2002), 13.

enabled him to achieve a unique blend of Arabic classics, modern French literature and Cartesian philosophy. As a result, throughout his career as professor, writer, and critic, Ḥusayn sought to maintain a balance between modernity and tradition.[4] The fact that he writes an introduction to a work of art with ideas on language and literary representations different from his own is worth considering. On the one hand, Ḥusayn's introduction to the emerging literary talent of Idrīs is an acknowledgment of the existence of a new literary trend in Egypt – and in some measure a support of it. On the other hand, Ḥusayn's critique could be viewed as an attempt to contain this new phenomenon by addressing what he perceived as a major socio-linguistic limitation.

Ḥusayn starts by enthusiastically introducing a new way of writing to the Arab readers. He sets out to enumerate the various aspects of Idrīs's literary talent, "finding," as he says, "great pleasure in

[4] A number of Ḥusayn's works dwell on this binary. Take for instance his masterpiece, *Du'ā' al-Karawān* (*The Nightingale's Prayer*). This story represents a common theme of honor crimes, but transcends the thinness of a classical revenge story by fusing it with scenes of modernity and life in the city, as well as with major modern concerns such as the position of women in a self-contradictory, male-oriented Egyptian society that confuses misogyny with religion. The brutal killing of Hanādī by a selfish and ignorant uncle represents the worst nightmare of traditionalism and shows how Muslim women are easily expendable at the hands of a ruthless patriarchy that uses notions of God and honor to justify its senseless crimes. The killing of Hanādī has sunk deep into the consciousness of the Egyptian nation and has offered a powerful literary antidote to what has been silently and complacently practiced on a regular basis in Egypt, especially in the south. In this drama of love versus hate, love triumphs in the end as the novel celebrates the secular and works out a compromise between the modern city and the traditionalist Upper Egyptian town. The episode when Zuhrā, the mother, and her two daughters, Hanādi and Āmna, are leaving Banī Warkān, their hometown, following the disaster of the father's death, best represents the tension in Ḥusayn's fiction between these two worlds:

They traveled from one village to the other and from one estate to the other; some people treated them kindly, while others were harsh with them. They never settled in one place, until they ended up in the vast city with its extended outskirts and large population. The city was divided into two halves by an iron road, along which a kind of frightful monster passes, sending sparks and fire into the air, with its loud sound and noisy whistle. They call it "the train." People ride it to travel from one place to the other, just as desert and country people sometimes ride camels, or donkeys, or use their own feet in most cases.

See *Al-Majmū 'a al-Kāmila li-Mu'allafāt al-Ductūr Ṭāhā Ḥusayn* [*The Complete Works of Dr. Ṭāhā Ḥusayn*] vol. 13. no. 1 (Dār al-Kitāb al-Lubnānī: Bayrūt, 1974), 139.

introducing this collection of short stories to the Egyptian reader, because its writer is one who makes us hold our hopes up high and believe that Egypt would be a more prosperous country and that its intellectual life would be more vibrant."[5] Ḥusayn regards Idrīs as a gifted young author whose experience in the medical field provides him with a diagnostic perspective on events and the ability to offer a unique "representations of people's lives, with all their pains and hopes, their contentment and discontent."[6] Idrīs's attention to the smallest details of the "body and soul" leads Ḥusayn to state that he has "never seen a representation of a street or a square, or of groups of people with different features, colours, and activities the way [I see it] in this young writer."[7]

But Ḥusayn's commendation of Idrīs is not without criticism. Ḥusayn concludes with two points he wishes Idrīs to consider:

> First, he should not let himself be completely swayed by literature at the expense of his medical vocation, because literature gets better every time it is resisted and abandoned by its writers. Second, he needs to show mercy to *al-Lugha al-'Arabiyya al-Fuṣḥá* (Standard Arabic) and allow his characters to use it. Oftentimes, some of our young writers make the mistake of thinking that a true representation of reality entails making characters speak the colloquial Arabic of streets and clubs. What really distinguishes good from bad literature is its transcendence of reality in a way that does not diminish its performative portrayal of it. A realist writer is not a phonograph that parrots and records whatever people say; nor is he a photographer who takes pictures of things as they are in real life. The difference between a writer and phonograph or a camera is that a writer adds something new to the representation, something that reaches the hearts and souls of readers ... Young writers should not deceive themselves, spoiling their talents and the literature they produce. In the end, I commend the author for his rich work and I look forward to reading more of work on the same calibre as this one, or perhaps even better ones which forsake colloquial Egyptian and use standard Arabic.[8]

Ḥusayn reopens here a central debate on literary representations and cultural expressions in modern Egypt: to what should a writer be

[5] Ṭāhā Ḥusayn, 'Introduction' in Yūsuf Idrīs, *Jumhūriyya-t- Faraḥāt* [*Faraḥāt's Republic*] (al-Qāhira: Maktaba-t-Miṣr, n.d.), 3.
[6] Ibid., 5.
[7] Ibid., 6.
[8] Ibid., 7.

faithful – a linguistic ideal or linguistic reality? Would a character like Faraḥāt, the protagonist of *Faraḥāt's Republic*, be better off speaking in the well-organized tongue of educated, standard Arabic, no different from that of Ḥusayn himself or, say, an Azharite preacher in a Friday prayers sermon? Or should one just accept Faraḥāt as he is, a truer-to-life image of what a repressed, bureaucratized, ill-educated Egyptian *Shāwīsh* of the 1950s would act and speak like?

Ḥusayn's discomfort with the disruptive presence of colloquial Egyptian is, in effect, an uneasy acknowledgment that there is more to high culture than linguistic sublimity. The question is not just one of representation, but of adherence to a traditional concept of representation, especially in connection with a specific understanding of realism. Ḥusayn's critique of Idrīs's so-called cultural immaturity is a defense of a cultural orthodoxy that believes that the end of linguistic propriety means the diminishment of art. His defense of the purity of the Arabic language, which is rooted in an imaginary aesthetic origin,[9] in fact raises an issue that is ubiquitous in the culture of modern Egypt: mimesis or the relationship between signs and their referents.

Both Ḥusayn and Idrīs, in their different ways, confront the same dialectic of diglossia in Egyptian cultural identity. It is clear from Ḥusayn's critique that the expressive substance of Idrīs's language is diametrically opposed to an imagined aesthetics of literary representation, which entails the use of *fuṣḥā* (standard Arabic), although many writers used colloquial Egyptian long before Idrīs.[10] But it is important to note that this supposedly degenerate aspect of Idrīs's diction is not simply a fall into impropriety or a sign of immature self-indulgence, as Ḥusayn seems to argue. Idrīs's colloquial Egyptian calls attention to a subcultural reality – namely, Egyptian Arabic as

[9] For more on the question of *'āmmiyya* vs. *fuṣḥā* and other stylistic matters in Idrīs's fiction, see Sasson Somekh, "Language and theme in the short stories of Yusuf Idrīs" (JAL Vol. 6, 1975). Somekh offers a fine analysis of the linguistic aspects of Idrīs's stories as well as the role of dialogue. Somekh was born to a Jewish family in Baghdad in 1933. They immigrated to Israel in 1951 due to the pressure that Jews were facing in Iraq, at which time Somekh began to learn Hebrew, with the goal of translating Arabic poetry. His MA work was in Semitic linguistics, and his PhD was in modern Arabic literature (Oxford, 1968) under the supervision of M. M. Badawi. His articles deal mainly with modern Arabic literature and writers, connections between Arabic and Hebrew literature, and the Cairo *geniza*.

[10] See for instance Maḥmūd Ṭāhir Ḥaqqī, *'Adhrā' Denshawai* [*The Virgin of Denshawai*] (n.p., 1906).

it is actually spoken – that has been oppressed and canceled by the taboos of cultural conventionalism. *Faraḥāt's Republic* contains nothing heroic or noble; instead, Idrīs dedicates himself to the lower depths and lost souls of his own society, and his use of Egyptian Arabic is a sign of this dedication.

In this novella Faraḥāt appears as a desperate and helpless victim of Egyptian bureaucracy at its worst. He is a half-educated *shāwīsh* (police sergeant) to whom defendants and plaintiffs arrive everyday with the strangest of alleged felonies and crimes. Idrīs's choice of Faraḥāţ and the standpoint from which he views him in order to comment on the nature of his job and the poverty of his surroundings – the standpoint of universal sympathy with the underdog – determines the pattern of his work down to the level of the most faithfully representative language, or to what Flaubert refers to as *le mot juste*. The social moments Idrīs depicts in all his fiction could only be represented in the language of the masses. In Idrīs, colloquial Egyptian becomes a language of the community, a language that can only be condemned by guardians of élitism, including Islamists, who continue to imagine their communities in idealized rather than practical terms. Idrīs's use of Egyptian colloquialism creates, in place of a critical commentary on the cultural decline of modern Egypt in the 1950s, a total identification with the culture of the present. Egyptian Arabic, unlike God's Qur'ānic Arabic, is the language of the people, one that becomes its epitome, and, as such, it is in effect the anti-theology and a source of secular liberation for a people who deserve to celebrate the present and not to feel embarrassed or ashamed to speak their own minds. By failing to recognize this, Ḥusayn – who in *The Days* opens up a new horizon of humanism in modern Egypt – is in danger of falling into the very trap of rigid traditionalism he confronted some thirty years prior.

If one is to make a judgment about literary expression, one must also take a view of what is expressed. In Idrīs's case, colloquialism includes a potential for freedom. In this spirit, and in opposition to a critical discourse in favor of regressive *fuṣḥā*, Idrīs is revolutionizing the cultural discourse and its limited understanding of mimesis. Significantly, he belonged to a group of Leftists and progressive writers from the 1950s who insisted on autonomously operative language emerging from the voices of the people – a language that follows its own impulses instead of exhausting itself in puritanical and fundamentalist rejection of the present; it derives its autonomy from its own internal relationship with the social moments it depicts. In this sense, art no longer needs to legitimate itself in terms of prescribed norms of decorum. The language of fiction is pictorial: its mode of articulation relies on its function as a vehicle of cultural expression for the representation of social themes rather than on the clarity of conservative diction and proper grammar. As such, the colloquial embodies an affective solidarity that might be rejected, if not ridiculed, in a social world in which formal rationality is the dominant principle. Thus with Idrīs we reach a new level of a revolutionary cultural expression where writing freely and irreverently embraces multitudinous shifts of style, form, and content; it does not apologize for lack of appropriateness or civility.

Thus only in a kind of unpretentious writing can the utopian motif be suspended, precisely because it is at this pivotal intersection between economic depression and the desire for a prosperous society that the utopian dimension of Faraḥāt's allegory manifests itself. This intersection is also the locus of freedom. In the unadorned language of vulgar realism befitting its character, Idrīs's work represents a world of happiness and fulfillment, almost a fantasy denied in the workaday world of bourgeois material life. *Faraḥāt's Republic* represents a secular redemption of the present, a desire to cancel it, or at least to transcend it. The story is only capable of imagining a superior cinematic world order in which, unlike the present world, power no longer stands in the service of the few.

Historically, then, *Faraḥāt's Republic* pursues a certain literary approach that differentiates itself, despite Ḥusayn, yet also because of him, from older categories of representation. Without trying to make facile connections between literary and political revolutions, it is useful to remember that Idrīs's generation represents a different kind of cultural engagement with tradition and responds to a new wave of socio-political changes in Egypt. Whereas in Egyptian politics, *Majlis Ḥukūma-t-al-Thawra* (the Revolutionary Command Council or RCC) of 1952 had designated a new republican age, a number of intellectuals, including writers, scholars, and journalists, and filmmakers were skeptical of that transition. The epochal new beginning that signaled Egypt's break with monarchy was to many nothing more than a well-orchestrated movement that devalued a tyrannical past in form while repeating it in content.

The writing of *Faraḥāt's Republic* thus coincides with a time in Egypt when Nasser's attempts toward the development of the welfare state come to a critical impasse. Written at this climactic time in Egypt's political history, *Faraḥāt's Republic* represents a microcosm of Egypt that intersects with a number of pivotal events: the emergence of the so-called Third World, the eve of African independence, the beginning of the end of colonization (at least in its most obvious, state-based form), the formation of postcolonial Arab governments, and the rise of Islamism. Those events have contributed to the creation of epistemological and cultural shifts, particularly in Egypt. During those times Nasserist nationalism and pan-Arabism gave rise to an awkward tension between two sentiments: a desire for a revolutionary social, economic and political change, and a creeping realization that the republic had failed to live up to its promise.

In fact, it was in 1954 that Egypt made its first strides toward a form of republicanism under Nasser's new regime, and it was during that time that European postmodernity began to exhibit its postwar power in many fields, e.g. the military, industry, commerce, and agriculture. In face of the onslaught of this postmodernity, Nasser's regime promised to bring independence not just to Egypt but to the entire Arab world while exercising ethical and rational control over the means of production. With the promise of solidarity among members of the so-called third world, social harmony did not seem far from possible, a "happy" republic (to invoke the literal Arabic meaning of Idrīs's protagonist, Farahāt) appeared achievable, and the utopia Egyptians had been dreaming of seemed almost a reality.

Unlike utopia in the works of early Western theorists such as More, Campanella and Bacon, utopia in the Egypt of the 1950s became a polemical socio-political concept. Early Western utopianists wrote works that never went beyond the realm of the fictitious. In very broad terms, most European classical utopianists attempted to translate eschatological notions of paradise into historical space and earthly possibilities. Even if they were critical of their socio-political conditions, their utopias remained largely ahistorical.

Although it shares major traits of European classical utopias, including the need for a life of dignity and prosperity as well as the desire for an organized state of social justice, Faraḥāt's film proposal differs from most of these representations of utopia in that it focuses mainly on economic promise. Islam already offers versions of utopia in this world and in the hereafter, as we have seen in Quṭb's polemics and Bākāthīr's *The Red Revolutionary*. *Faraḥāt's Republic*, by contrast, offers a utopian vision that manifests itself in a careful intersection of various cultural elements – economics, film, and politics – all illuminated by an unfailingly brilliant act of satire. This intersection gestures toward a longing and a hope for a better life inspired not only by a cynical rejection of a hideous present, but also by the promising prospects of filmic imaginary. *Faraḥāt's Republic* could be read at many levels: as an allegory of a failed utopia, a novella about a mediocre proposal for a melodramatic film, a parody of Nasser's regime, an ironic portrayal of fate, or a sarcastic comic narrative. Whatever perspective we take on it, it is a sign of an epistemological shift and the birth of a new cultural disillusionment with both Islamism and nationalism in Nasserist Egypt.

The events take place in a downtown Egyptian police station, where the narrator, a well-dressed, white-collar man, appears to have been brought in by the police to face some charges that are never specified. Making his way inside, escorted by a policeman, he steps across a threshold, feeling as if he were entering an underground trench. All of a sudden we find ourselves in a space unconnected to either the present or the immediate past, a space so cut off from time that readers might be tempted to anticipate another variation on the Platonic theme of the people of the cave. Idrīs describes Faraḥāt's surroundings with medical clarity: the slimy, indeterminate floor, be it mud or asphalt, exemplifies Idrīs's clinical precision in depicting a true-to-life scene while preparing the reader for the psychological transition to Faraḥāt's underworld.

In fact, the whole first page of the novella describes what could be characterized as a kind of Inferno – the policemen look like *afreets* of the dead and the taut facial skin of Faraḥāt is reminiscent of mummification or skeletal remains. The people there wander around as though under hypnosis like the inhabitants of the underworlds in Homer and Dante, in which the shades in Hades gather around eager for news of the world, or even stuck in time like al-Ḥakīm's people of the cave. Immediately, the narrative turns into an *Arabian Nights* scene of a storyteller and a listener, as Faraḥāt, reversing the expected roles of police interrogator and criminal suspect, shares with the narrator his quotidian life, frustrations and dreams.

Faraḥāt begins by telling the narrator that his life has been a constant struggle against lowlifes, criminals, and petty thieves. The police station where Faraḥāt works is a dystopia of complete squalor where, as the narrator describes it:

> ... the walls were covered half-way up with a blackness that resembled paint, while the other half was enveloped in a general gloom; white patches scattered here and there merely served to emphasise the ugliness of the rest. The floor was so slimy you could not tell if it was made of asphalt or plain mud. The all-pervading smell, whose quintessence defied definition, gave one a sensation of nausea.[11]

Even if in these dark depths, Faraḥāt has power over suspects awaiting arraignment (the narrator included), he still thinks that his is the most miserable of lives: "By the prophet, I am the victim, I swear it. It's not for nothing I've got old before my time ... I have seen cases where men murder for a stick of sugarcane, burn down a barn for a corn-cob ... People have gone mad."[12] To Faraḥāt, this madness has enveloped all aspects of society to the point that social manners and cultural tastes seem to have completely disappeared: as with Mahfouz's madman, the whisper of madness sounds loudly in his ear. Among the many aspects of a decadent morality in this dystopic version of modern Egypt, the film industry, according to Faraḥāt, has deteriorated the most. Faraḥāt's conversation with the narrator about film and his ideas for a good movie trigger the notion of utopia. The question of film arises when Faraḥāt interrupts his dialogue with the narrator to dismiss a woman bystander by saying that "the likes of [her] should not go to the cinema."[13] This in a nutshell is what the novella is all about: a tale of the storyline of a didactic film and an outline of its melodramatic plotline: the establishing shot/scene, a rising action, complication of plot, climax, and a falling action. Faraḥāt's passionate outline of this film idea confuses yet intrigues the narrator, whose attention is held for the first time since Faraḥāt began to force his utopian film narrative on him.

To understand the function of this utopian narrative, we must appreciate that like all utopias it grows out of a disappointment with the present. The very history of the writing and reception of Idrīs's text, culminating in his imprisonment immediately after its publication, confirms that, in the present that the novella portrays, something

[11] Yūsuf Idrīs, *Jumhūriyya-t- Faraḥāt*, 8.
[12] Ibid., 9.
[13] Ibid., 10.

must have gone seriously wrong. At this moment in history, Faraḥāt's satirical film proposal seems to set itself two complementary tasks: to postulate – in however simplistic a fashion that the postulate is expressed – a socio-economic order that would heal the festering wound of past despotism and colonialism, and to critique Egypt's current devastating economic conditions.

Faraḥāt's film proposal opens a new space for visual and textual intersection in the text, one that further complicates the question of technological modernity and the prospects of Egyptian utopia. Faraḥāt's modernity could only be imagined through a medium that this modernity created; in a kind of immanent critique, then, a desperate slave of bureaucracy, who spends all his time in the subcultural nadir of Egyptian society, envisions a plot for a film, and through it a vision of life, that responds fully, if absurdly, to the needs of the common Egyptian in an economically challenged postwar Egypt. According to Faraḥāt, his film proposal should replace what he considers to be an adolescent and futile quality of Egyptian film as a degraded product of the culture industry, which attracts people without educating them:

> Stories! The Cinema! What are these stories they make up? They might as well boil them up and make soup of them.
>
> Why don't you like it?
>
> Like it? How can I like it? A film must be really interesting – not all this clowning and dancing around that gets one nowhere.[14]

Faraḥāt does not, and indeed cannot, think of film as a technical reproduction of the visual *à la* Walter Benjamin. He is not alarmed by the rise of the film industry during Nasserism as a government tool for nationalist propaganda. He does not occupy himself with the technical aspects of film – from cinematography to camera movement and setting, sound, and editing. These elements do not interest him at all, since he sees film as a finished product offering the best recipe for economic progress. Thus, what he sees in film is nothing more than a didactic Horatio Alger-type narrative of rags-to-riches on the theme of integrity rewarded, a narrative that he believes life must imitate.

The film that Farahāt envisions is about an impoverished Egyptian man who stumbles upon an Indian maharaja's pearl, and instead of

[14] Ibid., 10–11.

running away with it, hands it back to the maharaja, who, in turn, offers him a generous reward. To everyone's surprise, the Egyptian man, who is in dire need of money, refuses the gift, with ultimately positive consequences. Farahāt's proposed film, then, is about moral choice. If you are poor but honest, your honesty will be miraculously rewarded. To Farahāt, film at its best must celebrate and promote ethics in order to fashion an image of a better life to be emulated by filmgoers. Life, as Oscar Wilde puts it, must imitate art, and film must represent the aspiration for a promising future as well as merely offering distraction from an unsatisfactory present. However, ironically, Farahāt's utopian narrative is itself a distraction from an unsatisfactory present, as its repeated interruption by that present – in the form of shocking crime reports – indicates. Caught up in visualizing his perfect society, Farahāt brutally dismisses victims who are trying to make some sense and order out of their own realities. These interruptions, and Farahāt's response to them, serve to create tension and suspense in the utopian narrative; but, more importantly, they symbolize the hideous present in which Farahāt lives and from which there is no escape. The first of these interruptions comes very early on:

It's about an Indian man who visits Cairo, a very well-to do man, one of those people who has as much money as we have poverty here. The man comes and puts up in one of those terrible posh hotels, let us say Mena House or "Shabat,"[15] and there is some poor wretched man like ourselves ...

Suddenly, all my senses are wide awake. I lean heavily over the barrier so as not to miss a word. A woman comes forward demanding help, half-screaming. She is fair-skinned and good-looking and her eyebrows are penned with exquisite care.

"What's up with you, woman?" Sergeant Faraḥāt growls at her. "What is wrong – Has the world come to an end? ... As I was saying, this Indian man checks out of the hotel and leaves behind a diamond which today would be worth at the very least 70 or 80 thousand Egyptian pounds. The poor Egyptian, seeing it, picks it up and hands it back to the rich Indian."

What diamond are you talking about you old humbug?

We both turn around to see who is talking. It turns to be a tall police sergeant carrying a file in his hands. He asks Faraḥāt in a scolding tone: "What have you done about the unidentified victim?"

[15] For an attempt at pronouncing the word for 'Shepherd's Hotel', see Idrīs, *Faraḥāt's Republic*, author's note, 12.

"What did you want me to do?" Faraḥāt fired back. "Walk round the streets saying 'Anyone lost a body?'"

Faraḥāt then ignores his fellow sergeant and turns to me to finish the plotline:

When the Indian man decides to reward the Egyptian for finding his jewel, the Egyptian swears by everything holy that he wouldn't accept a single *millieme* [cent/penny] from him. In vain the maharaja tries to persuade him to take the money. The poor Egyptian's repeated refusals only make the maharaja respect him even more. Time goes by and the rich fellow travels back to India still thinking how to reward this honorable Egyptian. He then decides that the best way is to reward him with a lottery ticket ... Do you know how much the first prize is for the lottery ticket? I won't tell you until we share a cup of tea.[16]

After a long series of similar interruptions, the narrator finally pleads with him to finish the story. Faraḥāt, delighted to hear that his audience is taking interest in the story, goes on:

The first prize is for one million Egyptian pounds. The Maharaja buys up all the one hundred tickets out there in order to make sure of winning, and when the draw comes along, one of the tickets naturally wins the first prize – a million Egyptian pounds free of tax. It never occurs to the man to be stingy and keep it for himself. So what does he do? He buys an enormous cargo ship which he loads up with the very best quality Indian silk, some ivory, a package of ostrich feathers, a collection of fine wool and Cashmere and high-end furniture. Then he sends the ship complete with its captain and crew to Alexandria. After that, he sends the contract of cargo ship sale and the bill of lading fully paid up to our friend in Egypt.[17]

A simple review of the logic of this story reveals its deliberate absurdity. First the maharaja plans to buy a winning lottery ticket in honor of the poor Egyptian. Then he buys up all the hundred pound tickets and wins the prize *himself* (presumably a very inefficient way of getting a million pounds, since, unless the organizers of the lottery are insane, the total cost of all of the tickets will be more than the prize). Then, he buys a cargo ship and hands it over to the Egyptian who, for some reason, has changed his mind and is now willing to accept a gift from the maharaja. When ship finally arrives in Alexandria and the poor Egyptian man accepts it as a gift, he somehow becomes an entrepreneur with amazing mercantile talent: he manages to sell all

[16] Ibid., 12.
[17] Ibid., 13.

the goods, uses the profit to buy yet another ship and in no time amasses an enormous fortune.

Once more, the utopian plot is interrupted, this time by the sight of a man "rushing in, wearing a *gallabiyya* [a traditional local Egyptian gown often worn by peasants in the Delta and Upper Egypt] and all covered in oil and stains, bold, with wooden clogs on his feet that make the most despicable sound."[18] The man, whose entry irritates Faraḥāt, is a shop owner who comes to report a "bastard boy" who has broken his irreplaceable, genuine Belgium-made pre-war crystal-glass windowpane. Assuming an official tone, Faraḥāt asks the man where his shop is. From the man's description, Faraḥāt knows the shop and asks which window is broken. When the man tells him it is the big one on the corner, Faraḥāt tells him that this corner is outside his jurisdiction and that he needs to go to the *Būlāq* police department instead and report it there. When the man begs him for help, Faraḥāt screams in his face and drives him out: "Beat it, may the *khamāsīn* [dry, hot, sandy local wind from the south] blow you away."[19]

Faraḥāt finally finds the time to finish his story. Every time he gets down to it, the narrator observes, Faraḥāt's features seem to "relax" and his eyes wander "about in the sky like two dreamy butterflies; his voice becomes free from all discord and is filled with a sweet casual elation."[20]

Faraḥāt's poor man soon becomes astronomically rich owing initially to his honest act of returning the jewel. Before long, he is able to buy all the ships in the city of Alexandria, both native and European. Then he takes the profit to buy

> an immensely large textile factory in which he employs about half a million workers. After one month, the profits from the textile factory pay for a glass factory. The glass factory profit pays for flour mills and rice-hulling factories, then some cotton ginneries, sugar refineries, a gas company, a paper company, a heavy machinery factory, and a steel factory. Soon, the day comes when he becomes the owner of all the factories in Egypt.[21]

In short, Faraḥāt's hero buys an Industrial Revolution, complete with steam ships and heavy industries. Hence, at play in this miraculous

18 Ibid., 14.
19 Ibid., 15.
20 Ibid., 15–16.
21 Ibid., 17.

purchase, is the circulation of capital, investment in raw material, agriculture, and economic growth, as well as the rise of economic tycoons. But that is not all. Faraḥāt's hero sets out to create his own republic. He buys 10,000 *feddans* of land: 5,000 to build factories on and 5,000 for the workers' housing, to make sure there is a healthy relationship between labor and income-based justice and social equity. "The person who does work worth five piasters will receive five piasters; the one who does work for ten gets ten, and so on."[22] Workers in *Faraḥāt's Republic* look different from the traditional miserable image of poverty and shabbiness we see in most factories, then and now. Their clothes are new and clean; they wear leather shoes, frequent nice cafés, have beautiful gardens, and gamble at highly accommodating casinos.

In Faraḥāt's cinematic republic, the workers are kind to one another and happy, with "no unpleasantness, no hard times"; everyone enjoys "laughing all day long and having fun."[23] In the evening

> they would go to the cinema. Cinema is so important. In every street there is a movie theatre and everyone has to go. As for the films, they are absolutely top-notch. The Republic has no police, because there is no crime and no need for a police force – save perhaps for a constable who instead of having to be out for eight hours on patrol sits at a glass kiosk right at the center of the street, visible and available for anyone who wants to speak with him.[24]

As the story proceeds, the interruptions that Faraḥāt experiences become raw material for his film. In the midst of his utopian contemplation, Faraḥāt is approached by four men "wearing felt skull-caps, every one of whom held a fistful of unkempt children in each hand and old beggars whom they dragged behind them, the *gallabiyya* of one child tied to that of the next."[25] The *gallabiyya*, a traditional symbol of nationalist pride and authentic peasantry, becomes for Faraḥāt a symbol of backwardness and poverty. No wonder in the next segment of his plot his cinematic republic cancels the *gallabiyya* entirely. After German machinery arrives at his society of happy workers, he tells the narrator that in this film the whole Egyptian

22 Ibid.
23 Ibid.
24 Ibid., 17–18.
25 Ibid., 18.

desert is cultivated by the hard work of engineers and workmen. Crucially, the transformation cannot take place without European machinery:

> Everything is done by machines – irrigation by machines, threshing by machines, fertilising by machines. There were even machines for gathering up the cotton and cutting the clover. The peasants who do the work have forgotten about things as *gallabiyyas*, skull-caps, yellow slippers and all that tomfoolery.[26]

Instead, clothing is modeled on the European fashion, namely, "it is all suits – khaki pants to the knees, clean white hats and shoes with double soles that never wear out."[27]

The equation of industrial modernity with utopia dominates Faraḥāt's narrative. For Faraḥāt, the ideals of modernity (embodied in technology serving the nation) constitute a basis for a valid critique of the social, political, and economic implications of this very modernity. Art performs a redemptive function in Faraḥāt's screenplay. For Faraḥāt, art represents a form of salvation from the pressures of daily life. But, as Idrīs makes clear, his nonsensical tale should be read as a cautionary tale concerning the fate of Egypt if it were allowed to reach the zenith of modernization. Idrīs's ironic representation of this utopian potential, in the voice of an uneducated police sergeant in love with his own cinematic imagination, brings to the fore the escapist tendencies of utopia. The sergeant's vision is the result of a naïve and uncritical understanding of the economy of modernity. Specifically, one can argue, as did the authorities after the publication of *Faraḥāt's Republic*, that the word "Republic" in the novella's title suggests that, whatever Faraḥāt himself intends, Idrīs has a contemporary utopia in mind, since in 1958 Egypt signed an agreement with Syria and changed its name to the Arab Republic of Egypt.

But "Republic" has philosophical associations as well, which may be relevant. Plato's republic is ruled by a philosophically trained elite guided by ethical principles, whereas in Faraḥāt's republic the guiding principles are entirely economic: it is a materialist anti-Platonic utopia dedicated to economic prosperity and entirely dependent on modern technology.

[26] Ibid.
[27] Ibid.

But there is another, very different, philosophical conception of a republic to which Faraḥāt's republic can be usefully contrasted: Kant's vision of the republic in *Toward Perpetual Peace*, where he defines republicanism as "the political principle of separation of the executive power (the government) from the legislative power."[28] To Kant, as to Idrīs, republicanism is the opposite of despotism, which he describes "a high-handed management of the state by laws the regent has himself given, in as much as he handles the public will as his private will."[29] From this perspective, Faraḥāt's utopian "republic" is the precise opposite of a true republic. With its mandatory indoctrination by way of film where "everyone has to go," and its panopticon-like observer in "a glass kiosk right at the center of the street" it bears a Foucauldian resemblance to a totalitarian "utopia" of power relations. In this, it is perhaps not dissimilar to the anti-modernist Islamist dystopia to which Faraḥāt's republic, with its naïve pretensions to progressive modernity, is a misguided response.

This initial optimism of Faraḥāt's screenplay of desire characteristic of the utopian genre is rooted in the hope that narrative can function as a tool of inspiration, as a will-to-power capable of provoking a denunciation of what is and an aspiration to what will be. But in the end, utopian narrative becomes its own narcissistic utopia, since it is predicated on the desire to achieve that which is already achieved in the act of utopian writing. Utopia thus becomes a textual desire whose satisfaction lies in the very act of expressing it. But the inner contradictions of Faraḥāt's utopian film project, as dramatized in the

[28] Immanuel Kant, 'Toward Perpetual Peace: A Philosophical Project', in Kant: *Political Writings*, ed. H. S. Reiss, trans. H. B. Nisbet (Cambridge: Cambridge University Press, 1970), 99.

[29] Ibid., 100. In the same essay, Kant denigrates democracy as a form of despotism, because according to him democracy "establishes an executive power in which all decide for all, and if need be, against one (who thus does not agree), so that all, who are nevertheless not all, decide; and this is a contradiction of the general will with itself and with freedom" (ibid., 101). To Kant, there is not really much difference between sovereign powers of autocracy, aristocracy, and democracy for all three are capable eventually of lapsing into different kinds of tyranny: "the power of a prince, the power of a nobility, and the power of a people" (ibid.). It is also important to mention that Kant wrote his essay in the immediate aftermath of the French Revolution of 1789, and that democracy in that sense belonged to a larger concept of sovereignty.

repeated interruptions by the real world, eventually lead to its collapse. Faraḥāt's impatient response to these interruptions – his scorn for the lower classes who supposedly are to be the beneficiaries of his utopia – underlines the irony of his absorption in his ideal narrative and his alienation from the realities of the world around him. Faraḥāt had originally thought that, in the narrator, he had finally found someone worthy of his vision, someone attentive and appreciative, and was even eager to tell him about the radio station that the not-so-poor any more man has made and linked up with every single house in his "republic." But in the end he discovers that his listener is "one of them," and he shuts the narrative down abruptly. At this point, the novella stops dead, along with the film proposal, as Faraḥāt ignores the narrator's pleadings to tell him more about the radio station, and goes on with his business of managing the police station. The fate of Faraḥāt's radio republic may not be dissimilar, Idrīs implies, to that of Nasser's.

There was, to be fair, another, positive, side to Nasser's socialist reform: namely, it prioritized its people's education, but always with the particular goal of making them into good laborers and obedient citizens. This is not new. As Raymond Williams notes, socialism from around the middle of the nineteenth century "began to distinguish itself from a whole body of associated and overlapping movements."[30] by emphasizing that "the central problem of modern society was poverty, and that the solution to poverty was production, and more production."[31] According to this principle, poverty came to be seen as humanity's worst evil, a view which encouraged military socialisms in the Middle East, and especially in Egypt, to consider production the absolute human priority; anyone who opposes this approach must be unrealistic and must therefore be dismissed as sentimental and naïve.

The origin of Nasserist utopianism, then, can be found in ideas that permeated Europe well before the Industrial Revolution, which could arguably be traced back to Francis Bacon's *The New Atlantis*. In fact, a comparison between Sir Thomas More's *Utopia* (1516) and Bacon's *The New Atlantis* (1626), illustrates how, in the span of 110 years, the concept took a dramatic shift from the socio-religious

[30] Raymond Williams, *Resources of Hope* (London: Verso, 1989), 213.
[31] Ibid., 213.

to the industrial, with statements like "conquest of nature" and "mastery of nature" defining Bacon's work.[32] This concept will even resonate later in Engels' unfinished work *Dialectics of Nature* (1883). Engels's thesis that "the hand and the brain grew together" implies a dangerous metonymy. This dialectic of mastery and control, which renders nature conquerable and masterable, is also, not accidentally, the classical rationale for imperialism.

Engels's socialist ideas were espoused and realized in the principles of so-called Third World governments of the postcolonial era, specifically in Nasserism. Like the case of Islamism in the regressive utopia of Bakathīr's *The Red Revolutionary*, the inherent danger in all despotic regimes is that they will eventually seek to reify their sociopolitical agendas and reduce utopian visions to a quick-fix for people's economic conditions, thus neglecting other conditions in need of reform and improvement in society: democracy, public diplomacy, liberal education, education, environment, and so on. Ironically enough, Nasserism eagerly embraced the heritage of the Industrial Revolution, and by implementing its principle of production over all, set itself on a path of emulating the very colonizers that Egypt had just expelled. That is, Nasserism subjected its own people to the mastery of the machine, the assembly line and the factory.

A utopia to Idrīs, then, cannot be conceived of undialectically – without insight that critiques it even at the moment of its articulation. Idrīs's subtle critique emerges from the understanding that Egypt's republican trajectory – like Faraḥāt's film proposal of a utopian republic – is at odds with itself, and to save the Egyptian Dream, this ethos must be rethought, not with the intention of overthrowing it altogether, but of rethinking its forms of emancipation. For Idrīs, utopia is necessarily tied to a commitment to transform the present rather than to repeat the past. Utopia must always refuse to be dictated by a course based on limited preconceived notions of economic gain. *Faraḥāt's Republic* is a work of transgression, and there is little wonder that it is the last work of fiction Idrīs wrote before he was jailed as a political dissident. The Heraclitan motto "Whoever does not hope for the unexpected will not find it" summarizes the irony of

[32] One would also see a connection to Descartes' project in his 1637 *Discourse on Method*, in which he writes of a reasoning that allows for humans to become "masters and possessors of nature" (René Descartes, *Discourse on Method* [Indianapolis, IN: Hackett Publishing Company, 1998], 35).

this powerful allegory, whose satirical stance is not itself an act of transgression, but a gesture toward a possibility for crossing the borders and re-delineating the horizons of socio-political thought in modern Egypt. To take such a transgressive gesture seriously – both in the postcolonial context and in the spirit of Idrīs – requires calling into question the *Aufhebung* of Nasser's Egypt: if the emergence of Nasserism meant the crushing defeat of colonial modernity, thus both cancelling and preserving the "modern" – is there then a dialectic of nationalist modernity subsumed in the very culture of Egypt's postcolonial film industry? If so, how would such culture mark itself at the nexus of Islam and modernity in Nasser's Egypt? The next chapter entertains this dialectic more closely.

8 *Islam and Secular Nationalism in a Film Age: Unveiling Youssef Chahine's* Gamīla Al-Gazā'iriyya

The history of cinema appears to be easy to do, since it is, after all, made up of images; cinema appears to be the only medium where all one has to do is re-project these images so that one can see what has happened.

Jean-Luc Godard, Histoire(s) du cinéma

The visual field is a turning point in the discourse of modernity. Martin Jay has argued that the "scopic regime of modernity" is nothing but the visual, and that since the Renaissance this "ubiquity of vision" has become a synonym of the modern.[1] This specific feature of modernity does not exclude the Arab world, especially Egypt, where various forms of the visual appeared in colonial and postcolonial epochs. The visual aspect of Britain's so-called civilizing mission was so crucial that it has been labeled "visualism."[2] Extending roughly from the early 1880s until the early 1920s, British visualism, which began as a kind of epistemology and affected the emergence of visual culture in Egypt, treated the Egyptian scene as an object of study. The link between visual culture and colonial domination, then, is not merely contingent; it is deliberate and strategic. European occupation in Egypt resulted in an immensely productive visual colonialism that ranged from maps, photographs, and paintings to museums. This kind of scientific activity began much earlier, with the famous *La description l'Égypte*, prepared by Napoleon's French Campaign of 1798–1801. With motives strictly European and reflective of a predominant Western Egyptomania, Cromer sponsored an archaeological campaign to rediscover the monuments of Pharaonic and Greco-Roman Egypt. Although most of those

[1] Martin Jay, 'Scopic Regimes of Modernity' in *Vision and Visuality*, ed. Hal Foster (Seattle: Bay Press, 1988), 3.

[2] Fabian argues that the science of anthropology grew in direct connection to European colonies and was so visually oriented that the task to "visualize" a specific culture was almost identical to understanding it. See Johannes Fabian, *Time and the Other: How Anthropology Makes Its Object* (New York: Columbia University Press, 1983).

discoveries were assembled in vast collections and shipped to British and French museums, Cromer established the Greco-Roman Museum in Alexandria in 1892, and the Egyptian Museum in Cairo in 1902, honoring the European founding fathers of Egyptology and celebrating a modern imperialistic remapping of Egypt's Pharaonic past. The Latin inscriptions decorating its colossal entrance stand as a strong visual reminder of the imperialist credo enunciated by Cromer in *Modern Egypt*, which was the subject of an earlier chapter: "Do not let us imagine that, under any circumstances, we can ever create a feeling of loyalty in the breasts of the Egyptians akin to that felt by a self-governing people for indigenous rulers."[3]

The emergence of an indigenous visual culture in Egypt, *pace* Cromer, complicates the relationship between Islam, culture, and history. In the absence of the industrial, socio-economic and artistic atmosphere from which modern European film emerged (with its movements of Cubism, Dadaism, Futurism, etc.), what Egyptian film imported from a colonial West remains in essence a *style*. Consciously or not, out of this style Nasser's July Revolution managed to establish a new genre of historical narratives and biopics for the first time in the history of Egyptian film.[4] Film is arguably the only artform in which Nasser's regime can claim important achievements. The connection between the Revolutionary Command Council (RCC) and film as a new form of expression can easily be perceived in the Egyptian context: both are modern, representing a historical break with the past and tradition. Moreover, film is a popular means of communication that appeals to the masses; it is therefore a perfect tool for political propaganda, particularly propaganda in aid of Nasser's struggle with the Muslim Brotherhood and its Islamist reconstruction of the past.

It is difficult – and especially difficult in the Arab world – to talk about film's relationship to modernity and history. Film emerged in the West roughly contemporaneously with major movements of European modernism, in which new conceptions of time and space had started to inform representation in literature and the arts. But, as Arnold Hauser argues, there is a "fundamental difference between film and the other arts … in its world-picture, the boundaries of space

[3] Ibid, 570.

[4] The classic biopic features an emphasis on one famous individual, a chronological temporal structure, quality lighting, smooth camera movement, and continuity editing.

and time are fluid – space has a quasi-temporal [element], time, to some extent, a spatial character."[5] In addition, as in the West, Arab film became more accessible to the general public than fiction and signaled not only the shift from print to visual modernity, but also a change in the perception of the real. Appealing to a broader audience, cinematic representations of historical events gave the impression of actually preserving those events due to the camera's ability to create the illusion of capturing the historical moment and of offering an approximation of, if not direct access to, the real.

As a fascinating new medium, film spread quickly, beginning to be exported to the Arab world soon after its emergence in the West. At the end of the nineteenth century, Egypt's contact with Europe grew stronger due to the inauguration of the Suez Canal in 1869, which made the country a vital navigation path for the entire world. After its occupation by Britain in 1882, while still under the rule of Turkey, Egypt – especially metropolitan Cairo and Alexandria – was considered by many Europeans to be the only country in the Middle East that was relatively developed and open to cultural advancement. Verdi's *Aida*, for instance, was commissioned by and first performed at Cairo's Khedivial Opera House in 1871 to commemorate the inauguration of the canal. But in the 1890s, film was transmitted to Egypt primarily as a technical and commercial product to display and sell rather than to develop and enrich artistically.[6] The expression "*Ṣināʿa-t- al-Sīnimā*" (film industry) was more common in Egypt than "film art," at a time when the novel itself, if we take Ḥaqqī's 1906 *The Virgin of Denshawai* as a rough start, had just begun its journey as a new form in Arabic literature, appearing almost contemporaneously with European film.

The first films ever screened in Egypt were, unsurprisingly, European: Lumière Brothers shorts (1895).[7] The screening was a success and

[5] Arnold Hauser, 'The Film Age', in *The Social History of Art: Naturalism, Impressionism, the Film Age*, vol. 4 (New York: Vintage Books, 1958), 239–40.

[6] See Alexander Astruc, "The Birth of a New Avant-Garde: Le Camera-Stylo." www.newwavefilm.com/about/camera-stylo-astruc.shtml (accessed on November 23, 2017). Astruc's essay was originally printed as "Du Stylo à la caméra et de la caméra au stylo" in *L'Écran française*, March 30, 1948. See also Seymour Chatman, "What Novels Can Do That Films Can't (and vice versa)," *Critical Inquiry*, 8 (Autumn, 1980), 121–40. Seymour's famous thesis is that novels describe but films present events.

[7] The film was shown at a café called Zavani, in Alexandria, in 1896.

encouraged a group of foreign merchants to create a space for film in Egypt primarily by importing films and building cinemas in which to show them. Before 1909, five cinemas were established: two in Alexandria and one each in Port Said, Asyūṭ, and al-Manṣūra, respectively.[8] Egyptian film is thus an illegitimate child of European modernity. Thanks to Britain and France, Egypt knew film before the Egyptian Museum was built. But then again, it is not surprising in a culture whose modernity is "the triumph of a pure visuality," as Martin Jay puts it, to disseminate its "triumph" to its colonies. It was not until after the first two decades of the twentieth century that Egypt made its own local imprint on film and made investment in the film industry on a par with France and Russia. But it is important to emphasize that Egyptian film has its own history and its own versions of classicism, realism, and modernism that differ from those as usually understood in Europe.

The declaration of independence in 1922, albeit nominal, incentivized Egypt to take major steps in revitalizing its film industry. In *Madkhal ilá Tārīkh al-Sīnimā al-ʿArabiyya* (*An Introduction to the History of Arab Cinema*), Samīr Farīd argues that the history of film in modern Egypt had seen two golden eras: the 1920s and the 1950s.[9] The first Renaissance began in the 1920s and lasted until the early 1930s and included all fields of art. It was a time that witnessed, in addition to the first full-length Egyptian film and the first cinematic journal, *Jarīda-t- al Sīnimā* (*Cinema Journal*): Ṭāhā Ḥusayn's provocative

[8] See Samīr Farīd, *Madkhal ilá Tārīkh al-Sīnimā al-ʿArabiyya* [*An Introduction to the History of Arab Cinema*] (Cairo: Maṭābiʻ al-Hay'a al-ʻArabiyya al-ʻĀmma lil-Kitāb , 2001); Yves Thoraval, *Regards sur le Cinéma Égyptien* [*Insights into Egyptian Cinema*] (Beyrouth: Librairie Orientale, 1986); see also M. Khan, *An Introduction to the Egyptian Cinema* (London: Informatics, 1969).

[9] Farīd divides the history of Egyptian cinema into ten stages, of which Chahine's *Gamīla al-Gazā'iriyya* occupies the seventh, namely, the period 1956–62, that is, from the Suez War to the Public Sector. Farīd's categories are arbitrary and mainly political, ignoring major thematic and stylistic shifts in Egyptian cinema that could have been useful in historical classifications. Those ten stages are: Stage 1: First Cinematic Show to First Cinematic Shooting (1896–7); Stage 2: Silent Cinema (1907–31); Stage 3: Sound Cinema (1932–5); Stage 4: Studio Miṣr (1936–44); Stage 5: End of Second World War to July Revolution (1945–52); Stage 6: July Revolution to Suez War (1953–5); Stage 7: Suez War to Public Sector (1956–62); Stage 8: Cinema Public Sector to June War (1963–7); Stage 9: June War to October War (1967–73); Stage 10: New Realism and After (1973–94) (Farīd, *Madkhal ilá Tārīkh al-Sīnimā al-ʿArabiyya*, 86–119).

Fī al-Shiʿr al-Jāhilī (*On Pre-Islamic Poetry*); ʿAlī ʿAbd al-Rāziq's work on the Islamic caliphate; al-Sayyid Darwīsh's inspirational music; Maḥmūd Mukhtār's architectural nationalism; Maḥmūd Saʿīd's paintings; ʿAbd al-Wahhāb's and Umm Kulthūm's songs; Aḥmad Shawqī's poems and historical plays; Ḥāfiẓ Ibrāhīm's poetry; Yūsuf Wahbī's and Nagīb al-Rīhānī's acting; Zakī Ṭulaymāt's first Institute for Acting; Naguib Mahfouz's maiden novels; Tawfīq al-Ḥakīm's first plays; the inauguration of Egyptian radio; and the opening of the Egyptian National Theatre. It also witnessed the emergence of political parties, including an official communist one, and the first free elections in Egyptian history.[10]

In 1922, two Egyptian actors, Fawzī Mūnīb and Gubrān Naʿūm, exhibited a short film in Alexandria called *al-Khātam al-Siḥri* (*The Magic Ring*). In the same year a group of actors showed *al-ʿAmma al-Amrīkiyya* (*The American Aunt*). All films of this era are secular in their themes and characterization. For instance, in 1923, Muḥammad Bayyūmī, a young Egyptian who had studied film-making in Germany, directed *al-Bāsh Kātib* (*The Civil Servant*). Produced by Amīn ʿAṭāllah, and shot in locations around Cairo, Bayyūmī's al-*Bāsh Kātib*, which precedes *Josef von Sternberg's The Blue Angel* (1930), is a thirty-minute melodrama about a government official who dates a belly dancer and steals money in order to run away with her. He is arrested and sent to jail.

The first Egyptian film to be shown abroad was *al-Baḥr Biyiḍḥak Līh?* (*Why is the Sea Laughing?*). Produced by Amīn ʿAṭāllah and directed by Alvise Orfanelli, the film was screened in Lebanon in 1924. In 1927, Sṭīfān Rustī, the first Egyptian known to make a feature-length film, directed *Layla*, another secular melodrama about an engagement gone wrong when the fiancé falls in love with an American woman and follows her to the US, leaving behind his pregnant and vulnerable fiancée. Around the same time, the Mīnā Cine-Club was founded by the Lāmā brothers, Ibrāhīm and Badr, who later screened their own production, *Qubla fī al-Ṣaḥrā'* (*A Kiss in the Desert*), shot in what was then called the Victoria Desert on the outskirts of Alexandria. In 1928, the Lāmā Brothers made *Fājʿa Fawqa al-Ahrām* (*A Disaster on the Pyramids*), which was followed by

[10] For more on Egypt's artistic modernism, see Afaf Lutfi al-Sayyid-Marsot, *Egypt's Liberal Experiment, 1922–36* (Berkeley: University of California Press, 1977).

another picture, *Muʿjiza-t- al-Ḥub* (*The Miracle of Love*), screened in 1930. Most of those cinematic productions remain largely unstudied to this day.

What Farīd calls the "second Renaissance of Egyptian cinema," the primary concern of this chapter, was shaped by the Revolution of 1952, also known as *Thawra-t- al-Taṣḥīḥ*, namely, The Revolution of Rectification. With this revolution, another political system, in fact another hierarchy of power, prevailed and with it the need for another kind of film. The socio-political agenda of Nasser's regime was quasi-Marxist, for its main aim emerging from *Taṣḥīḥ* was to achieve drastic changes in the Egyptian modes of production – changes capable of annihilating the class system. Nasser's regime, however, did not rest easy on Egyptian soil. Before long, an Islamist front began to form once again, as had happened during Fārūq's reign. Soon, Nasser found himself crippled by the threat of local violence. His regime was fighting two wars: an internal conflict waged by a number of Islamic groups that denounced his regime and accused him of being *shuyūʿī* (a communist), which in its Arabic connotation is tantamount to "ungodly" or "disbeliever," and an external anti-European campaign that aimed to form a unified Arab front against Britain, France, and the United States.

The RCC was determined to bring about a complete change in political, economic, social, and cultural affairs, and to pay attention to the arts, especially film. "Nasserism," argues Yves Thoraval, "if it does not bring about a complete cultural revolution, will give a boost to the cultural life of modern Egypt, helping to clarify and organize it, with the intervention of the government in various kinds of arts."[11] In 1955, the RCC established *Maṣlaḥa-t- al-Funūn* (The Organization of the Arts) to support the arts and, specifically, cinematic productions. In 1956, The Free Officers of the Revolution established *Wazāra-t-al-Thaqāfa al-Qawmiyya wa al-Tawjīh* (The Ministry of National Culture and Orientation), which directs *al-Majlis al-Aʿalá li-ḥimāya-t-al-Adab wa al-Funūn* (The Supreme Council for the Protection of Literature and the Arts). And in July 1957, the Ministry of National Culture and Orientation expanded its authority by founding *al-Hay'a al-Qawmiyya li-Daʿm al-Sīnimā* (The National Organization for the Subsidization of Film). In 1959 a specialized institute for film and the

[11] Thoraval, *Regards sur le Cinéma Égyptien*, 31.

arts, *Al-Maʿhad al-ʿĀlī lil-Sīnimā* (The Higher Institute for Film) was established.[12] As a result of this encouragement, between 1952 and 1962, Egypt witnessed a relatively large increase in the production of films, with over 513 films produced (see Appendix 3). That nationalist and patriotic films inspired and informed – if not dictated – by the July Revolution would inundate the Egyptian market was therefore more or less inevitable. Unlike the Fārūquian film of the "first Renaissance" whose focus was melodrama and comedy, the post-Fārūquian film of the "second Renaissance" was soon pressed into the service of forming a modern Egyptian identity.

With the establishment of the Ministry of National Culture and Orientation in 1956, the film industry was allotted an annual budget of 1.5 million Egyptian pounds. The ministry also organized annual festivals, with awards including best direction, best production, best script, best camera work, best sound recording, and best acting. Those awards reached a sum of 40,000 Egyptian pounds in 1959.[13] In addition to annual awards, foreign co-production was welcome, and censorship laws were changed to target Islamophobic, anti-Arab, or pro-Israel films.[14] Moreover, many films were sent for screening abroad in countries like Japan, China, India, Pakistan, and Indonesia. Indeed, *Gamīla al-Gazāʾiriyya* is said to have been a success when shown in the USSR in 1958.[15]

It would be erroneous, however, to argue that all of these films were solely dedicated to the service of the national cause. Many of them treat popular social themes like class struggles and gender issues, especially rags-to-riches plots, psychological dramas, and love

[12] See Farīd, *Madkhal ilá Tārīkh al-Sīnimā al-ʿArabiyya*, 104–10; see also Thoraval, 'La Révolution de Juillet', in *Regards sur le Cinéma Égyptien*, 31–43 as well as Khan 'The Contemporary Cinema: 1952–1969', in *An Introduction to the Egyptian Cinema*, 38–80.

[13] Khan, An Introduction, 38.

[14] Film censorship is a barometer of national sensitivity, one that always reveals the limits of the national imagination. What are the criteria, one might ask, that grant or deny access into the visual space of cinema and therefore decide the cultural and political image that the official system likes to draw for itself? Between 1955 and 1967, 323 foreign films were banned. Fifty of them were banned on the grounds of their pro-Zionist political messages, seventy-four for ridiculing Arabs and their culture, 120 for their blacklisted stars, four because they were shot in Israel, and one because it made fun of Islam (ibid., 39).

[15] Ibid., 40.

stories, as well as adventure films and romantic comedies. Some films of these types that might seem irrelevant to the national cause in fact owe their production to government support; but, in many of these cases, the hero of the film is a symbol of the nation. In any case, the second Renaissance of Egyptian film remained predominantly nationalist, emphasizing continuity with tradition, most notably in the historical film genre that can fall into three broad categories. The first category includes films against colonization that either portray nationalist heroic resistance or reveal its horrific practices.[16] The second category includes films that expose the oppression of the old regime, depicting the exploitation of Egyptian Fallāḥīn at the hands of a feudal monarchy.[17] But it is films of the third category that are most significant for an understanding of the particular nature of film under Nasser. Films of this category, while celebrating Islamic culture, de-emphasize its role, especially in its fundamentalist forms, as a central agent in the struggle for national liberation. Such films include Henry Barakat's 1961 *Fī Baytina Rajul* (*There is a Man in our House*). In this film Islam does no more than provide a cultural background to the film's main events. Stylized as a Hitchcock chase narrative, especially in its suspenseful theme music, the events take place in 1930s Cairo during the holy month of Ramadan in the house of a moderate Muslim family harboring a runaway secular nationalist (played by Omar Sharif) who has just assassinated the Egyptian Prime Minister for his involvement with the British. Another example is Youssef Chahine's *al-Nāṣir Ṣalāḥ al-Dīn* (*Saladin the Victorious*, 1963). Despite historical inaccuracies, the film was enthusiastically received as restorative propaganda in favor of Nasser as a valiant leader of the Arab-Muslim world, especially in the aftermath of the clash with the Muslim Brotherhood. It is clear from the title that the movie positions Nasser as a Muslim hero and the hope of the Arab-Muslim world in unifying all Arabs and bringing back their lost land.

[16] These films include *Muṣṭafá Kāmil* (1953); *Yaṣquṭ al-Istiʿmār* [*Down with Imperialism*] (1954); *Kilometre 99* (1955); *Al-bāb al-Maftūḥ* [*The Open Door*] (1956); *Allāh Maʿana* [*God is with Us*] (1956); *Sajīn Abū Zaʿbal* [*The Prisoner of Abū Za ʿbal's Penitentiary*] (1957); *Rudda Qalbī* [*My Heart is Restored*] (1957); *Arḍ al-Salām* [*Land of Peace*] (1957); *Port Said* (1957); *Ḥub min Nār* [*A Flaming Love*] (1958), and *Samrāʾ Sīnāʾ* [*The Dark Woman of Sinai*] (1958).

[17] Films *include Ṣirāʿ fī al-Wādī* [*A Struggle in the Valley*] (1953), *Arḍuna al-Khaḍrāʾ* [*Our Green Land*] (1956), *Al-Fitiwwa* [*The Bully*] (1957), and *al-Kharsāʾ* [*The Mute Woman*] (1957).

But probably the most important example of this category is, as we shall see, another film of Chahine's, his *Gamīla al-Gazā'iriyya* (1958).

The rapid growth of film contributed to the process through which cultural standards and assumptions were established, maintained, challenged, and reconfigured in Nasserist Egypt. In this context one cannot help but think of Benedict Anderson's argument that "the growth of what might be called 'comparative history' led in time to the hitherto unheard-of conception of 'modernity' explicitly juxtaposed to 'antiquity,' and by no means necessary to the advantage of the latter."[18] Anderson's definition of the nation as essentially an "imagined community" clearly applies to Nasserist Egypt, especially with regard to the nexus between modernity and vision in the grand nationalistic narrative of the July Revolution. Having said that, one must acknowledge that modernities of different societies have their own unique visual emphases. These emphases – like any emphasis – still fall within larger categories of cinematic representations of history. Extending Anderson's argument, the Egyptian filmmakers of a nationalist modern age must have negotiated between and, further, reconciled the expressions of modernity and tradition by asserting the Egyptianness (along with the Arabness, in certain cases) of European-inspired film art.

This cultural expression had to strike a delicate balance between Islamism and secularism. As soon as Nasser took power, Egyptian Islamists vehemently opposed his moderate Islamic agenda and his continued adoption of secularist politics. Islamists interpreted the abandonment of the *sharia*-based conservative society proposed by the Muslim Brotherhood (the project for which they supported the Free Officers' Movement in the ousting of King Fārūq) as a submission to intellectual colonization and as a surrender to the onslaught of Western Europe's secular modernity. Many Islamists, including Quṭb, opposed this perceived threat by producing texts in support of a Bākāthīrian return to "origins" and an adoption of a total Islamicization of Egypt.[19] But Nasser's most immediate nationalist

[18] Benedict Anderson, *Imagined Communities: Reflections on the Origin and Spread of Nationalism* (London: Verso, 1991), 68.

[19] For more on the growing discontent between Nasser and the Muslim Brotherhood elsewhere, see Mohammad Salama and Rachel Friedman, "Locating the Secular in Sayyid Quṭb," *Arab Studies Journal* (Spring 2012, No. XX. Vol.1): 104–31.

projects consisted of the modernization and secularization of Egypt in a manner that still honored Egypt's Islamic culture but incorporated both the pre-Islamic past and Western modernity.[20] Nasser's opposition to the Muslim Brotherhood gained him tremendous support among secular Egyptians, and especially among Egypt's working class. As Nasser turned a deaf ear to the Muslim Brotherhood's demands, the incompatibility between secular Nasserism and ultra-conservative Islamism began to widen. When Nasser rejected the proposed union between the mosque and the state in post-Fārūq Egypt, it was evident that he and the Muslim Brotherhood had an irresolvable disagreement not only on the meaning, definition, and understanding of Islam, but also on Egypt's cultural and socio-political manifestation of this understanding.

A video clip of a speech by Nasser to the Egyptian nation sums up the fundamental disagreement between his and the Muslim Brotherhood's visions of postcolonial Egypt. In this speech, Nasser acknowledges his intention to work with the Muslim Brotherhood and describes the essence of their different approaches to Islam. According to Nasser, al-Murshid al-ʿĀmm (public guide for the Muslim Brotherhood) requested that the ḥijāb be made mandatory and that every woman must walk in public wearing a *ṭarḥa* (Egyptian colloquial synonym for the ḥijāb). Nasser's response was that wearing a ḥijāb is a personal matter, not a governmental mandate. The public guide replied that Nasser would be abandoning his responsibility as a leader of a Muslim country if he allowed women to walk *sāfirāt* (sans ḥijāb) in Egypt's public sphere. Nasser responded as follows:

Sir, you have a daughter in Medical School and we know she does not wear the ḥijāb. If you are unable to force one woman, who is your own daughter, to wear the ḥijāb, how do you expect me to force ten million

[20] See Abd al-Moneim Said Aly and Manfred W. Wenner, 'Modern Islamic Reform Movements: The Muslim Brotherhood in Contemporary Egypt', *Middle East Journal* 36, no. 3 (1982): 342. For a detailed account of the Muslim Brotherhood's support for the coup, see Khālid Muḥyī al-Dīn, *Wa al-Ān Atakallam* [*And Now I Speak*] (Cairo: Markaz al-Ahrām lil-Tarjama wa al-Nashr, 1992); Muḥyī al-Dīn, *Wa al-Ān Atakallam*, 107, 137; see also his section *'al-Ikhwān min al-Mushāraka ilá al-'Udwān'* [*The Muslim Brotherhood's Turn from Allies to Enemies*], in the chapter entitled '*Naḥw al-Hukm Khuṭwa Khuṭwa*' (*Toward Governance Step by Step*), 196–9. For a fuller account of Quṭb's direct relationship with Nasser's government, see Muḥyī al-Dīn, *Wa al-Ān Atakallam*, 204–10 and 297.

Egyptian women to wear the ṭarḥa? [Audible laughter and applause from the audience.][21]

The ḥijāb debate grew more and more central to Egypt's cultural self-definition, and became, among other matters related to Islam and its history, an important topic in Egyptian films of the 1950s and 1960s.

Nasser eventually saw his only option as a suppression of the Muslim Brotherhood followed by a new cultural strategy: to deradicalize Egypt's public sphere and reverse the influence of Islamism. But this crackdown, which forced the Muslim Brotherhood to go underground, did not mean that it stopped amassing religious power and popular support among Egyptians. In fact, the persuasive rhetoric of Quṭb's arguments in his polemical writings, including *Ma ʿālim fī al-Ṭarīq* (*Milestones Along the Path*), as well as the organization's social charitable efforts in support of Egypt's poor and deprived populations, brought the Muslim Brotherhood unprecedented far-reaching support. This support grew to the point that calls for a "return to Islam" and statements such as Bākāthīr's "Islam is the Solution" became more credible to those in the mainstream of Egypt's politics, especially after the country continued its descent into economic despair, autocracy, and dictatorship.

During Nasser's regime, there was still room to practice religion and to become a conservative Muslim "brother" if one wished to do so, but condemning others as irreligious or labeling the society as ungodly became unacceptable. In opening public schools to all Egyptians, Nasser ensured that all secular subjects were offered, while religion subjects continued to be offered to Muslim and Christian students but were excluded from their final grade. He adopted similar policies within the existing private school system by offering religion courses. Examples of such secular colonial schools included Victoria College of Alexandria (established by Lord Cromer in 1902) and Lycée La Liberté (established by the Mission Laïque Française in 1909). These schools were built on the model of liberal European schools and marginalized religious teaching. In Nasser's view, religion – still restricted to Islam and Christianity – and other topics such as social service were to be offered as curricular classes taught within the school day. Religion in particular was assigned its own teachers, mostly Arabists, and taught in accordance with each student's

[21] Gamal Abdel Nasser, 'President Gamal Abdel Nasser on the Muslim Brotherhood' www.youtube.com/watch?v=TX4RK8bj2W0.

belief system. Religion, then, was to be offered in Egypt's public school systems as a complementary study, as a subject not central to a student's failure or success.

It was not just in academic curricula where Nasserism sought to de-emphasize hyper-religiosity and Islamist dogma. In using film and radio as organized propaganda in the process of nation-building, Nasserism sought to increase the scope of secular Arab nationalism in all aspects of life.[22] Nasser's strategy of claiming to represent a modern international Third World viewpoint echoes in many ways the anticolonial nationalist Muṣṭafá Kāmil's patriotic scheme of nationalizing Egypt in the early 1900s, especially after the massacre of Denshawai. For Kāmil, since the Muslim Brotherhood had not yet come into existence, the movement was exclusively Egyptianist. The situation was different for Nasser: Nasserism, though still centered in Egypt, invoked pan-Arabism with the aim of countering the pan-Islamism of the Muslim Brotherhood, while at the same time asserting the essentially Arab nature of Egyptian society in the face of ethnic diversity, which was seen as a threat to national unity. Paradoxically, then, the assertion of an overarching identity, larger than any one particular national identity, had become central to the national culture of modern Egypt under Nasser. In light of this paradox it is not surprising that Egypt mobilized its most powerful technology of communication and propaganda to focus on an episode in the epic of pan-Arabism, which, at first glance, had no connection with the project of national self-definition within Egypt. Youssef Chahine's *Gamīla al-Gazā'iriyya* is a visual anti-Islamist *and* anticolonial expression of Egyptian nationalism that does not focus on an event crucial to the history of the anticolonial struggle in Egypt, such as the massacre of Denshawai; its focus is on the Bouhired Affair, equally crucial to the history of the anticolonial struggle, but in Algeria. Chahine's specifically Egyptian, anti-Islamicist response to this affair provides a unique insight into the role of Islam in the culture of modern Egypt.

[22] See Youssef Chahine, 'Numéro Spécial: Youssef Chahine'. *Cahiers du Cinema* 506 (October 1996): 12–13. See also Chahine's interview in translation in Appendix II. Despite the more advanced goals of Nasser and the disruptive effects of his achievements, his strategy failed to develop a critique of modernity itself and in doing so inadvertently re-established European hegemony. Also, the dominant idea of democracy is contradicted by Egypt's lapse into militaristic tyranny following Nasser's regime.

Djamīla Bouhired (known among Egyptians and, therefore, in Chahine's film, as Gamīla) was a young Algerian *Fidā'iyya* (freedom fighter/redeemer) said to have been a member of the *Front de Libération Nationale* (FLN). She was caught carrying the correspondence of FLN leaders in the infamous Battle of Algiers, and was tortured in April 1957 during "interrogations" by the notoriously brutal French paratroopers. Among other atrocities, her torture consisted in having electrodes attached to her breasts, and Bouhired was eventually accused of planting a bomb at the Coq Hardi Café in Algiers and killing a number of French soldiers. She was condemned to death, but after demonstrations by French intellectuals, she was found innocent and was released.

The Bouhired Affair quickly became a *cause célebre* in both Algeria and France, in which it generated similar responses. Typical of these responses is a poem by Nūr al Dīn Bū-Djadra, "Djamīla Bouhired, Victim of Blind Persecution":

On the straw-mat in a dark cell
Lies a broken girl
She is thirsty.
She raises her hands, but they fall down.
Her closed eyes no longer have any spark.
Filth surrounds her.
It is a place where rats and lice roam unchecked,
Where many of her kind have met their end
She is a woman. Her name is Djamīla Bouhired.
Her pulse is weak. She can hardly move.
Her barely warm body tainted with blood.
She has been humiliated by blood-thirsty soldiers.
She lost her virginity while she was alone among the civilized
She lost her precious honor.
It was maimed, but it came back like fire
In the spirit of her cell mates who are still abused
What did she do to deserve all that torture?
Is there no iota of humanity left?
Yet, the Republic still speaks of
"Fraternity, liberty, and equality."
The principles nations adore.
Spit on them! The principles that make us a worthy nation!
The French republic is forever at a loss.
Roundabout ways and thorny issues
Prevent it from attaining happiness.

Significantly this poem was written in both Arabic and French, and to a large extent was based on an essay by the French doctor Étienne Burnet, since it is representative of both Algerian and French responses to the Bouhired affair.[23] These responses typically focus on Bouhired's torture, especially on its sexual nature, as a reproach to France, the supposed beacon of European enlightenment. There are many examples of French works, both literary and para-literary, that deal with Algeria's struggle for independence and its impact upon the metropolis, from the early 1950s, passing through the Algerian War, and culminating in the events of 1968 in which French intellectuals took it upon themselves to show that the French-Algerian War damaged the French republic, that the army was working *against* the Republic in collusion with the "colons." In so doing it was rejecting an ideal France, the France of Rousseau's social contract and the freedom of man. From this perspective, the question of torture, as a reproach to everything European civilization supposedly stood for, was crucial.[24]

This response is particularly evident in films of the French New Wave. Jean-Luc Godard's films, for example, are permeated with images of torture in stark condemnation of France's barbaric colonial past and postcolonial present.[25] His *Le Petit Soldat* (*The Little Soldier*), for example, features France's colonial violence coming home to roost in the torture of innocent French civilians engaged in protest against the French occupation of Algeria. Another example, is Alain Resnais's *Muriel* (1963), which juxtaposes two plots involving two overlapping wars: one plot involves an older couple during the Second World War, and the other a soldier involved in the torture

23 The poem was written in French and translated into Arabic by the same author. There is no available English translation. My translation is based on both versions. See Nūr al-Dīn Bū-Djadra, *Al-Ḥarīq: Qiṣṣa min Waḥī al-Thawra al-Jazā'iriyya* (*The Fire: A Story Inspired by the Algerian Revolution*) (Tunis: Dār al-Nashr, 1958.), French Sections, 6 and 7; Arabic Sections: 106–15, 128–9.

24 Besides *L'Affaire Audin* and *The Question*, several other important works pushed French intellectuals to confront the realities of torture in Algeria. Among them is *Pour Djamīla Bouhired* (1957), written by Jacques Vergès and Georges Arnaud, two French lawyers working at the Algerian bar. Arnaud and Vergès explained that they had written *Pour Djamīla Bouhired* to provoke an outcry against her treatment and prevent her execution.

25 See Mohammad Salama, 'Jean-Luc Godard and the Dilemma of Postcolonial Cinema', *Journal of Modern Art History Department Faculty of Philosophy University of Belgrade*. No. 10 (2014): 9–30.

and murder of a Djamīla-like Algerian woman, the Muriel of the title. Celia Britton argues that "[*Muriel*] provides a formal and historical core" which is, in fact, "an exploding nucleus ... the structurally and metaphorically explosive secret of torture."[26] Most such films, however, represent the war from a strictly French perspective. Torture is seen as the legacy of the Algerian War to be inherited and visualized by French film. Visually, torture subscribes to the Jamesonian rule of being pornographic, in the sense that it reveals the nakedness of the violated body of the other coupled with the flagrant nakedness of French morality. Torture becomes a metaphor for French colonial guilt, or for the political bankruptcy of de Gaulle's France, or even for the contradiction between the France of liberation and the France of occupation at the end of the Second World War. The specifics of the Bouhired affair, of the Algerian War, and of the struggle against colonialism throughout the Arab world, become secondary as torture becomes an all-embracing metaphor for the decline of the West.

In *L'an cinq de la révolution algérienne* Franz Fanon brings a very different perspective to the Bouhired affair, by shifting the focus from torture as an ahistorical crime against civilization to the more historically specific outrage of "unveiling."[27] Although Fanon does not refer to Djamīla Bouhired or any other episodes of Algerian female, it is obvious that his close connection to the scene of the war and his medical involvement with French soldiers must have provided the groundwork for his argument.[28] Fanon's most provocative chapter is "Unveiling Algeria." Dwelling on the most characteristic garment of the Algerian woman, her *ḥāyik* (a variation on the veil), Fanon discusses the peculiarly modern function of veiling in colonized Algeria. Fanon argues that the Algerian women's position as "unveiled" members of the FLN belies the colonialist misconceptions of French authorities. To believe, as the French claim to do, that unveiling Algerian

[26] Celia Britton, 'Broken Images in Resnais's *Muriel*': *French Cultural Studies*, 1, part 1, no.1 (February, 1990): 40.

[27] Fanon's book was translated into English in 1965. See Franz Fanon, *A Dying Colonialism*, trans. Hakon Chevalier (New York: Grove Press, 1965).

[28] Another important case involves Djamīla Boupacha, a female FLN member who went through the same process as Bouhired. Like Bouhired's, Boupacha's rape and torture was also scandalous. Boupacha's case inspired Picasso's portrait of her. Her case also inspired Simone de Beauvoir and Gisèle Halimi's *Djamīla Boupacha* (Paris: Gallimard, 1962).

women is a welcome sign of French penetration into Algerian society is nothing but a myth:

> [T]he authorities were strengthened in their conviction that the Algerian woman would support Western penetration into the native society. Every rejected veil disclosed to the eyes of the colonialists horizons until then forbidden, and revealed to them, piece by piece, the flesh of Algeria laid bare. The occupier's aggressiveness, and hence his hopes, multiplied ten-fold each time a new face was uncovered ... Every face that offered itself to the bold and impatient glance of the occupier, was a negative expression of the fact that Algeria was beginning to deny herself and was accepting the rape of the coloniser. (See footnote 22.)

What the French colonialists fail to understand is that, by unveiling, the Algerian Muslim woman has put on another veil more secretive than the facial one. If the "phenomenon of [de-colonial] resistance" is necessarily connected to a process of "counter-assimilation, of maintenance of a cultural, hence national, originality," Djamīla and her female cohorts, it appears, must have used colonial logic against itself.[29] If colonial France imagines that once an Algerian woman is unveiled she is automatically saved from the tyranny of a predominantly male-oriented Islamism, Bouhired's sham unveiling frustrates this imagining. The French army's acceptance of stereotypes about the veiling/unveiling of Muslim women provided an opportunity for a radical and highly successful modification in the Algerian strategy of combat: the engagement of women.

Fanon argues that this led to a unique moment of modernity: Muslim women's experience of the European city in Algiers. In the Casbah, Algerian women "adopted an absolutely unbelievable offensive tactic."[30] Overcoming a considerable number of taboos, young Algerian women entered the space of the enemy. Their missions were complex. First, they had to act as if they were secular, free, almost uninhibited, something that women never experience in conservative, predominantly male-oriented Muslim cultures. In the so-called modern European city, the Algerian woman is the anti-modern, though she has to look modern in order to destabilize the city:

> Every time she ventures into the European city, the Algerian woman must achieve a victory over herself, over her childish fears. She must consider the

[29] Ibid., 42.
[30] Ibid., 51.

image of the occupier lodged somewhere in her mind and her body, remodel it, initiate the essential work of eroding it, make it inessential, remove something of the shame that is attached to it, devalidate it.[31]

Chahine's *Gamīla al-Gazāʾiriyya* capitalizes on this Fanonian moment of devalidation by employing the theme of torture, as do the films of Renoir and Resnais and other French cultural productions, but not necessarily to shame post-Second World War France for the atrocities that it condoned; rather, he does so to invoke a different sense of collective responsibility among his own people. Seen through Arab eyes, the expressionistic torture scene that marks the climax of the film builds a strong resolve for vengeance among Arab nationalists. But for Chahine, as for Fanon, there is another theme which has an importance that it cannot have for the colonialist oppressors obsessed with their own sense of guilt and responsibility: the theme of unveiling. Ultimately though, the perspectives which Fanon and Chahine take on unveiling are very different, reflecting the very different factors at play in the decolonization of Fanon's Algeria and Chahine's Egypt.

Chahine's film, *Gamīla al-Gazā'iriyya*, which was released in 1958, was financed in large part by the Egyptian army, a fact that is noted in the film's dedication (Figure 1). In his 1996 Cahiers du Cinema

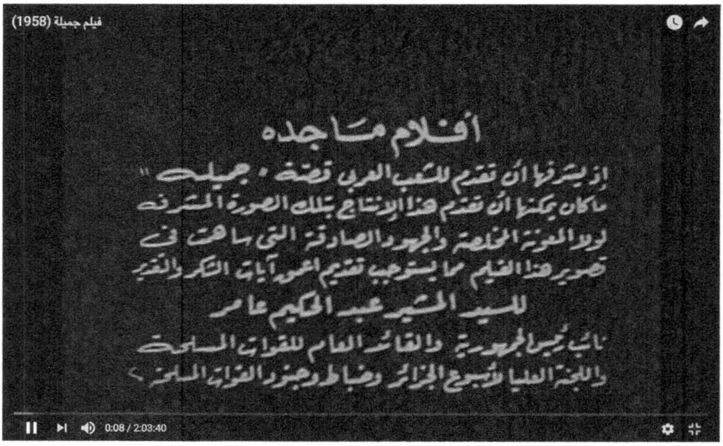

Figure 1 Opening Credits, Magda Films expresses gratitude and indebtedness to Egyptian Military Forces

[31] Ibid., 52.

interview, Chahine downplays the significance of the Egyptian army's role in the making of the film:

CHAHINE:	It was produced by the young Egyptian actress Māgda al-Ṣabbāḥi. Her brother was an officer.
INTERVIEWER:	Was there a lot of money put into this film?
CHAHINE:	I have to say that Māgda was rather generous; she was a competent producer. Maybe her army connections helped her. If I wanted 200 soldiers, she would bring them to me.[32]

Perhaps, in speaking to *Cahiers du Cinema*, the very source of *auteur* theory, Chahine feels obliged to minimize the role of an arm of the Egyptian government in shaping his artistic vision. But be that as it may, contextualizing Chahine's film in terms of a nationalistic movement that was dominant in postcolonial Egypt during Nasser's regime invites us to read it in light of its radically Egyptian contextualization of an Algerian theme. The attraction of an event like the Bouhired affair to the Egypt of Nasser is not its historical specificity, but the opportunity it gives for a powerful formal representation of what are, in essence, Egyptian concerns. *Gamīla al-Gazāʾiriyya* remains an Egyptian film that furthers the interests of an ideology that has broader aims than the independence struggle of one colony among many. The film becomes a marketable commodity for a secular, woman-empowering, de-Islamicized Egyptian.

This may serve to account for the following questions: why would an Egyptian film celebrate the feats of a young Algerian woman? And, why film? As we have seen, in Nasserist Egypt, the fascination with the technology of modernity constituted the utopian dimension of *Thawra-t al-Taṣḥīḥ* (*The Revolution of Rectification*). It is no surprise then, that the Egyptian government utilized an imported Western technology as a crucial historiographic instrument for re-envisaging history from a nationalistic perspective. In a state-run cinema, Egyptian filmmakers were interpellated, to use an Althusserian term; that is, they were called out or hailed to contribute to the national cause. The production of *Gamīla al-Gazāʾiriyya* coincided with a crucial national liberation moment in the Arab world as a whole and in Egypt in particular. The film not only portrays the Algerian struggle in a critical time

[32] 'Numéro Spécial: Youssef Chahine', *Cahiers du Cinema* 506 (October 1996), 12–13. For my full English translation of the interview with Chahine, see Appendix II.

of Arab modernity, but it also produces an alternative visual history of colonialism by celebrating female, secular heroism, in stark contrast to the Islamism of the Muslim Brotherhood. By so doing, it shows us how an event can be used as systematic visual propaganda to disseminate cultural imaginings of a collective Arab nationalism, which was so central to the nationalism of Nasserist Egypt. In this light it matters considerably what a given nation newly emerging from colonialization would imagine itself to be. This imagining depends on particular forms of self-definition, national mythologies, images of national history, and concepts of national mission. The national project of mainstream Egyptian film during Nasser's regime stemmed from the view that Egypt needs above all a political and cultural modernization emphatically secular in nature; the film spread a new spirit of national hegemony – one fashioned in anticolonial modernity – that was finally capable of carving its own path, independent of the West.[33]

Chahine's *Gamīla al-Gazā'iriyya* reflects this purpose; and in so doing it draws a complicated picture of two countries, their social and national concerns, and their people as subjected to the pressures of history. Just as the Denshawai event linked Ireland and Egypt (despite their obvious differences) in their struggles against Britain, so too the Bouhired affair made it seem as if the concerns of Egypt and the concerns of Algeria were one and the same (again despite their obvious differences). While seeking to further a sense of shared Arab

[33] By 1956, colonial presence in North Africa started to disintegrate. In March of the same year, Tunisia and Morocco obtained their independence, opening up two important strategic sources of support for the Algerian revolutionaries. In August and September, a group of about fifty Algerian leaders gathered at the Soumma Valley Congress to reorient Algeria's struggle for independence. At this meeting the FLN emerged as the dominant political representative of the Algerian people. The most important resolution of the conference was the reiteration that a ceasefire would not be discussed until the French authorities ceded independence. The French government then closed the Algerian assembly on April 11, dashing the last hopes of political resolution within Algeria's existing parliamentary system. Nasser saw that the time was ripe to strike against all forms of colonialism. On July 26, 1956, he nationalized the Suez Canal. On October 30, the Anglo-French coalition sent an ultimatum for the withdrawal of all troops within ten miles of the canal. The ultimatum going unheeded, the Anglo-French forces landed in Port Said, and on November 6 a ceasefire was called. The UN General Assembly asked Britain and France to withdraw their forces, accusing Israel, France, and Britain of collusion. By December 22, under US supervision, all British and French forces withdrew from the canal.

struggle stemming directly from a foreign presence in the Arab world as a whole, *Gamīla al-Gazā'iriyya* at the same time purports to present specifically Algerian characters who are shaped by changes in their own environment, by their own nation and history, and by the political and material realities of their own life under colonialism. Having heard Djamīla Bouhired's story broadcast on the Egyptian Radio programme, *Ṣawṭ al-'Arab* (*The Voice of the Arabs*), Chahine claims to have seen Bouhired as both a common Algerian woman, who was expected to fall in love, get married and have children; and as exemplary of the widespread Arab rage against colonial injustice.

As a mainstream film, *Gamīla al-Gazā'iriyya* employs a predominantly traditional visual style, adopting the codes of the biopic. Reshaped along the familiar lines of a normative plot, the story of Djamīla Bouhired is easy for its intended mass audience to follow, and more engaging than the complex historical event it displaces. But Chahine also adopts the bold, brash European style of 1950s newsreels in certain scenes, blending real and fictional newsreel footage, and flashbacks. The film begins with a rapid montage of newsreels and a voiceover summing up the struggle of the Algerians against their French colonizers, followed by a brilliant sequence in which a group of freedom fighters tries to smuggle a cache of arms – sent, significantly, by Egypt – into the Casbah behind the backs of the French patrols. He then makes an interesting stylistic shift to Gamīla's biopic proper. This shift allows for a smooth spatio-temporal gap, thus connecting Gamīla to world events and giving her a heroic aura similar to "real" history.

The energy of the opening sequence spills over into the first scenes, which depict Gamīla's shattered childhood; we see her family forced to evacuate their neighborhood (where she was born and where she spent all her childhood and adulthood years) and surrender it to French settlers, while she is compelled to live with her uncle in the ghettos of the Casbah. Gamīla is first portrayed as a kind and peaceful high-school girl who loves children and tries to make everyone around her happy by settling disputes among family members and classmates. Suddenly, an incident takes place that interrupts the normality of her life, forever altering her destiny. Amīna, one of Gamīla's classmates, plants a bomb in a French police station and gets arrested by the French military. Seeing Amīna swallow a pill to kill herself during her capture (Figure 2) shatters Gamīla's complacency, as she is forced to acknowledge the grim realities of her life and the lives of millions of Algerians. She decides to join the FLN, unaware that her uncle is also a member of the liberation front. Gamīla begins to work as a messenger, but because of her remarkable intelligence she is soon made an organizer. Her commitment to the cause only increases when her uncle dies at the hands of a cruel French lieutenant who kills him in cold blood despite seeing his prison release form, which he tears into pieces.

Figure 2 Gamīla watches as her friend Amīna's undercover identity as an FLN operative is exposed. Amīna swallows a suicide capsule and dies on the spot in the classroom after being surrounded by French military police

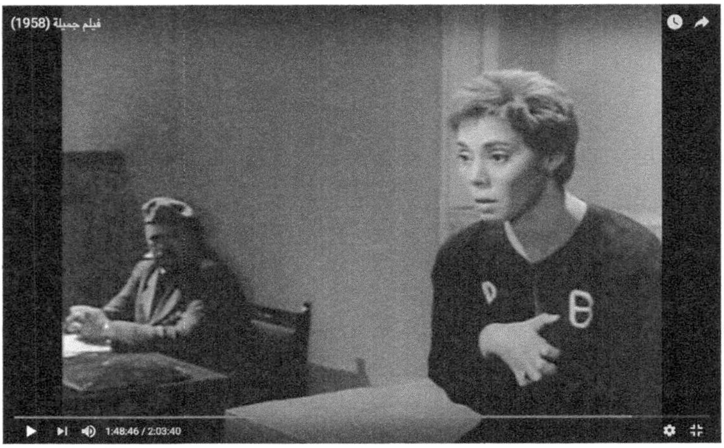

Figure 3 Gamīla stands militrary trial after being captured by the French military

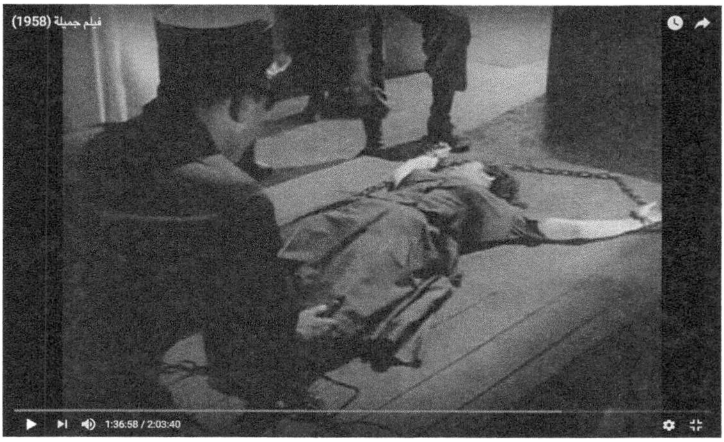

Figure 4 Gamīla pinned to the ground with both hands and feet shackled as French military torture her to extract information and root out all FLN members

After a number of successful resistance operations, Gamīla is wounded and captured by the French military while trying to lead her cohorts to a safehouse after a major operation. With Gamīla's capture, the *mise en scène* shifts to prison and the inhuman torture inflicted upon her (Figure 4). Despite torture and humiliation, and despite seeing her younger brother asphyxiated before her very eyes, Gamīla refuses to yield. The horrific effect of this episode is built up through Chahine's camerawork, specifically the use of the *noir* technique of *chiaroscuro* to imply the application of electric shocks to Gamīla's breasts (Figure 5). While in prison, her people decide to release her story to the foreign press to embarrass the French army and expose it to an international audience. In light of this publicity, the French military decide that to summarily kill her would make her a hero and would turn every Algerian man and woman more vehemently against them. A military tribunal, providing a façade of justice, is seen to be the best way to solve the problem, but her trial becomes a blessing in disguise for the cause of Algerian independence. A defense lawyer arrives from Paris, embarrasses the French military, and accuses the army of corruption. Although he fights courageously and convincingly for Gamīla, the court still sentences her to death (Figure 3). Chahine's film (which was completed before Djamīla Bouhired's acquittal) ends with Gamīla awaiting her death.

As a film made in Egypt about an Algerian woman, of what reality, one might ask, is *Gamīla al-Gazāʾiriyya* really the image? What are the criteria that grant or deny access into the visual space of film and

Figure 5 In a discrete shot, discrete as it could possibly be, Chahine uses the noir technique of chiaroscuro and shadows to show the French military's inhumane torture of Gamīla by applying electric shocks to her breasts

therefore decide the cultural and political image that the official system likes to draw for itself? One way to entertain these questions is to view *Gamīla al-Gazāʾiriyya* as an alternative version of anticolonial struggle that ultimately gets subsumed under a nationalist meta-narrative, which ultimately reflects the Egyptian nationalist project more than the Algerian one. Chahine begins his film by presenting the blatant brutality of the occupier and exposing the structure of foreign expropriation. In what is perhaps the shortest visual history of the Second World War offered on film, an Algerian man is anxiously waiting to be reunited with his son, who had been drafted by the French army, only to find that he has become an amputee. Inserted between two shots of newsreel, the effect of this scene increases resentment toward the French occupier, reminding the audience of facts that are not only gruesome, but also historically and politically valid, i.e. Algerians were asked to give life and limb to a colonizer that does not even grant them basic human freedoms. The Second World War is thus a crucial event in the rise of nationalism in North Africa. According to some records, by the end of Second World War "over a million Algerians had been killed out of a population of 9 million, 800 villages were destroyed, and over three million peasants were dislocated (Figure 6)."[34] As if these sacrifices

[34] Hassan S. Haddad and Basheer K. Nijm, eds. *The Arab World: A Handbook* (Wilmette, IL: Medina Press, 1978), 41.

Figure 6 Algerian peasant dispossessed of his land as *Pieds-Noirs* settlers move in

were not enough, the voice of the narrator grows angrier when he says that France took back its promise of liberation: "France betrayed us," he shouts in clear modern standard Arabic, "we paid the price of her victory. We lost 45,000 people to liberate her, to dignify her, only to lose our own dignity. We restored life to her, we restored freedom to her, only to lose our own. We were betrayed. Yes, we were betrayed. But, enough is enough. We will be betrayed no more." In an interesting variation, Gamīla herself then picks up the voiceover from the narrator and begins to tell her own story. At this point, the (hi)story of Gamīla becomes the occasion for Chahine to reinforce a national theme by documenting an event that took place beyond Egypt's national borders, but in such a way that it becomes a representation of something already at home – in Egypt, not in Algeria.

The "Egyptianism" of Chahine's treatment of his ostensibly Algerian topic is clear from the many liberties that he took with the historical record. Chahine's film does not speak the dialect of Algerian Arabic, but rather speaks in colloquial Egyptian to its national citizens. The film is shot in Egyptian studios and on Egyptian locations. The whole cast in the film – including the French military – are Egyptian actors. Even the hero's name, Djamīla Bouhired, is different in Chahine's version; it is mispronounced – and miswritten – in the Egyptian dialect as "Gamīla Buḥrīd." But perhaps most important is Chahine's focus on a heroic woman and the particular form this focus takes. *Gamīla al-Gazā'iriyya* was banned in Algeria both before and after independence. One reason may be that Algerian nationalists believed that the War of Liberation was a collective endeavor that does not acknowledge the singling out of heroes. To them, Djamīla is one of millions who fought in the war; she is therefore no more heroic than any other Algerian citizen. But, according to Chahine, there may have been a different factor at play: "After the Algerian Revolution, it is still banned. Why? *Because it is the woman who starts the revolution.*"[35] Chahine's claim might find support in Pontecorvo's later film *The Battle of Algiers*, an international classic highly regarded by the Algerian government, but one that emphasizes male heroism. Significantly, Chahine, in his representation of the ideal citizen as a death-defying woman, recapitulates the trope of the land as woman so prominent in the literature of modern Egyptian nationalism. Perhaps even more significantly, from the perspective of the specifically Egyptian conflict between Nasserism and the Islamicism of the Muslim Brotherhood, the woman, like Mukhtar's *Nahḍa-t Miṣr*, is unveiled.

In *Gamīla al-Gazā'iriyya* veiling is not as focalized and as strategic as it is in Fanon, or in Pontecorvo. In fact, at most five veiled women are shown – each time in passing – throughout Chahine's film. Gamīla and most of her friends are not veiled. This is crucial. The intentional unveiling of Gamīla confirms the RCC's resolve to guard Egypt against the perverse threat of Islamism; the veiling of a female Algerian hero will send the wrong message, allowing the Egyptian spectator to think that it is the Muslim/Islamist fighter, not the national citizen, who should receive the credit for launching the war of liberation.

In light of this unveiling – itself situated amidst the mutually informing and conflicting tensions of foreign and local modernity, Islam(ism), and cultural production – the question is not why and how an elite filmmaker like Chahine participates in the construction of national identity; it is how the construction of national identity can take place. In other words, what are the conditions for the possibility of national identity? What is it between Egypt and Algeria that propels Chahine to direct this film? To ask such a question is to pose yet

35 Youssef Chahine, "Numéro Spécial: Youssef Chahine," 13.

another question: what is the condition of Egyptian national identity? If Chahine's film produces a national image, is it also a product of a certain condition that governs its emergence? Or, to ask the question more bluntly, what is the Egyptian event that predicated the depiction of the Algerian event of Djamīla Bouhired in Egyptian film?

If *Gamīla al-Gazā'iriyya* is indeed propaganda for Egyptian nationalism, why would Chahine use a non-Egyptian event? Why not use an event from Egypt's history of colonial resistance? If the discourse of nationalism teaches us anything it is that language works best through subtle and subliminal messages. The film uses a non-local event – foreign but not completely alien – to deepen the sense of national belonging and to raise awareness of the atrocities of occupation. Another factor is the urgent need to create and to maintain an image of a perpetual enemy necessary for the propagation of the nationalist project. Egypt, though no longer occupied, needs to be in a perpetual state of readiness to face external threats. In *Gamīla al-Gazā'iriyya*, Egypt is repeatedly glorified in scattered phrases like "receiving weapons from a sisterly Arab Nation," or "how dare they attack Egypt, the pulsating heart of the Arab World?"[36] There is emphasis too on the Egyptian radio station, *Ṣawṭ al-ʿArab* which becomes "the only" viable source of information to the Algerian army up on the mountain. In this way, Egyptian film has become a medium to infiltrate preferred models of national identity, namely pan-Arabism and anticolonialism. Under the tutelage of Nasser, Egypt's state-run film acts as a medium for maintaining order and as a call for solidarity. The aim was to create a new consciousness by allowing nationalism to masquerade under a newly formed Arab body whose freedom from all sorts of colonial domination is an inalienable right. It was also to invent a nation, an *imagined* political community *à la* Anderson that relates more to a sense of modernity.

To achieve this sense of the modern, the Egyptians and the Arab world would need to be shown that the power of the RCC is neither totalitarian nor institutional, like the power used by colonial forces to ensure the continued subjugation of its subjects, as evidenced by the Denshawai event. Nor is it the general oligarchic system of domination exercised by one small group over the nation. In *Falsafa-t- al-Thawra*

[36] Chahine, *Gamīla al-Gazā'iriyya* (*Djamīla, the Algerian*) (Cairo: Māgda Films, 1958).

(*Philosophy of the Revolution*), Nasser makes it clear that his government's mission is transitional:

As to our role in this, it is just that of the guardian, no more no less, guarding for a definite and specific period of time. Our nation now looks like a caravan that veered off from the original path it was taking, its journey became longer, difficulties cropped up, bandits overtook it, a mirage misled it. And so it scattered, every group went in a different direction. In this situation, our mission is to recollect and regroup all those who lost their way and put them back on the right path, then let them continue their journey. This is our role. I cannot conceive for us any other role but this.[37]

Building on this awareness of its role as a guardian, Nasser's regime recognized that modern Egypt needed above all an effective new political and cultural medium – namely film – that would put an end to national sympathies with Islamism. Through the image of an unveiled young woman agreeing to give her life for the nation the government sought to naturalize and normalize the struggle for independence. The deployment of Egyptian troops all over the Arab world, including Yemen, Sudan, Syria, and Algeria, speaks for Nasser's project to reproduce a homogeneous Arab nation, one that speaks the same language, suffers the same wounds, and lives under the same laws. Nasser sees anticolonial struggle as a call for national liberation, not as an Islamicization involving the outright rejection of European modernity and the persistence of decadent and irrational forms of pre-modern tribalism; it is the mutually constitutive – and indeed dialectic – relationship between the modern and the counter-modern. In the film, Gamīla's statement "we should use their weapons against them" makes it clear that the cultural forms of the colonized do not simply replace the colonizer's, but metamorphose into something else: a dialectic that, despite aiming at negating the modernity of the colonizer, still preserves its tyrannical aspects only to sublate it and claim it as its own. Ironically enough, Egyptian film art becomes an interesting example of this dialectic of nationalist modernity, a product of European modernity used against itself.

What emerges from Chahine's *Gamīla*, then, is a well-conceived political project. What we call pan-Arabism, the national demand for solidarity to integrate the Arab world into a single unified nation, is nothing but a decree licensed by one army and one government

[37] Nasser, *Falsafa-t- al-Thawra* [*Philosophy of the Revolution*] (Beirut: Maktabat al-ʿIrfān, n.d.), 69–70.

responding to its own particular historical situation; but it is one that is meant to appear independent of these very entities. The relation between Nasser's political project and the epistemological discourse of the 1950s, through which Egyptian citizens are perceived collectively as a population existing in relation to a larger concept of government, is crucial. Indeed, if we try to answer the question about the vision of the society regulated by the Nasserist regime, we will find in Chahine's film, and almost all films of the period, a canonical phrase: "*Taḥyya al-Thawra*" (long live the revolution). This phrase is liable to seem quite vague and can more aptly be understood in terms of a carefully constructed opposition – and a choice – between two political visions of Egypt: a nationalist revolution that continues to renew itself and a temporarily disruptive Islamism, between a secular orderly society and a rigid society of religious orders.

It is easy to say, then, that what Nasser's government disseminated, or tried to inculcate through popular culture, especially the modern means of film and radio, is everything that went un-inculcated in the life of the Egyptian society, including Islamism – everything that could be said to have lacked conformity, ranging from the dissident organization of the Muslim Brotherhood to non-religious political opposition. Nationalizing popular taste and channeling anticolonial visual culture was therefore a primary concern for Nasserism. But does it stop there? What are the contours and nuances of such concern? This question is raised by the naively Nasserist utopia of *Faraḥāt's Republic*, complete with panopticon and compulsory film attendance. Is not this visual mode of social control through mass media in fact what the police state is all about: a great effort toward the formation of the social body, an elimination of enemies, within and without, and a secure governing of the population? For despite its image and sound, film acts in silence, flowing without interruption, talking to solitary, isolated individuals wherever they are. The difference between a pre-cinematic mode of nation-formation – in fact pre-media forms of power in general – and modern media lies in this modern community of audience, here formed through the reach of the imaging and imagining that is film. Walter Benjamin's discussion of tactics of distraction in Nazi Germany is very useful here:

> Reception in a state of distraction, which is increasing noticeably in all fields of art and is symptomatic of profound changes in apperception, finds in the film its true means of exercise. The film with its shock effect meets

this mode of reception halfway. The film makes the cult value recede into the background not only by putting the public in the position of the critic, but also by the fact that at the movies this position requires no attention. The public is an examiner, but an absent-minded one.

In addition to this Benjaminian formula of public apperception, the practical principles for the effective conduct of the nationalist revolutionary state will also presuppose some way of conceiving how these citizens, with diverse social and economic visions of their own society – citizens who are members of particular groups and communities, who have different interests, needs, aptitudes, and abilities – are to be integrated into one unified society.

The problem that the first Egyptian republican government had to confront in its task to regulate the Egyptian state is how to establish a system in which various tools of integrating the masses can be employed. The awareness of a divergent film audience in the newly republican, post-Fārūquian political order presupposes, either explicitly or implicitly, a unified framework whereby film viewers have to be integrated into Nasser's republic. And this is exactly what the film audience constitutes. Films like *Gamīla al-Gazā'iriyya* in a public communication system like film are therefore indispensable to the development of a sense of conforming citizenship in a complex society like Egypt, with its diverse ethnicities and varied interreligious and intra-religious sensibilities, namely, the coexistence of Copts and Muslims and the coexistence of varied groups of the Islamic faith with one another and also with non-Muslims and non-religious citizens. With Gamīla awaiting her death dauntlessly – and unveiled – it could be argued that the film's goal was not just to reinforce nationalism, but to promote secular citizens' heroism and martyrdom precisely in order to maintain and stabilize a rational sense of order during a crisis of a different order, the social crisis represented in the agitation of the Muslim Brotherhood, which was contributing to the rising tensions within social and political groups, most notably fueling the turmoil between Muslims and Christians.

Through state-run propagandist film, Nasserism did not treat the Egyptian public as organic elements and forces contributing to the vigor and growth of the state's greater welfare and strength. Nor did it perceive of them as useful individuals who can partake positively in Egypt's modern national project and carry it safely through the postcolonial and the postnational. The aim was rather to create a community of citizens, a raw material shaped in accordance with the regulatory principles of the state's rational will. The result was a republic of poverty and fear, not prosperity and prospect, one in which hope became a desire for utopia, a seed that eventually flowers in autocracy, militarism, and despotism, which inevitably persisted past Nasser, through Sadat, Mubarak, and now el-Sisi. The illusion of stability and progress has only worsened and turned into a phantom as Egypt's utopia remains suspended, "a mirage under construction,"[38] to borrow Mitchell's powerful phrase describing fake projects and amusement parks like Toshka and Dreamland promised by Mubarak, a desire left unfulfilled as the dreams of common Egyptian citizens continue to be deferred (if not squandered) in the crooked hallways of Islamism and despotism. One thing remains clear: Nasser rid Egypt of the overt power of the Muslim Brotherhood by forcing them to go underground, if only temporarily. But in the process of de-Islamicizing postcolonial Egypt, Nasser, inadvertently or not, set out on a precipitous course of nationalism and military absolutism as Egypt continued to stagger culturally, politically, and economically under the yoke of a ferocious and predatory postmodernity.

[38] Mitchell, *Rule of Experts*, 303.

Appendix 1 – The Whisper of Madness

What is madness?

It appears to be a mysterious case: just like life and death, you can know a great deal about it if you look at it from the outside, but from the inside the essence remains secret. Our man knows he was a resident of the sanitarium for some time. He now remembers his own past the same way all sane people do; he is also well aware of the present. But this short interval of his life – thank God it was short – perplexes his mind; he really cannot make any sense of it at all. The whole thing was for him like a journey to a marvelous ethereal world, so foggy and full of many featureless faces that haunt his memory. No sooner does he try to shed a light of remembrance on them than they vanish and sink into darkness. Sometimes his ears would catch sounds like murmurs, but as soon as he tries to concentrate on them, they vanish and retreat, leaving behind them only silence and confusion. That magical time with its pleasure and pain is now lost forever; even those who witnessed it have kept silent about it for an obvious reason. It is completely skipped from memory as if it had never happened. No single truthful historian could tell us about its wonders. How did it all take place, we wonder? When? How did people come to realize that this reason of his had become something other than reason and that he had become an abnormal individual that had to be confined and isolated from the community as if he were a carnivorous beast?

He was a quiet man, so quiet that his quietness could be described as absolute. Perhaps this is why he tended to like quiescence and indolence and to avoid socialization and activity. Therefore he gave up school early in his life, refused any employment, and opted to live on a humble income. His greatest pleasure was to sit down in a remote corner of a coffee shop, locking his hands to his knee, and spend long hours motionless and silent. With sleepy eyelashes and heavy lids, he observed tirelessly and dauntlessly people passing by.

That seat was his pleasure. But underlying his stagnant inactive appearance, his psyche and imagination were active and warm. His quietness was on all levels, internal and external, physical and mental, sensory and imaginative. He was a statue of flesh and blood that appears to be observing people, whereas he is isolated from life altogether.

Then what?

Suddenly something happened to the stagnant water as if a stone were thrown into it.

How so?

One day, while he was safely sitting on his chair by the street, he saw many workers scattering pleasant-looking golden sand all over the road in anticipation of a grand procession. For the first time in his life something attracted his attention and made him wonder why they were scattering sand. Then he thought that the sand might blow into people's nostrils and cause detriment to their health. Besides, once the procession was over, he saw the same workers quickly brush the sand away anyhow, so why scatter it in the first place? Perhaps the whole matter is too trivial to think of or bother about, but his question seems to him to have been the gravest reality of his life, so he thought that he was dealing with one of the greatest issues of the universe. He found the whole process of scattering sand then sweeping it away after scattering it, in addition to the harm it causes, to be quite baffling. He felt so confused that he wanted to laugh, something that he seldom did throughout his life, so he laughed ceaselessly until his eyes overflowed with tears. But his laughter was not just a passing excitement: it changed his life and took him out of his utmost silence to a new state. He spent that day between confusion and laughter saying to himself in bewilderment, "they scatter it, then they harm people, and finally they sweep it away. Ha, ha, ha!"

The next morning, he had not yet recovered from his confusion. He was standing before the mirror dressing when he caught sight of his necktie. Before long, a new confusion haunted him: Why does he have to tie his neck in such a manner? What is the use of this necktie anyway? Why do we have to spend all that effort choosing its color and fabric? No sooner had he said that to himself than he found himself laughing again, closely observing his necktie with perplexity and astonishment. Then he started to look at all his clothes as if they were unfamiliar to him. "What is the wisdom behind shrouding ourselves in such a funny way," he says to himself, "Why don't we take them off and throw them on the ground? Why don't we just look the same way God created us?" However, these questions did not stop him from putting on his clothes until he was done. Then he made his way out of the house as he usually did.

He could tolerate his long life of clouding silence no more. How could he be quiet while all these garments were stifling him against his wish? Yes, against his wish. He flew into a rage while walking, and hated to go on being yoked by his clothes against his wish. Isn't man free? He meditated for a while, then said enthusiastically, "Yes, I am free." He was full of the ecstasy of feeling free, and the light of freedom filled all aspects of his soul. Yes, he was free. Freedom overtook him like a revelation that gave him a great sense of undoubted security. He was free to do whatever he liked, however he liked, whenever he liked, without submission to any power whatsoever, any external force, or any internal drive. In a second, he was able to solve the question of human will and saved it with excellent vigor from the toils of reasoning. A feeling of happiness and distinction overwhelmed him. He started to look down on the people who go about feeling predetermined and shackled, unable to cause benefit or harm to themselves, people who cannot stop once they walk, and cannot go anywhere once they stop. But he can walk if he wills to walk or stop whenever he wishes to stop, mocking any sort of power or law or instinct. This great feeling of free will prompted him to try his superhuman power, so he decided to stop suddenly, saying, "Here, I can stop without any reason whatsoever." He looked around for a few seconds and wondered if he could raise his hands to his head. Sure, he could do that, and here he was, raising his hand with utter unconcern to the people around him. Once more, he wondered if had enough courage to stand on one foot. He said to himself, "Why could I not, and what could stand in the way of my freedom?" Quietly and nonchalantly, he started lifting his left foot off the ground as if he were doing an exercise and as if he were the only person on the street. His heart leapt with joy and he was so filled with boundless confidence that he started to regret not having thought of this freedom much earlier in his life, so that he could have enjoyed it longer. He went on his way as if encountering life for the first time.

One day, on his way to the café, he stopped by a restaurant where he used to dine occasionally. On the sidewalk of the restaurant, he saw a table loaded with delicious food, where a man and a woman were sitting on either side eating and drinking in mirth. Not very far from them sat a group of young paupers, almost naked except for some shabby rags, their faces and skins covered with thick layers of dust and dirt. The incongruity between the two sights made him uncomfortable and his newly gained sense of freedom aggravated his sense of annoyance, so he decided not to let it pass. But what could he do? His heart replied in determination and faith, "the kids should eat with the others." The man and the woman won't spare any part of this chicken for anybody. That is true. But if he managed to throw the chicken on the ground, so that it would catch the sand, no power whatsoever would stop those kids from taking their share of it. Is there any reason why he should not do that? Of course not. Hesitation might have been possible in the past, but not now ... He approached the table calmly, his hand reached the dish, and he picked up the chicken and threw it at the feet of the naked kids. Then off he went, as if nothing had happened, careless of the roaring curses and swearing reverberating in his ears. On the contrary, he began to laugh one more time until his eyes were overflowing with tears, and then he sighed with a great sense of comfort, and regained his deep feelings of security, confidence, and felicity.

At last, he reached the café and sat conveniently on his chair as usual, but this time he could not lock his hands against his knee or surrender to his habitual silence; somehow his psyche could not be motionless anymore; it had lost the ability to be immobile. So he rebuffed his chair, and started to rise, but at that very moment he saw someone whose face was familiar to his eyes, though they had never been acquainted before. Like him, the man was one of the café regulars. His body was muscular and his cheeks inflated. The man walked with his nose in the sky in provocative arrogance, looking down on everybody and everything that met his eyes. Every pulse, every move he made speaks of unbearable hubris, as people disgust him the same way that vermin would cause disgust to a sensitive person. As if he were looking at him for the first time, now he could see his ugliness and abnormality as plain as the Sun, so he started laughing again in the same manner, his eyes observing the back of the bully's neck emerging from his shirt so wide and so full, so provocative. He wondered, should he let him go in peace? God forbid?

He was now used to freedom and had promised himself not to let his free thoughts down. He shook his shoulders in dismissal, and approached the bully until he almost touched him, raised his hands in the air, and with all his might he swung them down on the man's back. The slam was so loud that he could not help laughing. However, this time, it did not pass peacefully as did his other moves. The man was so angry that in his rage he started beating him violently until the people sitting by separated them. He ran away from the café breathlessly, never feeling angry or in pain. On the contrary, it was a pleasurable experience for him. So he smiled again: the happiness he felt diminished the pain. He no longer cared for anything other than his own freedom, which he had managed to win back and would never again give up. So he threw himself into a tide of dangerous adventures with an unyielding will: hitting people on their backs, spitting in their faces, and kicking others in their stomachs and their backs. He also got his share of defensive fists and curses; he broke his glasses, lost the button of his fez, and tore his shirt, but nothing stopped him from going on his dangerous path, with the same old smile that never left his face, and the same ecstasy that never died down. If death were to comes his way, he would face it unafraid.

It was almost sunset when his roaming eyes caught a glimpse of a beautiful young woman holding the arms of a handsome man; the woman was wearing a transparent chiffon dress and her nipple almost poked through her silky gown. Her well-shaped breasts attracted his eyes, which grew wider and wider in wonder. He loved what he saw, and the woman was approaching gradually until she was only one yard away from him. His mind – or his madness – started thinking at an astronomical speed, it soon occurred to him to snatch this wild nipple. If a man ever had to do this, let him be that man. He blocked their way, and with the speed of lightning, he reached her nipple and pinched it. Showers of punches and fists overtook him, and many people surrounded him, but in the end they let him go, perhaps dismayed by his lunatic laugh, or panicked by the staring look of his eyes. They left him anyway. Again, he survived, but he was getting worse. He had an increasing ambition for more adventures. Then he took a look at his own clothes and was shocked to see them torn and shabby. Instead of taking pity upon himself, he started to remember what he thought of when he stood before the mirror early that morning. A distant look appeared in his eyes. He started to question again why he allowed himself to be incarcerated in these tight shreds that were gripping his chest, his abdomen, and his legs. He could no longer put up with them. Relentlessly, his hands began to tear them apart piece by piece until they were all gone. He stood as naked as God created him. His hysterical laugh triggered again, he giggled, then went on his way ...

Appendix 2 – An Interview with Youssef Chahine

Interviewer: Before *Gare Centrale* (*Cairo Station*), among the films you've directed, which ones really began to exist? *Ciel d'Enfer* (*The Blazing Sun*) had a much greater influence ...

Chahine: More popular. Already, *Le Fils du Nil* (*Son of the Nile*) had been a success. When it was presented at the *Cinema Rivoli* (Rivoli Movie Theater), in Cairo, it was fully booked. The Egyptian public wasn't familiar with this type of film, with an unknown actor as the star. Creators often forget that it is the young people who make up the public. But its success didn't last long, because three days later the theater was burned down.

I: Was this before Nasser's rise to power?

C: Yes. That had to be in 1951. I don't remember the exact date, but it was right before the July Revolution of 1952; there was an extraordinary rush of good feeling. You could finally go somewhere without being afraid that King Farouk would snatch away your girlfriend. At this time I had to work to live, in order to eat. I even worked in advertising for Fox.

I: You worked on American films? On *La Terre des Pharaons* [*Land of the Pharoahs*] for example?

C: No, but on a film by William Dieterle. The Cinémascope had just been invented. I had just finished *Ciel d'Enfer*. I had worked in the Luxor studios and the assistants were all gone. I was annoyed: in order to have the status of director, I needed to understand a new invention, which, it seemed, was going to turn everything upside down. I was contacted by the officers whom I happened to know, to make a film about the army. I refused. It was through them that I met William Dieterle. I understood the principle behind the Cinémascope, but I wasn't an expert in lenses and I was really curious. So I attended a film shoot of Dieterle's, simply in order to understand. The first day,

"Numéro Spécial: Youssef Chahine." *Cahiers du Cinema* 506 (October 1996): pp. 12–13. My translation.

I was sitting on a little chair just behind Dieterle. Once, he turned to me and said to me in English with a very pronounced German accent: "Go tell this caravan that I want it to be a little bit further back." So I explained to him that I wanted to do what he wanted, but a caravan of camels doesn't back up all that easily. The assistants, who were older than I, were looking at me; they were all working with me. I tried to rise to the challenge, and in four minutes, his take was ready. Where they normally shot two takes a day, Dieterle was shooting eight. Seeing how well I managed, he wanted to keep me around him. Then *Ciel d'Enfer* was presented at Cannes, where I had been present for *Le Fils du Nil*.

I: And how was *Le Fils du Nil* received?

C: The people wondered why the film was so white. In fact, the laboratory had gotten the wrong copy and had sent a much lighter copy to Cannes, that we had pulled because of the takes in the small Egyptian villages that were too dark. An official from the festival came to see me and told me that he didn't want to know how much I had suffered to make my film. Nor did he want to know who had made a mistake in the choice of the copy. I took two hours of his life from him, and that was enough – I couldn't ask him to make any other concessions. After that adventure, he refused the slightest copy error on the part of the laboratories, and was more vigilant as to my comings and goings. In fact, I gave in to the same conditions at the Venice Film Festival. I went there with my film – twelve cans which were bloodying my hands. When I arrived, they asked me what I was doing there, whom I was representing.

I: There was no selection?

C: The films were chosen by country. At the time, the Cannes Festival wanted to have an international dimension and was always wanting to add a new flag to its list of winners. The organizers accepted you willingly. So I went to present *Ciel d'Enfer*. I think this film was more controlled. It was Omar Sharif's first film.

I: How did you meet him?

C: In a movie theater. Then a second time at a place where we were having tea. I sent my assistant to look for him and asked Omar if he wanted to make movies. He was extraordinarily handsome. I told myself that with such an actor, the battle was half won. I remember the presence of Jean Cocteau that year at Cannes. He always encouraged Egyptian films. Cocteau invited Omar Sharif to join his group.

A: How was *Ciel d'Enfer* received?

C: It was well received and I wasn't expecting it. Even today, I never had it in my head to win a prize. All my work took time to be recognized, accepted. In the beginning, it was folklore: if I had walked in *babouches* on the Croisette, that would not have gotten their attention. Then, little by little, they began to notice. *Gare Centrale* was screened in Berlin. I didn't receive a prize and I was a little surprised and actually hurt. Six months later, I shot *Djamila l'Algérienne* [*Djamīla, The Algerian, Gamīla al-Gazā'iriyya*]. The producer and star who played Djamila [Gamīla], Magda al-Ṣabbāḥī, made the case for me to the jury as the director of *Gare Centrale*, and she added that I played the role of the limping man. At first, they did not want to believe it, but then they recognized my laugh. At that moment, I regretted not having been able to go to Berlin. But at that time, the producer had only offered to pay for half of my ticket, and I did not know where to get the other 120 francs I needed. However, I bought a tuxedo from a young man in a Greek café so I could go to Cannes. If they had seen me in a tuxedo in Berlin, they would have seen very well that I didn't limp, they would have understood that I had played a role. *Gare Centrale* was very poorly received in Egypt. At the film's premiere, they spit in my face: "What is this shit – who cares about a lame person?" With this film, I was told I presented a bad image of Egypt.

I: Did you already have problems with censorship at that time?

C: Yes, especially with the censors responsible for the festival programming. After *Gare Centrale*, I went through a rough patch with five films. I did not understand it: I thought I had talent, but I was only getting rejections for films I wrote, played, and directed, which made me doubt myself. That was a rather disastrous period in my life. After that, I took the advice of my colleagues. They suggested I make a melodrama based on a foreign film that had just come out.

I: There were a lot of remakes of American films in Egypt…

C: There was nothing but that. Some went almost as far as to copy take for take in certain films. They became Arab-speaking American films. But that worked and brought a lot of money. I wanted to make my own films, not just American-inspired remakes.

I: However, *Ciel d'Enfer* was already a different take from familiar Egyptian film productions.

C: Yes, but it was still a rather well-made melodrama. The public discovered a freer cinema: the scenes were shot on locations, not on the studios, and that made a difference and showed what things were real. Besides, this was already the case in *Le Fils du Nil*, which was a success.

I: Weren't you the first filmmaker to use significant exterior scenes in Egyptian cinema?

C: Yes, the producer sent us six francs for the staff, for transportation, renting cows, and for the ten peasants who were working with us... That was very little. But what a learning experience! How do you make a flood without money? That stimulates your imagination.

I: In *Ciel d'Enfer* and *Les Eaux Noires*, there was an important social dimension there.

C: Yes, very important, but it wasn't a deliberate political choice. I was born a socialist, I was born poor and I suffered a lot to get to a point where I could express certain things. How can you not have sympathy toward a scorned peasant, toward the maltreated worker? When I heard that before Nasser came to in power, the country was doing better, I didn't believe it. The people who thought that way had no memory, or rather they had gotten in the habit of being the slaves of others. For a rather long time, I have had in me this sense of freedom. I wanted to pass it on, to at least teach respect for others. I didn't understand, for example, how you could scorn a person who grows wheat for you or who makes your machines function. And I still refuse to understand it. This social dimension of my films was spontaneous. The revolution took place. But I did not agree with all the changes that it instituted: Nasser nationalized film. They replaced the expert with an officer. It was a matter of a military socialism, and the Soviet Union was not a particularly fabulous example. Many years afterwards, I went to work over there. They had simply replaced the money with which you could get yourself a prostitute by an important place at the heart of the party. But in society, man had not changed: he was still as bad, indeed even worse. After *Gare Centrale*, I fell into a terrible state of depression.

I: Naguib Mahfouz had participated in *Gare Centrale*?

C: No. A young man had brought the basic story, the miscellaneous fact. He and I embroidered from this miscellaneous fact. I only had a very little rapport with Mahfouz. When I shot *Djamila* [*Gamīla al-Gazā'iriyya*], I didn't know what was happening over there. I had very little news from Algeria. All that I knew of this country [France] was Julien Duvivier's *Pépé le Moko*. Then the director argued with the producer. He called me to ask me to make the film. He was so insistent that I had to accept. I didn't want them to bother me too much with the story. Who are the good guys? The Arabs. Who are the bad guys? The French. So I wanted my film to show that, in a believable manner.

I: Was this during the Algerian War?

C: Yes, it's the first film on the conflict.

I: Was it produced by Algeria?

C: No. It was produced by the young Egyptian actress Magda al-Ṣabbāḥī. Her brother was an officer. One thing struck me. Jacques Vergès was already participating in the trial. He had become the husband of the heroine of the film. A Frenchman was defending Algerians.

I: Was there a lot of money put into this film?

C: I have to say that Magda was rather generous; she was a competent producer. Maybe her army connections helped her. If I wanted 200 soldiers, she would bring them to me. We argued, however, in front of 200 soldiers. In one scene, after having witnessed the massacre of her parents, she swore to be a combatant to the end. Then, in the following scene, she came back to a plaintive attitude, playing the scene in tears. I was against it; you can't go backwards that way in the script. Since she didn't want to understand it, I kicked her in the rear in front of 600 soldiers. She insulted me. That was not important, as long as she obeyed me. After that, we got along very well. During this nationalistic epoch, this film provoked a wild movement in Egypt. It was banned in Algeria.

I: Because of the French presence?

C: It is still banned today. After the Algerian revolution, it is still banned. Why? Because it is the woman who starts the revolution? However, she's not the only one in the film.

I: Was *Djamila l'Algérienne* shown in France?

C: Yes, it was screened several times at the Cinémathèque. I went to present this film at the Moscow Festival. In *La Mémoire*, I recall a conversation with Henri Langlois, who called to warn me that the French Embassy wanted to ban the film. I noticed in fact that the organizers of the festival were furiously pushing back the screening time. I did not understand. I said to Henri Langlois: "But aren't you French?" He responded, "Me, yes. Them, no." I then asked him who was at the French Embassy. He said: "They're idiots." This type of experience opens your eyes. Each festival is a real battle. The film finally got permission for a special projection one day after the end of the festival. All the same, they managed to fill the room. It was a delight. In a whole career, there are moments of delight and, right after, moments when they spit in your face. You have to resist all that, a point that's all. Whether you achieve success or its opposite, you have to keep on. I don't see myself doing anything else.

Nor do I want to do it anywhere else but in Egypt. When someone asks me to do a film in France, I answer that they don't need me in France. Egypt needs me. I experience this feeling of belonging to other people. That is very important. It is true that I got angry with the group that surrounded Nasser; he had become totally fascist at certain times. That was in 1964.

I: Was this before your departure to Lebanon?

C: Yes, after I directed *Saladin* in 1963. Nasser gave me the State Prize. Six months later, they asked me to make the film that they wanted. I refused. I was the director, and I could not submit to this type of proposal. They told me that they were going to ban the film. It was *Gens du Nil*, about a dam being constructed with the Soviets. This film came out later. It was banned in Egypt and in Moscow. I had become the corner grocer. The Muscovites were impressed by the countryside of Nubia, the trees, the Sun's reflections. They asked me why I hadn't come to their country to film the main street of Leningrad. In fact, they even asked me to modify the film. But the film had ended for me, so they rejected it. I then presented it in Egypt. They didn't appreciate my filming of the Soviet engineer walking in front of the Egyptian engineer. That meant that the Russians were more important than we were. I explained it this way: it was because the Egyptian actor was lazy, walking more slowly [*laughs*]. I had to reshoot the scene with other actors.

Appendix 3 – Feature Films Produced in Egypt from 1927–1962

This table is based on readings of various references on Egyptian film, such as Samīr Farīd's Madkhal's *ilá Tārīkh al-Sīnimā al-ʿArabiyya (An Introduction to the History of Arab Cinema)*, Thoraval's *Regards sur le cinéma égyptien (Views on Egyptian Cinema)*, and Khan's *An Introduction to the Egyptian Cinema*

Year	Number of films
1927–8	5
1928–9	3
1929–30	3
1930–1	3
1931–2	5
1932–3	6
1933–4	6
1934–5	4
1935–6	12
1936–7	16
1937–8	14
1938–9	11
1939–40	14
1940–1	10
1941–2	17
1942–3	23
1943–4	16
1944–5	28
1945–6	67
1946–7	53
1948–9	58
1949–50	35
1950–1	32
1951–2	70

(*cont.*)

Year	Number of films
1952–3	58
1953–4	80
1954–5	49
1955–6	34
1956–7	38
1957–8	60
1958–9	59
1959–60	31
1960–1	52
1961–2	52

Bibliography

'Abduh, Muḥammad. "The Necessity of Religious Reform" In *Modernist and Fundamentalist Debates in Islam*. Edited by Mansoor Moaddel and Kamran Talattof. New York, NY: Macmillan, 2000: 48–81.

Ahmed, Jamal Mohammed. *Intellectual Origins of Egyptian Nationalism*. London: Oxford University Press, 1960.

Al-'Aqqād, 'Abbās Maḥmud. *Afyūn al-Shu'ūb: al-Madhāhib al-Haddāma (The Opium of the Masses: On Destructive Doctrines)*. Cairo: Maktaba-t- al-Anglū al-Miṣriyya, n.d.

Al-Bannā, Ḥasan. *Mushkilātunā fī Ḍaw' al-Niẓām al-Islamī (Our Problems in Light of an Islamic System)*. Cairo: n.p., n.d.

Al-Ḥakīm, Tawfīq. "Preface." In *Muqaddima-t- al-Malik Ūdīb (Oedipus King)*. Beirut: Dār al-Kitāb al, n.d.: 11–53.

Ahl al-Kahf (The People of the Cave). Cairo: Dār al-Hilāl, 1954 (1933).

Al-Mabkhout, Chokri. *Sīra-t- al-Ghā'ib Sīra-t- al-Ātī: al-Sīra al-Dhātiyya fī Kitāb al-Ayyām li- Ṭāhā Ḥusayn (A Biography of the Absent, A Biography of What Is Yet to Come: Autobiography in Ṭāhā Ḥusayn's The Days)*. Tunis: Dār al-Janūb, 1992.

Al-Musawi, Muhsin. *Al-Mawqif al-Thawrī fī al-Riwāya al-ʿArabiyya al-Muʿāṣira (The Revolutionary Position in the Contemporary Arabic Novel)*. Baghdad: Manshūrāt Wazāra-t- al-Iʿlām al-ʿIrāqiyya, 1975.

Al-Musawi, Muhsin. *The Postcolonial Arabic Novel: Debating Ambivalence*. Leiden: Brill, 2003.

Al-Nowaihi, Mohamed. "Towards the Reappraisal of Classical Arabic Literature and History: Some Aspects of Taha Ḥusayn's Use of Modern Western Criteria." *International Journal of Middle East Studies*, vol. 11, no. 2 (April 1980): 189–207.

Allen, Roger. *The Arabic Novel: An Historical and Critical Introduction*. Syracuse, NY: Syracuse University Press, 1982.

Anderson, Benedict. *Imagined Communities: Reflections on the Origin and Spread of Nationalism*. London: Verso, 1991.

Anderson, Perry. "Modernity and Revolution." In *Marxism and the Interpretation of Culture*. Edited by Cary Nelson and Lawrence

Grossberg. Urbana and Chicago, IL: University of Illinois Press, 1988: 317–33.

Ansar, Zafar Ishaq. "Contemporary Islam and Nationalism: A Case Study of Egypt." *Die Welt des Islams*, New Ser., vol. 7, no. 1/4. (1961): 3–38.

Badawi, M. M. *Modern Arabic Drama in Egypt*. Cambridge: Cambridge University Press, 1987.

Bākāthīr, 'Alī Aḥmad. *Al-Thā'r al-Aḥmar (The Red Revolutionary)*. Cairo: Maktaba-t-Miṣr, 1949.

Baring (Earl of Cromer), Evelyn. *Modern Egypt*, Vol. 2. New York, NY: MacMillan Company, 1908.

Beinin, Joel. "Formation of the Egyptian Working Class." *MERIP Reports*, no. 94 (February 1981): 14–23.

Benjamin, Walter. "The Author as Producer." In *Understanding Brecht*. Translated by Anna Bostock. New York, NY: Verso, 1973: 85–103.

Berque, Jacques. *Egypt: Imperialism & Revolution*. Translated by Jean Stewart. London: Faber and Faber, 1972.

Bhabha, Homi. *The Location of Culture*. London: Routledge, 1994.

Boullata, Issa J. and Terri DeYoung, eds. *Tradition and Modernity in Arabic Literature*. Fayetteville, AR: The University of Arkansas Press, 1997.

Bourdieu, Pierre. *Le Monde Diplomatique* (December 8, 1998). http://mondediplo.com/1998/12/08bourdieu

Britton, Celia. "Broken Images in Resnais's *Muriel*." *French Cultural Studies*, vol. 1, part 1, no. 1 (February 1990):34–46.

Brown, Richard Harvey. *Society as Text*. Chicago, IL: Chicago University Press, 1987.

Bū-Djadra, Nūr al-Dīn. *Al-Ḥarīq: Qiṣṣa min Waḥī al-Thawra al-Jazā'iriyya (The Fire: A Story Inspired by the Algerian Revolution)*. Tunis: Dār al-Nashr, 1958.

Burnet, Etienne. "Djamila." *Le Petit Matin*. November 1957.

Butler, Judith. *Loss: The Politics of Mourning*. Edited by David Eng and David Kazanjian. Berkeley, CA: University of California Press, 2003.

Cachia, Pierre. *The Days, Taha Hussein: His Autobiography in Three Parts*. Translated by E. H. Paxton, Hilary Wayment, and Kenneth Cragg. Cairo: The American University in Cairo Press, 1997.

Cahiers du Cinema, 1996. "Numéro Spécial: Youssef Chahine." 506, October.

Chatterjee, Partha. *Nationalist Thought and the Colonial World: A Derivative Discourse*. Minneapolis, MN: University of Minnesota Press, 1993.

Darrāj, Fayṣal. *Al-Riwāya wa Ta'wil al-Tārīkh [The Novel and the Interpretations of History]*. Casablanca: al-Markaz al-Thaqāfī al-'Arabī, 2004.

Derrida, Jacques. *Of Grammatology*. Translated by Gayatri Chakravorty Spivak. Baltimore, MD: The Johns Hopkins University Press, 1976.

Eban, A. S. "The Modern Literary Movement in Egypt." *International Affairs*, vol. 20, no. 2 (April 1944): 166–78.

Faḍl, Ṣalāḥ. *Taḥawwulāt al-Shiʿriyya al-ʿArabiyya (Transformations of Arabic Poetics)*. Cairo: Al-Hayʾa al-Miṣriyya al-ʿĀmma lil-Kitāb, 2002.

Farag, Alfrid. *Dalīl al-Mutafarrij al-Dhakī ilā al-Masraḥ (A Smart Viewer's Guide to the Theater)*. Cairo: Dār al-Hilāl, 1966.

Feldman, Noah. "Democracy Loses in Egypt and Beyond." *Bloomberg Review*. Accessed July 3, 2013. www.bloombergview.com/articles/2013-07-03/democracy-loses-in-egypt-and-beyond

Gibb, H. A. R. "Studies in Contemporary Arabic Literature: II. Manfalūṭī and the 'New Style.'" *Bulletin of the School of Oriental Studies*, vol. 5, no. 2. (1929): 311–22.

"Studies in Contemporary Arabic Literature." *Bulletin of the School of Oriental Studies*, vol. 7, no. 1. (1933): 1–22.

Gibbon, Edward. *The Decline and Fall of the Roman Empire*, Vol. 2. New York, NY: The Modern Library, 1932.

Goldschmidt Jr., Arthur. *A Brief History of Egypt*. State College, PA: Pennsylvania State University Press, 2008.

Gramsci, Antonio. *Selections from the Prison Notebooks of Antonio Gramsci*. Edited and translated by Quintin Hoare and Geoffrey Nowell Smith. London: Lawrence & Wishart, 1971.

von Grunebaum, G. E. *Medieval Islam: A Study in Cultural Orientation*. Chicago, IL: University of Chicago Press, 1953.

Modern Islam: The Search for Cultural Identity. New York, NY: Vintage Books, 1964.

Habermas, Jürgen. *The Structural Transformation of the Public Sphere*. Translated by Thomas Burger. Cambridge, MA: MIT, 1991.

Haddad, Hassan S. and Basheer K. Nijm, eds. *The Arab World: A Handbook*. Wilmette, IL: Medina Press, 1978.

Ḥaqqī, Yaḥyá. *Fajr al-Qiṣṣa al-Miṣriyya (Dawn of Egyptian Narrative)*. Cairo: n.p., 1960.

Ḥasan, Muḥammad. *ʿAbd Allāh, al-Hakīm wa ḥiwār -al-Marāyā (Al-Hakim and the Dialogue of Mirrors)*. Cairo: Dār al-Qibāʾ, 2000.

Haykal, Muḥammad Ḥusayn. *Zaynab, al-Ṭabʿa al-Sādisa*. Al-Qāhira: n.p., 1967 (1921).

Hauser, Arnold. *The Social History of Art: Naturalism, Impressionism, the Film Age*, Vol. 4. New York, NY: Vintage Books, 1958.

Ḥusayn, Ṭāhā, *Fuṣūl fī al-Adab wa al-Naqd (Essays on Literature and Criticism)*. Cairo: Dār al-Maʿārif, 1945.

Ḥusayn, Ṭāhā. "The Modern Renaissance of Arabic Literature." *Books Abroad*, vol. 29, no. 1 (Winter 1955): 4–18.

Husayn, Ţahā. *Al-Majmū'a al-Kāmila li-Mu'allafāt al-Ductūr Ţāhā Ḥusayn (The Complete Works of Dr. Ţahā Ḥusayn)*. Dār al-Kitāb al-Lubnānī: Beirut, 1974.

Ḥusayn, Ţahā. *The Days, Taha Hussein: His Autobiography in Three Parts*. Translated by E. H. Paxton, Hilary Wayment and Kenneth Cragg. Cairo: The American University in Cairo Press, 1997.

Hussein, Suzanne Taha. *Les 'Souvenirs' de Madame Suzanne Taha Hussein (Memoirs of Madame Suzanne Taha Hussein*. Edited by J. P. Lachèse. Translated by T. K. Kraft. Paris: Mélanges Institut Dominicain d'Études Orientales [MIDEO], 1982.

Idrīs, Yūsuf. *Jumhūriyya-t- Faraḥāt (Faraḥāt's Republic)*. Al-Qāhira: Maktaba-t-Mişr, n.d.

Jameson, Fredric. "Third World Literature in the Era of Multinational Capitalism." *Social Text*, 15 (Fall 1986): 65–88.

Signatures of the Visible. New York, NY: Routledge, 1992.

Seeds of Time: Utopia, Modernism, Death. New York, NY: Columbia University Press, 1994.

Jay, Martin. "Scopic Regimes of Modernity." In *Vision and Visuality*. Edited by Hal Foster. Seattle, WA: Bay Press, 1988.

Downcast Eyes: The Denigration of Vision in Twentieth-Century French Thought. Berkeley, CA: University of California Press, 1993.

Joyce, James. "Drama and Life." In *James Joyce, Occasional, Critical, and Political Writings*. Edited by Kevin Barry. Oxford: Oxford World Classics, 2000.

Kant, Immanuel. "Toward Perpetual Peace: A Philosophical Project." In *Kant: Political Writings*. Edited by H. S. Reiss, translated by H. B. Nisbet. Cambridge: Cambridge University Press, 1970.

Khan, M. *An Introduction to the Egyptian Cinema*. London: Informatics, 1969.

Le Sueur, James D. *Uncivil War: Intellectuals and Identity Politics during the Decolonization*. Philadelphia, PA: University of Pennsylvania Press, 2001.

Lewis, Bernard. *The Middle East and the West*. London: HarperCollins College Division, 1968.

Lukács, Georg. *The Theory of the Novel: A Historico-Philosophical Essay on the Forms of Great Epic Literature*. Translated by Anna Bostock. Cambridge: MIT Press, 1971.

Macherey, Pierre. *Pour Une Théorie de la Production Littérature (For a Theory of Production Literature)*. Paris: François Maspero, 1966.

Maghraoui, Abdelslam M. *Liberalism without Democracy: Nationhood and Citizenship in Egypt, 1992–1936*. Durham, NC: Duke University Press, 2006.
Mahfouz, Naguib. *Hams al-Junūn (The Whisper of Madness)*. Cairo: Maktaba-t-Miṣr, 1938.
Man, Paul de. "Autobiography as De-facement." *MLN*, vol. 94, no. 5. *Comparative Literature* (December 1979): 919–30.
Mansour, Fawzy. *The Arab World: Nation, State, and Democracy*. Tokyo: United Nations University Press, 1992.
Mernissi, Fatima. *Islam and Democracy: Fear of the Modern World*. Translated by Mary Jo Lakeland. New York, NY: Basic Books, 2002.
Mitchell, Timothy. *Rule of Experts: Egypt, Techno-Politics, Modernity*. Berkeley, CA: University of California Press, 2002.
Nancy, Jean-Luc. *The Experience of Freedom*. Stanford, CA: Stanford University Press, 1993.
Nasser. *Falsafa-t- al-Thawra (Philosophy of the Revolution)*. Beirut: Maktaba-t- al-'Irfān, n.d.
Nasser, Gamal Abdel. "President Gamal Abdel Nasser on the Muslim Brotherhood." Accessed on July 3, 2013. www.youtube.com/watch?v=TX4RK8bj2W0
Oxford University Press. "OED Online." Accessed June 2017. www.oed.com/
Owen, Roger. *Lord Cromer: Victorian Imperialist, Edwardian Proconsul*. Oxford: Oxford University Press, 2004.
Plato. *Phaedrus and the Seventh and Eighth Letters*. Translated by Walter Hamilton. New York, NY: Penguin Books, 1973.
Quṭb, Sayyid. *Ṭifl min al-Qarya (A Child from the Village)*. Beirut: Dār al-Shurūq, 1946.
Social Justice in Islam. Translated by John B. Hardie. Washington, DC: American Council of Learned Societies, 1955.
Rushdie, Salman. *The Satanic Verses*. London: Viking, 1988.
Sacks, Jeffrey. *Iterations of Loss: Mutilation and Aesthetic Form, al-Shidyaq to Darwish*. New York, NY: Fordham University Press, 2015.
Said, Edward. *Reflections on Exile and Other Essays*. Cambridge: Harvard University Press, 2000.
Shafīq, Munīr. *Al-Islām fī Maʿrakat al-Ḥaḍāra (Islam and the Civilization War)*. Lebanon: Dār al-Naāhir and Tunis: Dār al-Burāq lil-Nashar, 1991.
Shukrī, Ghālī. *Thawara-t- al-Mu'tazil: Dirāsa fī Adab Tawfīq al-Hakīm (The Revolt of the Recluse: A Study of Tawfīq al-Hakīm's Literature)*. Cairo: Maktaba-t-al-Anglū al-Miṣriyyā, 1966.

Smith, Wilfred Cantwell. *The Meaning and End of Religion*. Minneapolis, MN: Fortress Press Edition, 1991.

Starkey, Paul. *From Ivory Tower: A Critical Study of Tawfiq al-Hakim*. Oxford: Ithaca Press, 1987.

Steiner, George. *After Babel: Aspects of Language and Translation*. Oxford: Oxford University Press, 1975.

Ṭāhā Badr, 'Abd al-Muḥsin. *Taṭawwur al-Riwāya al-'Arabiyya al-Ḥadītha fī Miṣr: 1870–1938 (The Development of the Modern Arabic Novel in Egypt: 1870–1938)*. Cairo: Dār al-Ma'ārif, 1968.

Thoraval, Yves. *Regards sur le Cinéma Égyptien (Insights into Egyptian Cinema)*. Beyrouth: Librairie Orientale, 1986.

'Usfūr, Jābir. *Zaman al-Riwāya (The Time of the Novel)*. Damascus: Dār al-Madá lil-Thaqāfa wa al-Nashr, 1999.

Wahbah, Majdī. *Al-Adab al-Muqāran (Comparative Literature)*. Giza: al-Sharika al-ʿĀlamiyya li-l-Nashr, 1991.

Williams, Raymond. *Keywords: A Vocabulary of Culture and Society*. Oxford: Oxford University Press, 1983.

Resources of Hope. London: Verso, 1989.

Index